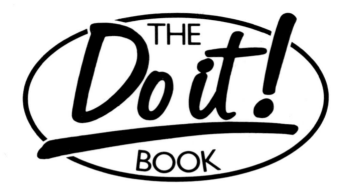

Consultant Editor
Bob Tattersall

Collins

Published in 1985 by
William Collins Sons & Co Ltd
London · Glasgow · Sydney · Auckland
Johannesburg · Toronto

9 8 7 6 5 4 3 2 1

© 1983, 1984, 1985 Elizabeth Whiting & Associates
and Rose & Lamb Design Partnership

First published by William Collins Sons & Co Ltd as
separate titles in *The Do It! Series.*

ISBN 0 00 411992 4

Printed in Italy by
New Interlitho, Milan

CONTENTS

Acknowledgements

Consultant Editor
Bob Tattersall has been a DIY journalist for over 25 years and was editor of *Homemaker* for 16 years. He now works as a freelance journalist and broadcaster. Regular contact with the main DIY manufacturers keeps him up-to-date on all new products and developments. He has written many books on various aspects of DIY and, while he is considered 'an expert', he prefers to think of himself as a do-it-yourselfer who happens to be a journalist.

Contributors
Dek Messecar is a professional joiner and furniture designer/maker, who has had experience of all aspects of DIY.

Beverley Behrens trained as a designer and has been involved in many aspects of art and interior design and decoration.

Robert Henley has been writing popular articles on electricity for over 20 years. Once a complete amateur himself, who had never used a pair of pliers or a screwdriver until he married, he has since rewired two homes.

Design
Mike Rose and Bob Lamb

Publishing Editor
Robin Wood

Copy Editors
Dek Messecar and Alexa Stace

Picture Research
Liz Whiting

Illustrations
Rob Shone
Rick Blakely
Anne Lamb
Su Martin

Photographs
Pictures from Elizabeth Whiting Photo Library, photographed by John Bouchier, Steve Colby, David Cripps, Michael Crockett, Clive Helm, Graham Henderson, Ann Kelley, Neil Lorimer, Michael Nicholson, Julian Nieman, Spike Powell, Tim Street-Porter, Ron Sutherland and Jerry Tubby.

Pictures on page 11 courtesy of Dulux Paints; pages 18, 30 and 33 courtesy of Berger Paints; page 78 courtesy of Timber Research and Development Association, UK; page 89 courtesy of Sikkens UK Ltd; page 96 courtesy of Blackfriars Paints, Bristol; page 143 courtesy of Shelfstore Ltd; page 221 (UK edition) courtesy of Carl Boyer & Associates: Leisure Shower Cubicles, Leisure Vanity Basin; pages 255 and 258 (UK edition) courtesy of Tony Byers.

INTRODUCTION

The interest in DIY grows apace. Each year more and more people start to tackle jobs that previously they would have left to a professional tradesman. It's easy to see why. DIY saves money; it is, in the opinion of many enthusiasts, the best way of ensuring a first-class job; and—most important of all—it becomes easier as the home improvement industries launch products and devise methods that bring a wider variety of projects well within the range of the do-it-yourself man or woman.

The Do It! Book features the latest methods and material, and it deals with the subjects that are most popular with do-it-yourselfers.

It is split into a series of chapters, all of them self contained and providing a first-class introduction to the subject. I feel that the text and illustrations explain the various tasks with a clarity never before bettered, while the colour photographs show you the sort of effect you can achieve. In addition, each chapter offers its Ten Top Tips, and gives advice to ensure that you do the job safely as well as effectively.

The book is aimed at a wide range of skills. No matter whether you are a beginner making your first hesitant steps at do-it-yourself or someone with more experience wanting to widen your range, I am sure you will find this book invaluable. It is the perfect companion for anyone who wants to . . . well, Do It!

Bob Tattersall

PAINT IT

CONTENTS

Introduction

Painting is the least expensive and the easiest way to change or brighten up your home, and today's paints offer a wide variety of colours and finishes from which to choose.

This chapter tells, clearly and simply, how to tackle household painting jobs. With a little patience, practice, and methodical approach, anyone can paint the interior of their home. For the more ambitious, there are full instructions on how to do your exterior painting as well.

This chapter of the book is divided into two sections: one for the inside and one for outside painting. There is also information on the tools and materials you'll need, and advice on ladders, steps, scaffolding and safety.

The point to be stressed with all the jobs described in this book is the importance of preparation. Flaws in surfaces are accentuated by coats of paint rather than hidden by them. Remember that no painted finish can be any smoother than the surface to which it is applied.

Another important point is that manufacturers' instructions and recommendations sometimes vary between brands, even for quite similar products. If in doubt, always follow the manufacturers' instructions.

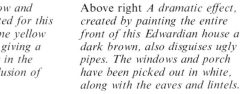

Above *Buttercup yellow and white gloss were selected for this small kitchen. The same yellow is echoed in the blind, giving a sunny feel. Reflections in the gloss help create an illusion of space.*

Above right *A dramatic effect, created by painting the entire front of this Edwardian house a dark brown, also disguises ugly pipes. The windows and porch have been picked out in white, along with the eaves and lintels.*

Right *A cool and restful choice of colour scheme enhances this elegant room. The ceiling and walls are painted in light blue, with cornice, woodwork and unused fireplace all picked out in white silk.*

TOOLS AND MATERIALS

Brushes

Good brushes are essential for good results and, with proper maintenance, will last for years. Buy the size you need for each job when you are buying the paint so that you build up a complete set, say 10mm, 25mm, 50mm, 75mm, and 150mm wide. The best brushes have natural bristles that are significantly longer than those of cheaper ones. They also have more bristles per brush and have a firmer 'spring' when you flex them. There are two specialized brushes that will prove useful:

The *cutting-in brush* is trimmed at a slight angle and is invaluable for painting straight lines, up to corners, glazing bars of window frames, and all awkward edges.

The *radiator brush* (or crevice brush) is used to get paint to parts of the wall covered by radiators or perhaps by a large object too difficult to move.

Care and Cleaning

New brushes should be washed in water and a little washing up liquid and allowed to dry before using them for the first time; this helps remove loose hairs. When dry, flex the bristles back and forth vigorously between thumb and finger.

To work properly, the bristles must be free to slide against each other. When paint has worked its way to the top of the bristles, the brush is 'bound up' and the only remedy is to clean and dry it. Have a second one handy when painting.

To clean brushes, get off as much of the paint as you can by using the brush on plenty of newspaper. Then, if it is *oil-based paint*, choose a container just large enough to hold the brush and pour in enough white spirit or proprietary brush cleaner to cover the bristles completely. Plunge the brush up and down vigorously.

Run a wire brush through the bristles from handle to

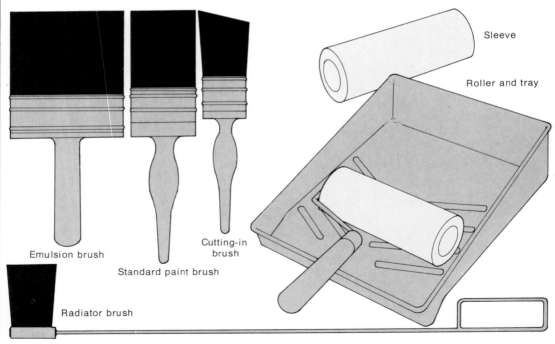

Emulsion brush

Standard paint brush

Cutting-in brush

Radiator brush

Sleeve

Roller and tray

tip on each side to remove any paint that is too dry to dissolve easily. Change the white spirit and repeat.

Wash the brush in warm water and a little washing up liquid. Rinse in clean water. Repeat the process, rinsing several times until the bristles are free of detergent. Shake out as much water as possible, smooth the bristles into shape and store flat; never leave standing on the bristles.

When using oil-based paint, brushes may be stored overnight (between coats, for instance) with the bristles immersed in water. Don't immerse the metal ferrule as it may rust.

If you have been using *water-based paint*, the procedure is the same, but leave out the step with white spirit and use the wire brush during washing.

If a brush has become hardened by paint left in it, soak it in paint stripper (water soluble) or proprietary brush restorer until soft, and then clean as described above.

Rollers

Rollers are useful for painting large areas such as walls and ceilings. Buy a good quality lambswool or mohair roller, and take care of it. Generally speaking, long-pile rollers are used for rougher surfaces, such as pebbledash, and short-pile for smooth surfaces. However, different piles produce different textures on smooth surfaces with some paints.

A good roller should have an easily removable sleeve (for cleaning) and some have an extension handle for painting ceilings etc. without ladders. A tray is used to 'charge' the roller with paint. It has a sloping section on which to work the roller up and down to distribute the paint evenly.

To clean a roller, use up the paint on newspaper, remove the sleeve and immerse it in water or white spirit as appropriate. Wearing rubber gloves, rub the pile thoroughly while it is submerged. Finish by washing in lukewarm water and washing up liquid and then rinsing thoroughly. Shake off as much water as possible and leave it standing on end to dry.

Paint Pads

Paint pads are an alternative if large brushes and rollers seem too heavy. They are usually used with water-based paint on large surfaces such as walls and ceilings, but can be used with oil-based paints.

The best pads have a mohair pile on a layer of foam attached to a plastic handle. The foam is to allow the pile to follow the surface being painted, not to soak up paint; only the pile

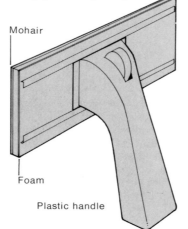

Mohair

Foam

Plastic handle

should be charged. The easiest way to avoid overloading the pad is to use a tray with a roller that picks up paint and transfers it to the pile as the pad is moved across the top of it. These trays are inexpensive and may come with the pads.

Properly loaded, paint pads leave an even film of paint with each wipe. If the paint streaks or drags, you are probably pulling the pad too quickly for the paint to spread evenly. Clean pads after use the same way as rollers.

Other Tools

Paint kettles are recommended when painting with a brush, especially from a ladder. They keep the can free of the bits and stray hairs that inevitably result from dipping the brush in it. Fill them to a depth of half the length of the bristles of the brush you're using. This helps to avoid overloading the brush.

Paint shields are flat pieces of plastic used to keep paint off window panes when painting the glazing bars. They are specially shaped to allow the paint to cover the join between putty and glass (important for weather proofing).

Paint stripper is a chemical liquid used to remove old paint. In preparation for repainting, it is more usual to use a *blowtorch* or *hot air paint remover*. This is a difficult and sometimes dangerous job and it is usually enough to scrape off unsound areas and rub down well.

Scrapers are stiff, metal-blade spatulas used for removing old wallpaper and flaking paint.

Filling knives are similar to scrapers but have flexible blades and are used to apply filler to cracks and holes in surfaces.

Abrasive paper is used to smooth surfaces before painting and also to roughen gloss paint before painting over it. Aluminium oxide paper doesn't clog easily and lasts longer than glass paper. When rubbing down between coats to make a very smooth finish, 'wet and dry' cloth-backed silicon carbide is best as it can be rinsed in water to prevent it becoming clogged with paint as you work.

Always wrap abrasive paper around a block of wood for flat surfaces. For large curves, staple the edges together to make a loop around your hand or use any object of a convenient shape as a sanding block.

When painting over old gloss paint, you can use a chemical product called *liquid sander* to prepare the surface without rubbing down.

Dust sheets will protect anything that may get splashed or dripped on. Fabric ones are best because they are absorbent, but polythene, although slippery, will do. Newspapers tend to move around when walked on or if there is a draught.

Automatic-feed brush, pad or roller machines are available. They have a reservoir for paint and use compressed gas to force it up a tube to the brush. They are quite expensive, and it is debatable whether they save as much time and effort as one may imagine.

Spray painting. There are small spray guns that use an aerosol propellant to spray paint from a jar. These are not expensive and are useful for many special effects.

Steam wallpaper strippers may be inexpensively hired and are very effective for removing stubborn wallpaper.

Paint stirring attachments for electric drills are inexpensive and save time and effort.

Tips

Don't use paint stripper to clean rollers or pads.

In case your brush gets 'bound up', have a second one handy.

Use white spirit on a lint-free cloth to remove last traces of dust before painting.

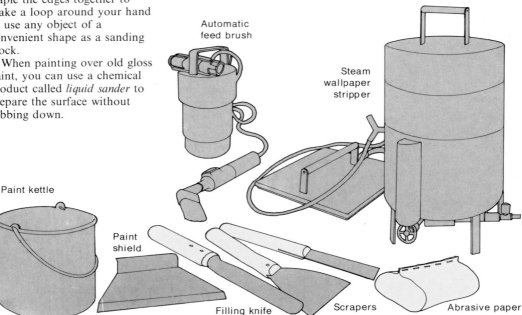

Automatic feed brush

Steam wallpaper stripper

Paint kettle

Paint shield

Filling knife

Scrapers

Abrasive paper

Types of Paint and Fillers

Paints for household decoration fall into two general categories.

Oil-based paint is thinned with white spirit and is used on wood and metal, although you can use it on walls and ceilings. It is available in matt, eggshell, and gloss finishes, although only gloss should be used for exterior painting. Oil-based paint is actually a 'system' of three different coatings: primer, undercoat and top coat. If you use a 'non-drip' top coat, apply it with a minimum of brushing and don't stir it beforehand.

Water-based paints are a vast range of emulsions for interior and exterior use on plaster, lining paper, brick and cement. Interior grades come in matt and silk finishes as well as thick resin mixtures that give texture to walls and ceilings. Exterior grades range from matt finish to masonry paints that contain granulated quartz or mica and have a sandy appearance.

Micro porous versions of both oil- and water-based paints are becoming available. These are said to be more resistant to flaking and peeling, especially on wood outside. These must be used with micro porous primers and undercoats and are not effective if used on top of old paint.

As well as conventional paint, there are specialized paints for specific purposes:

Radiator enamel is designed not to discolour with heat.

Stove paint will withstand the heat of stoves and fireplaces and comes in a range of colours.

Glass paint comes in transparent colours for a stained glass effect.

Tile red is used for roof and floor tiles and brick.

Multi-coloured paint gives a speckled effect.

Epoxy resin paint is available for floors and surfaces where durability is needed.

Matt black can make chalk boards on most smooth surfaces.

Artists acrylic paint is used for stencilling.

Damp proof paints may help overcome dampness problems in masonry, but they do not cure the causes. However, full instructions for dealing with damp come with these products.

Bitumen (tar) paint is for waterproofing the inside of gutters.

Knotting is a coating applied to knots in wood before applying primer or paint. Otherwise, resin from the knot will bleed through later. There are proprietary products or you can use shellac.

Thinners are simply the appropriate solvent for each type of paint. Instructions on the can almost always state whether the paint should be thinned and what to use for brush cleaning.

Primer is a coating used to take up absorbency and give a uniform surface to paint on.

Undercoat is used under oil-based paint to give an opaque colour and good surface.

Primer/sealer is an oil-based primer used to bind surfaces and stop old paint colours or wallpaper bleeding through.

Masonry sealer is a primer for brick and cement.

Wood preservative is a product for protecting exterior wood from rot and decay.

Universal stainers are tubes of coloured pigment that can be used with most types of paint to mix your own colours.

Filler is the term given to materials used to repair cracks or depressions in wood, plaster or metal.

For wood and plaster, the best fillers are resin based, sold as powder to be mixed with water or already mixed. These are hard, smooth, easy to rub down when dry, and also have the advantage of not shrinking as they harden. This means they can be applied flush with the surface, not proud as with cellulose filler.

Large areas of damaged plaster should be repaired with plaster or one of the DIY plastering systems that is applied by brush and remains soft long enough to give several attempts at smoothing it.

Metal should be filled with a two-part resin filler of the type used to repair car bodywork.

Mastic is an oil-based filler used to seal joins in exterior wood against moisture.

Using Steps and Ladders Safely

Indoors

Before tackling the painting job you have in mind, you should give some thought to the problem of reaching it. Time spent making good arrangements to reach the work can mean the difference between a satisfying job and a frustrating (and dangerous) experience.

Low walls and ceilings require only a small set of steps or step ladder. For *high walls and ceilings* two step ladders and a plank make a better platform. This speeds the work as larger sections can be covered.

Stairs present a complication. It is possible to hire purpose-built ladder systems for stairs, or you can use an arrangement of long ladder, step ladder and planks.

Any plank that spans more than 1.5 metres should have another plank secured on the top of it.

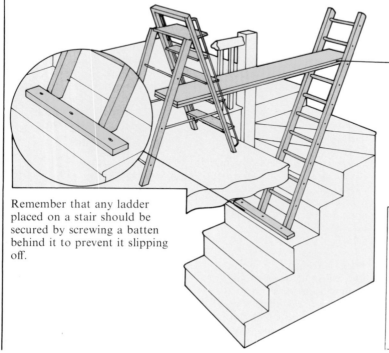

Remember that any ladder placed on a stair should be secured by screwing a batten behind it to prevent it slipping off.

Tips

Examine ladders (especially wooden ones) for loose rungs or damage *before* using them.

Don't stand too high on a ladder. Keep your waist below the top rung.

Outdoors

You will probably need extending ladders and possibly scaffolding. These are readily available for hire and are not expensive. Even if you are considering buying your own, it is a good idea to hire first so you can be sure of buying the right type. One

point to note is that aluminium ladders are far easier to handle than wooden ones. Examine the ground where you will erect your ladders or scaffolding *before* you hire, as some systems can make allowance for unevenness and others cannot.

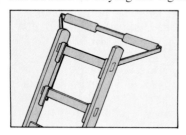

A *ladder stay* is useful on high walls, both to steady the ladder and give more area to work on.

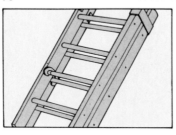

Extending ladders should never overlap less than four rungs when extended.

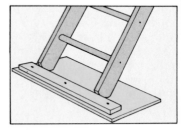

On soft ground, secure the ladder on a board with a batten fixed behind.

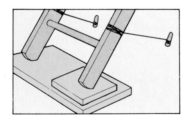

Long ladders must be secured at the bottom by rope or batten. On uneven ground, make a level base by using well-secured blocks or planks.

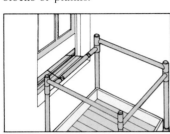

Scaffolding towers must be secured to the building near the top to prevent them from toppling over.

Erect extending ladders by placing the foot against the bottom of the wall and 'walking' it up. Then extend the ladder and pull the foot away from the wall $\frac{1}{4}$ of the height.

INTERIOR PAINTING

Colour and texture can be used to enhance or subdue features of a room. A low ceiling can be 'raised' by painting it one or two shades lighter than the walls. A high ceiling will appear lower if painted a dark tone. In the same way that colours appear lighter as the area increases, light colours increase the apparent size of the area they cover. To help balance a long narrow space, contrast the light colours of the small walls with significantly darker long walls. Highlighting picture rails or cornices can help the proportions of a tall room, while contrasting colours on the woodwork will seem to bring the walls closer in a large low-ceilinged room.

Choosing colours by using colour charts is unreliable, as it is difficult to know how the colour will be affected by the light and size of the surface to which it is applied. The best solution is to test some paint on a small area.

Mixing your own colours with tubes of pigment and base colour of paint allows you to experiment in this way. The main thing is to remember how much of which pigments you have added to each sample (writing in pencil on the wall is convenient) and to let the samples dry before making the final choice.

Ready-mixed colours. Buy the smallest can available and use it on a test area. Some manufacturers supply very small samples for this purpose. They are inexpensive and the price may be refunded when buying the full-size cans.

With all ready-mixed colours, you should buy at least enough for the job as there is often some variation between batches. It is also important to stir thoroughly unless the manufacturers' instructions specifically forbid it.

Left See how contrast between woodwork and walls can bring out detail that would be lost in a single-colour scheme. This staircase has become a sharply defined feature, rather than merging with the wall.

Right A mural in matt and silk finish water-based paint. Designs should be marked out in pencil after painting background colours. Use a straight edge or chalk line for straight lines, and a pencil tied to string for uniform curves. A cutting-in brush is invaluable for this kind of detail. Apply the paint as heavily as possible to keep the number of coats to a minimum.

Colours mixed in the paint shop have a nasty habit of holding a concentrated area of pigment in the can.

Types of paint. Traditionally, oil-based paint has been used on wood and metal, and emulsion paint on plaster and lining paper. This generally holds true with the modern synthetic versions of these types of paint. Emulsions have largely been replaced by vinyl based and latex based paints, which are more washable and in some cases may be used on wood. Oil-based paints have been replaced by several synthetics (such as alkyd) and are generally more hard wearing and long-lasting as well as being more expensive. However, both traditional types are still available. Detailed descriptions of the suitability of any paint for particular surfaces and the correct solvent for thinning and brush cleaning usually appear on the can.

Textures. A major advantage of the wide choice of paints today is the various textures that can be applied to any surface. Paints for wood are available in gloss, silk or eggshell, and matt finish. Paints for walls and ceilings come in these finishes, and also as thick resin mixtures to be stippled or trowelled on, or used with a patterned roller to give a rough plaster effect.

This textured paint has the advantage of covering small cracks and imperfections with a minimum of preparation. You should remember, however, that the surface must be sound enough to accept the paint, and that once on, it is very difficult to remove, stipples and all. It can be overpainted and damaged portions can be touched up, so it is best regarded as permanent, once applied.

Preparing Walls and Ceilings

The first step is to assess the state of the walls and ceiling. Although no longer common, there could be *whitewash* or *distemper* on them. The way to find out is to scrub an area with warm water to see if the colour comes off and the bare plaster is reached. If it does, you must wash off as much as possible and apply a coat of oil based primer/sealer to the whole surface.

If there is *wallpaper* it is best to remove it. However, if the paper is in good condition or has been overpainted already, you may prefer to leave it on. But this does not apply to vinyl wall coverings which must be peeled off and the backing paper removed in the normal way as described below.

Wallpaper

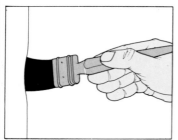

Repair any loose edges with wallpaper paste.

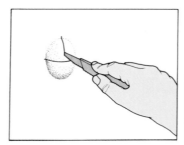

Cut through any bubbles with a sharp blade.

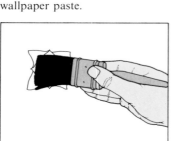

Paste under the flaps and stick them down.

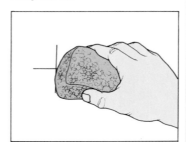

Remove any excess paste from the surface. Leave paper to dry.

Removing wallpaper (see also page 52)
Score the surface of the paper with a stiff wire brush. Using a large paintbrush, soak the paper with warm water containing a little vinegar. Scrape off with a stiff scraping knife, being careful not to dig into the wall. Work on a large area and keep re-soaking until the paper comes off easily, leaving little residue. For stubborn paper, hire a steam stripper. Wash off all traces of old paste before painting.

Plaster, concrete and brick

New walls need several weeks to dry before painting. Seal plaster with primer/sealer (or a thinned coat of the paint you intend using) and seal brick and concrete with a proprietary masonry sealer. This will neutralize any alkali in the mortar that could affect the paint.

Old, unpainted concrete and brick should be washed and, when thoroughly dry, sealed with masonry sealer.

Previously painted surfaces need washing with a mild solution of household detergent and water. This must be thoroughly rinsed and allowed to dry.

Any flaking paint should be scraped back to a firm edge.

Rub the area with abrasive paper to feather the edges of the surrounding paint.

If the previous paint is gloss finish, it must be rubbed down or treated with liquid sander to key the new paint.

Filling

Now is the time to fill cracks and depressions in the surface. First, brush all dust and loose material out of the damaged area and, in the case of hairline cracks, widen them slightly with a knife as filler isn't effective for cracks less than 1mm wide. Use a flexible knife and filler as described in the Tools and Materials Section.

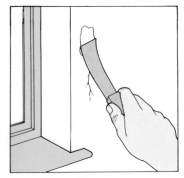

Scoop some filler on to the end of the knife and press the blade flat over the fault, sliding away to leave the filler in the hole. You may need several attempts to ensure the filler is pushed right to the bottom without air being trapped underneath.

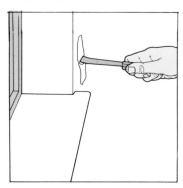

Holding the knife almost vertical, scrape across the top to remove the excess.

Professionals try to clean all the surplus away (including the ridges around the edges) leaving the repair flush. It's worth the extra time spent on the wet filler as rubbing down afterwards is messy, time consuming, and hard work.

Large, deep faults should be filled in layers 3mm thick. These will dry quickly enough for you to apply another layer every so often while dealing with the other repairs. This helps with faults that are wider than the filling knife, as the surface is built up gradually around the edges, reducing the area to be scraped off flush. Remember to clean the surplus from around the edges each time you fill.

Very large areas of damaged plaster should be repaired with plaster or one of the DIY plastering systems that is applied by brush. These are used in layers up to 3mm thick and take 24 hours to dry between coats, so, if the fault is deeper than this, use ordinary filler to build up the surface until only a thin "skim coat" is needed. The brushed-on plaster stays soft long enough to be smoothed with a plastic spreader.

Keep working the surface (re-wetting if necessary) until you're satisfied with the finish.

To get a neat edge on outside corners, hold a polythene wrapped piece of wood against one side and flush with the edge. Then fill as if it were a crack. Carefully slide the wood away when filler begins to set.

Priming

When the filler is completely dry, rub the areas with abrasive paper to ensure they are smooth. Then all repairs and bare patches must be primed with primer/sealer or a thinned coat of paint to be used.

Seal coloured wallpapers with oil based primer/sealer or the pattern will bleed through water based paint no matter how many coats are applied.

To prevent rust stains, prime metal (nail and screw heads) with oil based primer before using filler or water based paint.

Painting Walls and Ceilings

Water-based emulsion paint

Using a brush: Choose the largest one that is comfortable to use for the large areas and a cutting-in brush for edges and corners. Stir the paint thoroughly and pour enough to fill a large paint kettle to a depth of half the length of the bristles of the large brush.

Ceilings: Start at the window end of the room. Begin in a corner and work across in a strip about 50cm wide. As one strip is completed, start from the first side again, overlapping just enough to cover evenly but not building up a ridge. Water-based paints dry quickly, and the idea is to keep the wet edge fresh enough to accept the new paint. It may help to close doors and windows to slow the drying and to paint in narrower strips.

Water-based paint can be overlapped when touch-dry, so if you have trouble keeping the edge fresh, paint large areas separately and join them when the paint is no longer tacky. If the second coat is applied in the same way, make the joins in different places from those in the first coat to reduce shading.

If the walls are not going to be painted, use the cutting-in brush around the edge of the ceiling to make a neat join with the wall. However, if you are decorating the walls, paint over the join with the ceiling by 10mm or so to be sure there won't be any bare patches where they meet. Keep a damp cloth handy to wip any splashes off the wall.

Walls: Begin at the top corner of a wall near a window so you will be working away from the light. You can work in horizontal or vertical strips, paying particular attention to making a neat join with the ceiling. Make sure you keep the wet edge fresh.

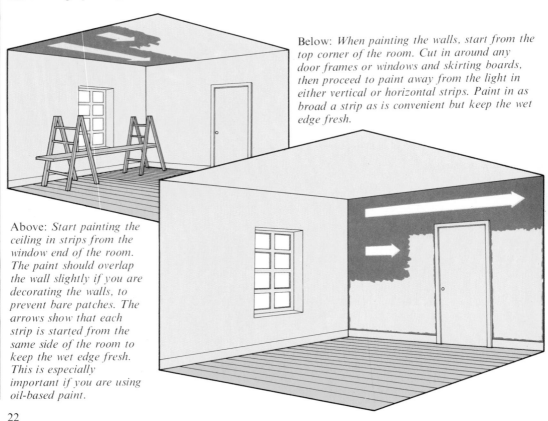

Below: *When painting the walls, start from the top corner of the room. Cut in around any door frames or windows and skirting boards, then proceed to paint away from the light in either vertical or horizontal strips. Paint in as broad a strip as is convenient but keep the wet edge fresh.*

Above: *Start painting the ceiling in strips from the window end of the room. The paint should overlap the wall slightly if you are decorating the walls, to prevent bare patches. The arrows show that each strip is started from the same side of the room to keep the wet edge fresh. This is especially important if you are using oil-based paint.*

Cutting in around door and window frames, skirtings and other edges may be done either before the main areas or between coats.

Two coats are usually sufficient but, if the colour change is great, more may be required. Don't worry about the patchy appearance of the wet paint; this will dissappear when the coat is dry. Shading is another matter. It is caused by greater thickness of paint on some areas than others. If shading is noticeable when the paint is quite dry, another coat is necessary, and you should avoid overlapping in the same places as in the previous coat.

Using a roller: The same procedure applies as for a brush. The main difference is that all cutting in of edges and corners (where the roller won't

reach) is done first. Pour paint into the tray leaving half of the slope uncovered. Dip the roller in the paint and roll it on the slope until it is evenly charged.

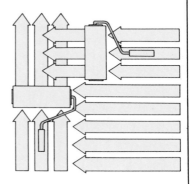

Roll the paint onto the wall in overlapping strokes about 30cm long and then change direction to cover the area completely. You will soon be able to judge how far to spread each roller full of paint.

Oil-based paint

Painting walls and ceilings with oil-based paint takes longer than with water-based as it takes more effort to spread it. However, it needs longer to dry. Each surface must be completed without stopping as it is not possible to overlap dry edges without showing brush marks. Do ensure good ventilation as the fumes are heavy. Use the undercoat recommended for the colour you intend to use. If the surface is porous, prime with undercoat thinned 10% with white spirit. If you are painting over wallpaper, remember that it will be difficult to remove the paper later. Two coats of top coat will be necessary.

In addition to new fittings, the transformation of this coldly lit bathroom is helped by the reflections and highlights in the gloss finish paint. Use moisture-resistant paint for damp rooms such as kitchens or bathrooms.

23

Interior Woodwork

Bare wood requires three separate layers—primer, undercoat and top coat. *Primer* soaks into the wood and takes up all its absorbency. This gives a uniform surface on which to apply the undercoat. *Undercoat* builds a thickness of a suitable colour on the surface and it also adheres well both to the primer and top coat. *Top coat* protects what is underneath. These are three different materials and are formulated to be used together.

New wood needs to be sanded smooth and sharp edges should be slightly rounded. Then remove the surface dust with a rag dampened with white spirit. Seal knots with shellac or proprietary knotting.

Primer should always be stirred first. Brush well in to the wood paying particular attention to end grain and any areas of greater absorbency. Allow to dry completely.

If you prefer, a water-based acrylic primer can be used, but the water will rise the grain of the wood, so the surface will not be smooth.

Undercoat should be stirred well. Use the colour that is recommended for the top coat you have chosen. Brush it on as heavily as possible without sagging or running. One coat is usually enough for interior wood, but for a better finish, apply two thin coats, rubbing down lightly after each one. Allow to dry completely.

Top coat should be stirred unless the instructions say otherwise. Oil-based paint doesn't brush on as quickly or as easily as water-based paint.

Use steady brush strokes to spread it evenly to avoid runs.

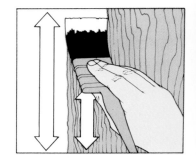

Brush on the top coat smoothly in the direction of the grain of the wood. Then go across the grain to evenly distribute the paint. Finish off with very light strokes with the grain again and towards the area just finished.

Old paintwork, if it is sound, only needs washing with a mild detergent solution and rinsing with water. Gloss must be rubbed down with fine abrasive paper or treated with liquid sander. Top coat may be applied directly unless you are changing the colour. In which case, undercoat should be used first.

If there is any flaking of the old paint, use a scraper to remove unsound areas. Then feather the edges of the surrounding paint with abrasive paper. When only sound paint remains, coat the areas of bare wood with primer and fill and paint as for new wood.

Windows

When painting next to the glass, always be sure to cover the join between the glass and the putty. Use a cutting-in brush and, if desired, a paint shield to keep the lines straight. Runs and splashes may be

Filling

Fill splits and dents with a resin filler using a flexible knife described earlier. For a superior finish, fill open grain and end grain. This is done by mixing the filler to a creamy consistency, spreading it across the grain of the wood, and then scraping the surplus away with the knife, leaving the filler in the grain. Do a small area at a time to be sure the filler doesn't set before you scrape it off.

When the filler is completely dry, smooth the entire surface with fine abrasive paper, being careful not to rub through the primer on corners. Remove the dust and apply a coat of primer over the filler.

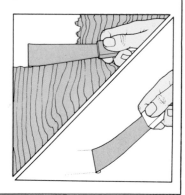

scraped off the glass when the paint is dry. There are scrapers made specifically for this purpose.

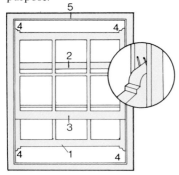

Sash windows should be painted in this order. Leave them open to dry, and insert matchsticks between the sashes and frame to prevent them from sticking together.

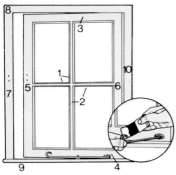

Casement windows are painted in this order. Leave the stay until last so you can adjust the window and hold it still without touching it.

Doors

Remove all fittings and wedge the door open. Use a narrow brush for mouldings and the edge of the door.

Flush doors should be painted in several horizontal strips,

30cm or so wide. Start at the top, brush the paint in all directions and then finish off with light upward strokes. Work quickly and blend each section with the strip above. A large brush is useful as it speeds the work and minimizes join marks in the paint. Use a small brush for the edges.

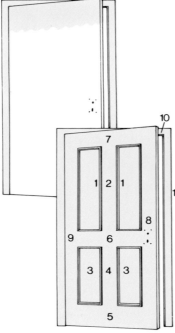

Panel doors are painted in this order. Paint the panels from the edge toward the centre of each. Extend the paint slightly over the rails (horizontals) and stiles (verticals) and finish off neatly along the joins to follow the grain of the wood.

Skirting boards

It is important to remove dust and hair from skirtings and the surrounding floor. Use a cutting-in brush for the join

with the wall and a larger brush for the rest, unless the boards are quite narrow. To protect the floor, you can use a piece of card or paint shield pressed into the corner between the skirting and floor, moving it along as you paint.

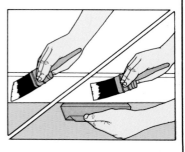

If there is carpet and you don't want to remove it, either use a cutting-in brush to get as near to it as possible, or use a paint shield. Wipe the shield clean of paint each time you move to another position.

Floors

Generally speaking, paints meant for walls and woodwork are not durable enough to be used on floors. However, a little-used room or the edges of partially carpeted stairs may be painted as for woodwork. It is important to remove any wax that may be present with white spirit and wire wool.

There are paints made specifically for wood or concrete floors. These should be used according to the manufacturers' instructions. Bear in mind that a finish can be no harder than the material beneath it, so painted wooden floors are likely to show dents and scratches. Epoxy floor paint gives good wear on concrete and tiled floors.

Furniture and Metal

Wooden furniture should be prepared and painted as for woodwork. Pay careful attention when filling and rubbing down to keep the surface smooth. Also apply the undercoat and top coat thinly, rubbing down lightly after all but the final coat.

Wicker and basket weave are best painted with an aerosol spray or aerosol-powered spray gun. Apply in very light 'mist' coats until sufficiently covered.

Aerosol touch-up paints from auto accessory shops come in a huge range of colours and are ideal if the area is small, but may prove expensive on a large project. You must remember that these paints are cellulose based and cannot be used over oil-based paint.

Metals require specific primers before they can be painted. Most paints may be applied to metal, once it is primed, but water-based paints should be avoided. Also, be sure to use a primer that is suitable for the top coat. The instructions on the can will advise you.

Radiators and hot water pipes should not be painted with water-based paints as they cannot withstand the heat without softening and, perhaps, crazing. Use either oil-based paint or one of the heat-resistant enamel paints designed for the purpose.

Rub down with fine paper or wet and dry and remove any loose paint. Any areas of bare metal should be primed with a suitable primer. Rub down patches of rust to remove as much loose rust as possible, and treat with a rust inhibitor. Choose one that also acts as a primer to save time. Once prepared and primed, use undercoat and top coat in the normal way. Do not clog up bleed valves.

If you are repainting sound paint, simply wash the surface and rub down to key the new paint. Undercoat isn't necessary unless you are changing the colour.

Brass and chrome can be lacquered to prevent tarnishing. If possible, it's best to use a clear polyurethane aerosol spray, but you can use a brush. Prepare the metal with a metal polish and then clean well with white spirit. Wipe thoroughly with a clean, dry cloth.

Top far left *This old wicker chair and new bedside table have been sprayed with sax blue automotive paint to match the wallpaper border.*

Top left *If you can't hide it, make a feature of it. An unsightly pipe becomes a bright pipe!*

Above *By using the same colour and finish paint, you can blend ugly pipes and fittings with the wall behind. The contrasting colour and texture of the fan help the illusion.*

Left *Give an old chest of drawers a new lease of life with bright colours or a mural of your own design.*

Far left *A working fireplace would be painted with heat proof stove enamel, but this unused one has been given a lift with the same emulsion used on the walls. The white gloss on the mantel has been extended into the hearth to complete the picture.*

Special Effects

Beyond painting rooms and furniture an even colour, there are many different effects that can be achieved with paint, Stencilling, antiqueing, dragging, spattering, marbling, wood graining, tromp l'oeil, and mural painting have all be practised by professionals for years.

While some techniques require a good deal of skill, there are many that anyone can use to add interest to decorating. Try experimenting with colour: paint the knobs on your green chest red; use contrasting colours on different panels of the same door; the possibilities are endless.

Above *A modern white bathroom that has been individualised by a simple stencil. Kits of stencil plates, brushes, and full instructions are available from art shops. Artists' acrylic paints are useful for matching colours of fittings etc.*

Top *A bright red front door is quite a special effect, even without a cat! The easiest way to do this kind of design, is to trace a picture onto graph paper. Scale up to size and tape this onto the door with a sheet of carbon paper behind. Trace over the design and paint to the lines.*

Above *The use of strong colours is stimulating for the children using this playroom. Also, DIY furniture benefits from the added flair of a well designed colour scheme. Notice the chalk board that has been inexpensively made using matt black oil based paint.*

Left *Glass paint is available in transparent colours. This can be used freehand or with a simple stencil. Another alternative is to paint each pane a different colour, although this will reduce the light significantly.*

Special Effects

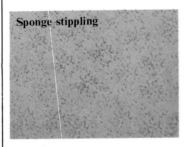
Sponge stippling

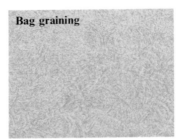
Bag graining

Four points to remember:
1. Choose paints that are suitable for the surface.
2. Don't mix incompatible paints.
3. Allow the first coat to dry thoroughly.
4. Practise the technique until you achieve a level of consistency.

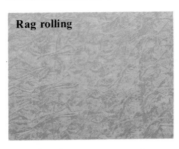
Rag rolling

Sponge stippling is suitable for water-based matt or silk finish paint. Paint the surface with the base colour and allow 24 hours to dry. Then apply one or more speckled 'glaze' coats by the following method.

Place a small amount of the glaze colour in a dish and dab the flat side of a slightly dampened natural (not synthetic) sponge in it.

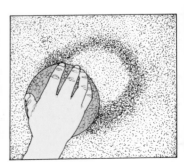

Now gently dab it on paper until it leaves a delicate speckled print.

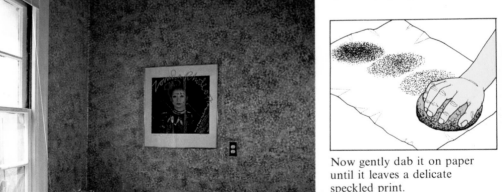

A cream base colour stippled with yellow, blue, and red.

Begin working on, for example, the wall until the pattern starts to grow fainter, and then recharge the sponge and dab it on the paper again before resuming. When this coat is finished, allow it to dry before applying any further coats. If you have made a mistake and sponged on too much paint in some places, this can be corrected by sponging on some of the base colour, after the glaze coat is dry.

Bag graining is suitable for water-based matt or silk finish paint. This effect is produced by brushing a glaze coat over a base coat and then using a rag-filled plastic bag to create a pattern that allows the base coat to show through.

Two people are necessary—one to brush on the glaze coat, and one to do the graining. When the base coat is completely dry, dilute the glaze colour 50/50 with water and stir well.

Using a large brush, one person should start painting the wall in vertical strips about 60cm wide, working from top to bottom. As soon as a small area is covered, the second person must lightly press the bag over

the wet surface. This is done by placing and lifting the bag, without skidding, each time overlapping slightly the area just finished.

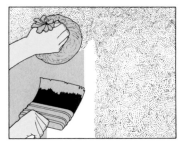

As one strip is finished, the first person must quickly begin the next, being careful not to overlap onto the previous one. Then, following closely behind, the second person should overlap slightly to keep the texture even. It is important to work quickly and not to stop until a wall is finished, as the graining cannot be done when the paint starts to dry. If the glaze coat seems to be getting darker, wipe the excess paint from the bag with a cloth. Be sure to mix enough glaze colour before starting.

Rag rolling is suitable for oil-based eggshell finish paint. This effect is achieved by brushing a glaze coat of oil-based eggshell, thinned 50/50 with white spirit, over a base colour.

Two people are necessary—one to brush the glaze colour, and one to rag roll it off. Brush on the glaze colour in 60cm wide vertical strips. As oil-based paint takes longer to dry than water-based paint, the person brushing on the glaze coat can work one or two strips ahead.

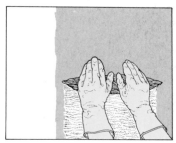

As soon as one strip is finished, fold a 30cm square rag into a sausage shape about 15cm long. Starting at the bottom, roll the rag up the wall, not allowing your fingers to touch the paint. (Wear rubber gloves to keep your hands clean.) When the rag becomes saturated, refold it and continue. When it's completely soaked, change to a fresh rag.

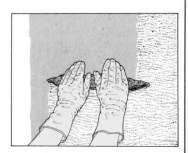

When the first strip is finished, begin at the bottom again and roll up a second strip, slightly overlapping the first. Leave 5cm or so unrolled at the edge of the strip of glaze, and brush on the second strip slightly overlapping the first. Begin rolling at the bottom as before, overlapping the edge of the two strips. Re-roll any areas where the glaze is too thick, and be sure to finish each wall without stopping. Rag roll some paint on to areas where the glaze is too thin.

EXTERIOR PAINTING

There are two main points to bear in mind when considering painting the outside of your home. One is that the main purpose of the paint is to protect what is constantly being attacked by the elements. Water, wind and sunlight will make short work of exposed wood and ferrous metal, so it is important to do the job properly and to keep outside paintwork in good condition. Secondly, the job is almost certainly larger than it looks. Walls that look small and accessible from the ground appear quite different from the top of a 6-metre high ladder.

As with interior painting, you should begin at the top and work down. It is usual to start with the gutters and eaves, followed by the walls, and the woodwork and drainpipes. However, if you are using scaffolding that is difficult to move, devise a plan that allows the maximum amount of work to be done on each section, before moving to the next.

With all exterior painting, the weather must be warm and dry. Rain, frost or condensation will spoil wet paint, so if the weather is doubtful, it is better not to start.

Begin with the side of the house that is warmed by the sun first. This will give the best chance of painting after the dew has evap-

The beauty of this traditional timber cladding and trellis work is well worth the maintenance required. Micro porous paint is best for new wood.

The main feature of this flat fronted building is the windows. The bottom row of windows are balanced with those higher up by extending the white gloss over the brick. Notice the wrought iron railing is painted with the same brown gloss as the wall.

A dark colour around the bottom of the walls can help to hide the inevitable spattering of dirt that is thrown up when it rains.

orated. Continue around the house, following the sun, and stop painting at least two hours before sunset to prevent condensation settling on the wet paint. Remember that the surface of the wet paint will be slightly colder (because of evaporation) than the surrounding air, so avoid very humid days when condensation may be a problem.

Choose paint for masonry walls according to the texture you want to achieve. Oil-based paint must be gloss as it is more moisture resistant than eggshell finish. Emulsion is matt finish and the easiest to use, but not as durable as some of the water-based resin paints that contain mica chips. These *masonry paints* are available in thin emulsion-like liquids and also thick mixtures that give a stucco effect. However, it is worth noting that these are not as easy to apply as emulsion and are very hard on brushes.

If you are considering using micro porous paint, you must also use a micro porous primer. Remember there is no point in using it over old paint.

Finally, it is impossible to successfully paint damp materials. Any areas of recurring dampness should be investigated and the cause found and cured.

Preparing and Painting Walls

New masonry

Whether of brick, stone, concrete, cement rendering or pebbledash, this is prepared in the same way. Use a stiff brush to remove dust and loose material from the surface, and watch out for white crystals that may appear on damp areas. If you find any, wire brush them off and remember where they were, as you must check for their return for at least a week before painting. Keep brushing them away until the area is completely dry.

Treat *moss and mould* with a solution of household bleach mixed 1 part bleach to 4 of water. Brush it on generously and allow two days for the bleach to neutralize before painting.

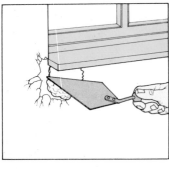

Fill *cracks and holes* with a sand and cement rendering mix after brushing out loose material and wetting the area. Allow to dry.

Finally, *seal the whole surface* with a proprietary masonry stablizer. This will neutralize any alkali in the wall and ensure good adhesion of the paint. It also has the added advantage of making the first coat of paint go further because it makes the surface less absorbent.

Previously painted masonry

This is prepared according to the type of paint that was used before.

Oil-based paint is best washed and prepared with liquid sander, or you can use household detergent, remembering to rinse thoroughly and then rubbing down to key the new paint. On rough surfaces, rubbing down is impossible. Scrape off any loose paint and fill cracks with exterior-grade filler.

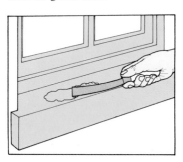

If the edges of bare areas are obvious, use filler to bring the level up to that of the sound paint. Finally, prime areas of filler with primer/sealer. If the texture of the filler is noticeable, brush undercoat on the repairs to blend them in.

Emulsioned walls should be washed with water as strong cleaners may damage the paint. When dry, fill with exterior-grade filler and seal the repaired areas with primer/sealer.

Cement-based paints are not washable and should be dry-brushed until a sound surface is reached. Repair faults and seal with masonry sealer.

Masonry paints are resin-based and contain granulated quartz or mica. Although water-based, they are waterproof when dry, and they tend to peel off rather than flake. Scrub with water and a stiff brush. Test corners and crevices with a scraper to make sure the paint is adhering well to the wall. Scrape off any loose areas and fill and prime as necessary.

Painting exterior walls

Having selected your paint, you may use a brush or roller.

For a roller, use a deep rectangular tray that hangs from a ladder or scaffold pole. This will carry more paint and you can load the roller with one hand and roll it up and down the inside vertical face of the tray.

A stiffer brush or long pile roller is best for rough surfaces.

Start painting at the top and work down in sections you can reach, trying to keep the wet line going. If possible, make the joins between sections where they will show least, i.e. along pipes or in line with windows. Try not to make the joins in exactly the same places on subsequent coats. Cut in around windows, edges and difficult places before painting the main area.

It is better to finish for the day having completed a wall rather than start another and leave it unfinished overnight. Apply the paint generously to keep the number of coats needed to a minimum.

Order of Painting:
1. Gutters and Eaves
2. Walls
3. Drainpipes
4. Windows and Doors

When choosing colour schemes for exteriors, the most important thing to consider is the environment. What looks right in one situation may not be suitable in another. Use of extreme colours or designs may be fun but could offend your neighbours – they see more of the outside of your house than you do.

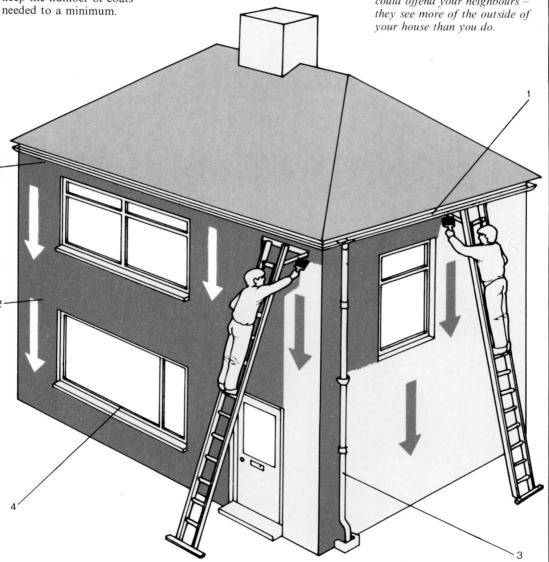

Woodwork and Metalwork

First assess the condition of the wood you intend to paint. It's possible that moisture may have penetrated and started to rot it, even though the paint on the surface appears sound.

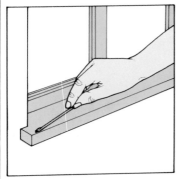

Prod the wood in search of soft areas and uncover and dry out any sodden parts.

Rotten wood must be removed and the area treated with wood preservative. Choose one that can be painted over. Apply it liberally by brush and be sure to treat the entire area including the masonry and anywhere the rot may have penetrated. Also, scrape the paint away from the surrounding areas and treat these as well. Apply two coats and allow to dry thoroughly.

The surface must then be made good with exterior-grade filler or new wood, not forgetting to treat any new wood as well.

New wood should be sanded, and treated with wood preservative. Then prime with a primer that is compatible with the paint you intend to use (i.e. microporous etc.). Fill faults with an exterior-grade filler and prime the repairs.

Previously painted wood. Scrape off loose flaky paint, fill if necessary, and prime the repairs. Wash and rub down sound paint or treat with liquid sander.

Weather sealing. The next step (whether new or old wood) is to seal all the joins between pieces of wood, wood and masonry, and wood and glass. The best material for this is oil-based mastic, sold in cardboard tubes. It is completely waterproof and remains flexible enough to accommodate movement of the wood without breaking the seal. Primer should be applied before mastic (or putty). Careful sealing of all the joints will ensure the damage does not happen again.

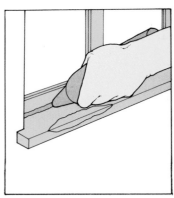

Squeeze mastic from the nozzle of the tube, working it well into the joins. Wipe off any excess with a cloth dampened with white spirit. Leave it for 24 hours to form a skin before painting.

Once prepared, primed and weather sealed, undercoat and paint as for interior wood. Apply at least two full top coats to everything; three are better.

On *wooden walls*, paint along as many boards as you can at a time, keeping the wet edge fresh to avoid join marks in the paint. Always work from the top downwards, whether the boards are horizontal or vertical.

Exterior metal

Metal window frames that have been painted before should have loose paint removed and be checked for signs of rust. If the paint is sound and there is no rust, wash and rub down with wet and dry and water, or treat with liquid sander. Rinse with clean water. Then undercoat and paint with gloss finish oil-based paint.

If there is rust, remove as much of it as possible with a wire brush. Treat the area with a *rust inhibitor.* Be sure to choose one that does not affect painted surfaces. When dry, wash and rub down sound paint or treat with liquid sander, and undercoat and paint as above.

New metal window frames should be already primed by the manufacturer. Clean them with white spirit on a cloth to remove any traces of oil or grease. Undercoat and paint as above.

Aluminium that has been painted before should have loose paint removed and the sound paint washed and rubbed down or treated with liquid sander. After rinsing and drying, prime bare areas with a primer suitable for aluminium (see advice on the can) and then undercoat and paint. One top coat is sufficient for aluminium, providing it is well applied.

Aluminium that has never been painted must be rubbed down with wet and dry and water with a little detergent. Rinse, dry, and prime with a suitable primer. Then undercoat and paint as above.

Gutters and drainpipes of steel or cast iron need good maintenance if they are to last. Remove loose paint and rust with a wire brush, and treat bare metal with a rust inhibitor. Wash and rub down sound paint, or use liquid sander and rinse. The inside of gutters should be painted with bitumen paint and the outside undercoated and painted with oil-based gloss.

Plastic drainpipes and guttering may be painted after washing and rubbing down with fine sandpaper to key the paint. Primer and undercoat are not necessary, nor is painting the inside of gutters. Remember that, once painted, they will need repainting regularly to keep their looks.

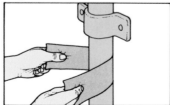

An easy way to rub down drainpipes is to wrap a sheet of wet and dry around the pipe and pull side to side.

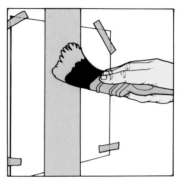

When painting drainpipes, hold a piece of card (or tape it to the wall) behind the pipe to keep the paint off the wall.

Wrought iron fences and railings are quite resistant to rust, but paint won't adhere to rusty areas. So it is necessary to remove loose paint and use a *rust converter.* This is a thin liquid that combines with rust and changes to a black colour. As it is thinner than a rust inhibitor, it is easier to apply to complex shapes. Use primer on bare areas and liquid sander on sound paint. Rinse and paint as usual. Don't be tempted to paint fences and railings with a spray as most of the paint will be wasted; use a brush and oil-based gloss paint.

Tips

If there is a large amount of wood and metal work to be painted, prepare only as much as you can prime in a day. Don't leave wood or metal bare to the weather.

TOP TEN TIPS

1 Estimating the amount of paint, primer, undercoat, etc. you need, is difficult to do accurately as rough surfaces require more paint than smooth ones. However, each can of paint has a guide to the coverage you can expect for each coat.

This is usually given as the number of square metres covered by each litre of paint. When you are buying the paint read the label of each can to see how many litres you need. Remember to allow this amount for each coat.

For oil-based paint on woodwork, one door takes about one-tenth of a litre for each coat. For windows, skirtings, etc., try to visualise the area compared with the door. Remember to allow for two coats.

To calculate the area of walls, multiply the length (L) of each wall (not forgetting alcoves or sides of chimney breasts, etc) by its height (H). Add the results together to give the total wall area. Subtract the area of windows, doors, etc not being painted, but don't forget gables, etc, for exterior walls. A room's ceiling area is usually equal to the floor area (multiply the room's length by its width).

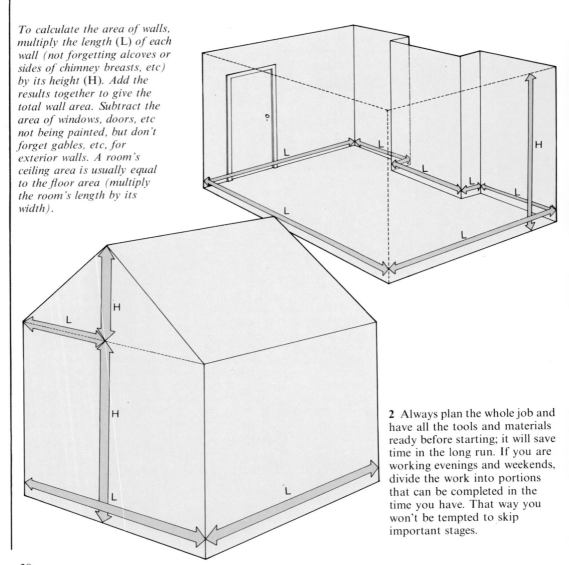

2 Always plan the whole job and have all the tools and materials ready before starting; it will save time in the long run. If you are working evenings and weekends, divide the work into portions that can be completed in the time you have. That way you won't be tempted to skip important stages.

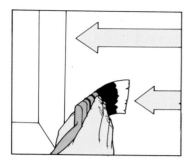

3 To prevent a ridge of paint building up on corners and edges, always brush or roll paint outwards over edges, never inwards.

For narrow edges, always use a small brush or a large brush edgeways on.

4 Cut in to corners neatly, holding the brush this way.

5 Drips in paint that is too dry to brush over can only be rubbed down with wet and dry when the paint is hard. Don't be tempted to overpaint runs and drips while they're tacky.

6 Oil-based paint takes several days to harden after drying. Leave shelves and window sills free of books and vases etc. to avoid marks in the paint.

7 Old paint that is full of bits can be strained through nylon tights. Be sure to stir thoroughly first.

8 Don't use machines (electric sanders etc.) to rub down old exterior paint. Old primers may contain lead which is toxic and must not be inhaled.

9 To prevent a skin forming on top of paint that is going to be stored for some time, make sure the lid is on tight and store the tin upside down. Then, when the tin is opened later, the skin will be at the bottom and the fresh paint at the top.

10 To rescue an old tin of paint that has a thick skin on it and is full of dirt and hardened pieces of paint, don't cut the skin away. Instead, replace the lid and turn the can upside down and remove the bottom of the can with a can opener. Then you can pour (or scrape) out the useable paint.

Safety Tips

Don't leave ladders and scaffolding unattended where children may play on them.

Don't leave them outside where a burglar could use them. Take them down and chain and lock them to a railing or pipe.

Rags soaked in oil-based paint or thinners can be a fire risk. Dispose of them by burning or put them in a metal container with a tight fitting lid.

Cans of paint and other products contain safety warnings about first aid in case of accidents. Read them *before* you need them.

Turn off all electricity before removing switch covers and light fittings.

Be sure to use non toxic primers and paints where they may be chewed by small children or pets.

When using mechanical sanders, always wear goggles and a face mask.

Don't wear loose clothes or a tie while using power tools.

PAPER IT

CONTENTS

Introduction

Wallpaper was invented as a cheap way of applying designs to walls. Since then, there has been produced a huge variety of other materials (such as fabric, metal foil, cork, wood, yarn, plastics, grasses, felt, glass fibre, etc.) whose purposes range from mere decoration to insulation, sound deadening, fire retarding, light control and improving a surface before decorating.

This chapter will help you find your way through the maze of products that have become known as wall coverings. There are colour illustrations to give you ideas about how they can be used, and straightforward instructions to show you how to hang them yourself.

Right *Here, a bold pattern vinyl wall covering contrasts with the stairs to make an attractive reading corner.*

Above *Lightweight wallpaper lends a delicate atmosphere to bedrooms. This traditional pattern creates an authentic setting for the old furniture and picture frames.*

Left *These walls and ceiling have been covered with striped fabric on a paper backing. To disguise the joins between ceiling and wall, a wood cornice has been put up after the wall covering.*

TOOLS AND MATERIALS

Here is a checklist of the tools and materials you will find mentioned later in the chapter. Each item is followed by a brief description or explanation of its purpose. How many tools you will need depends on the type of wall covering you choose and also on how large a job you're going to tackle. For a small papering job, the minimum would be shears, plumb line, hanging brush, seam roller, metal straight edge, and trimming knife. You will also need a supply of sponges, cloths, newspapers and a few plastic buckets.

Don't skimp on materials such as adhesives, sizes and fillers. Always use the type recommended by the wall covering manufacturer and follow the specific instructions about drying times.

Pasting table: Any table with a wipe clean surface will do, but a folding, purpose-made pasting table is easier to move around and keep near the work. It should be at least 2 metres long and longer if possible.

Pasting brushes and rollers: A proprietary pasting brush is better than a paint brush as the bristles are coarser and stiffer. It is important to spread adhesives as evenly as possible as any lumps or ridges may show in the surface of the wall covering.

An ordinary short pile roller may be used when the job calls for pasting the wall rather than the wall covering. A normal paint tray is best for loading the roller.

Hanging brush: These, also, are made for the purpose and it is best not to use a substitute.

Use the brush for smoothing down paper and vinyl coverings and also for pushing folds into corners. Choose the largest brush that you can comfortably handle.

Felt and rubber rollers: Soft rollers are needed for smoothing fabrics, metal foil, and veneer coverings.

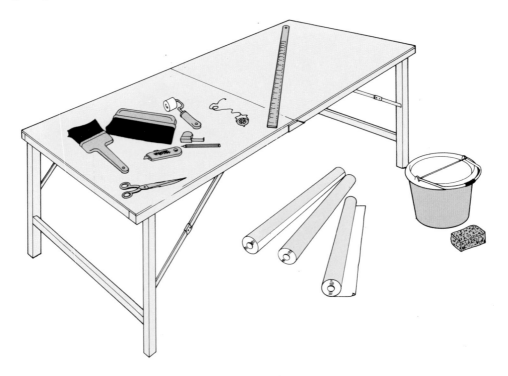

Seam rollers: These are hard plastic wheels approximately 25mm wide that are used to flatten joins between lengths of paper or vinyl. This is done when the adhesive is set but not yet hard. They should not be used on embossed papers, foils or fabrics.

Trimming knife: Choose a knife with replaceable blades, as a sharp edge is essential. Curved blades are best for wall covering materials.

Straight edge: A metal straight edge, such as a steel rule, is necessary for cutting straight lines, usually through two overlapping layers of material, to produce a butt join.

Shears: Don't be tempted to use household scissors. Paperhanging shears are shaped to crease paper into corners for marking and have edges designed for cutting wall covering materials.

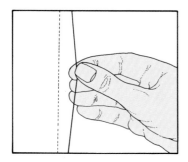

Chalk line: A reel of non stretch string that is used for marking straight lines. It is held taut against marks on the wall or ceiling, pulled away from the surface near the centre, and allowed to snap back, leaving a straight line of chalk.

Plumb line: This is a string with a weight on the end, used to mark vertical lines on walls. Any small object (such as a nut or washer) may be used as a plumb bob. The best bobs are flat so they can hang near the wall without touching, making accurate positioning easier. The line can be rubbed with chalk and used as described above.

Scrapers: Stiff, wide metal blades with handles, used to strip old wallpaper and loose paint during preparation. There are also modern scrapers of various shapes for different purposes.

Filling knives: These look like scrapers, but the blades are

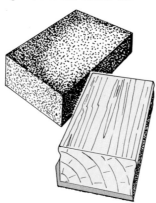

flexible. They are used to apply filler to holes, dents and cracks in walls and ceilings.

Sanding block and abrasives: The only sanding down that you will have to do before hanging wall coverings is when you fill cracks and holes or when the surface is gloss paint. On flat areas, always wrap the abrasive paper around a wood, cork or rubber sanding block.

There are a wide range of modern sanding blocks available that help getting into awkward corners and edges and also abrasive-coated sponge blocks that can be rinsed in water during use to prevent clogging. Glasspaper or aluminium oxide coated paper is sufficient for preparing surfaces for most wall coverings.

Metal foil wall coverings need a very smooth surface as they show every flaw in the surface beneath. Fill any cracks carefully and rub down well with fine grade 'wet and dry' abrasives. These are cloth (instead of paper) backed and are rinsed in water frequently during use to avoid clogging.

Fillers: If you have cracks and holes in the walls or ceiling, you will need to fill them. Even hairline cracks will show through the wall covering eventually. The best filling compounds are resin based rather than cellulose based. These are available ready to use or as a powder to be mixed with water and have the advantage of not shrinking as they harden. Instructions for using filler appear in the *Preparation* section.

Pastes, adhesives and sizes: Different wall coverings need different adhesives. Lightweight papers use a cold water paste, but waterproof papers and vinyls need a paste that contains fungicide to prevent mould growth beneath the wall covering.

If you apply lining paper under a waterproof paper or vinyl wall covering, then the lining paper must also be hung with paste containing fungicide.

The rule to follow with adhesives is to choose the wall covering before the paste. The manufacturers' instructions will usually state which type of adhesive to use, and the instructions on the adhesive will specify the correct 'size'.

Size is applied to surfaces during preparation to take up all excess absorbency. This prevents the adhesive soaking in and leaving 'dry spots' under the wall covering.

Chemical wallpaper strippers: When removing old wallpaper, these jellied water-based compounds cling better and dry more slowly than water. They are only necessary when the

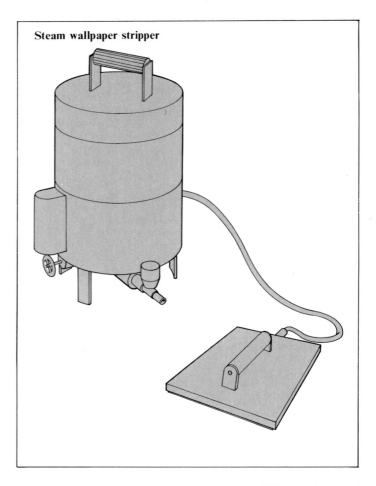

Steam wallpaper stripper

soak and scrape method (described in the *Preparation* section) is ineffective. However, they are less effective than steam wallpaper strippers. *Steam wallpaper strippers* are labour saving machines for removing wallpaper. They are inexpensive to hire and are widely available.

Primer/sealer: Primer may be necessary to prepare a newly plastered wall or ceiling that hasn't been decorated before, or

any areas of filler used to repair cracks and holes. You can use common oil-based primer, usually used to prepare wood or plaster for decorating, or water-based acrylic primers are available. These have the advantage of drying more quickly and not causing the smell common to oil paint.

Masonry sealer: Common primer for cement, concrete or brick that controls dust and neutralizes alkali that could effect wall covering adhesives.

Using Steps and Ladders Safely

Before tackling the job you have in mind, give some thought to the problem of reaching it. Take the time to make good arrangements to reach the work; it can mean the difference between a satisfying job and a frustrating (and dangerous) experience.

Low walls will require only a pair of steps, but papering a ceiling needs a platform running the full width of the room.

The most difficult area to work in is usually the stair well. It is possible to hire purpose built ladder systems for stairs, or you can use an arrangement of long ladder, step ladder and planks.

Planks that span a distance greater than 1.5 metres should have a second plank secured on top of them for safety.

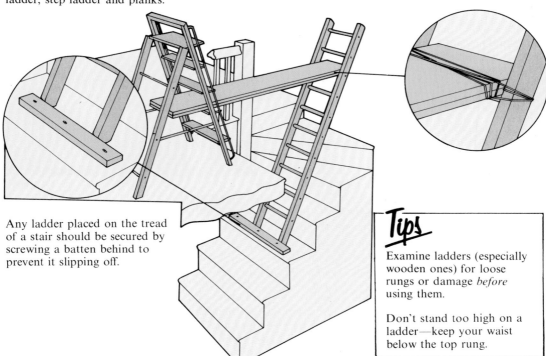

Any ladder placed on the tread of a stair should be secured by screwing a batten behind to prevent it slipping off.

Tips

Examine ladders (especially wooden ones) for loose rungs or damage *before* using them.

Don't stand too high on a ladder—keep your waist below the top rung.

WALL COVERINGS

When buying a wall covering, the first consideration (apart from price) is how much wear and tear the covering will be expected to take. This includes being rubbed by passing traffic in halls and stairs, and the cleaning required in different situations, such as kitchens and bathrooms.

Look around the walls for the places that get the most wear, and choose a wall covering that can take that kind of treatment without losing its looks.

You can use borders to break up walls and use different wall coverings above and below the border. For instance, a heavy washable or painted paper below the border will resist scuffing and dirt and the wall above the border (where wear is light) can be covered with a more fragile (or cheaper) covering.

Bear in mind that moist rooms (such as kitchens and bathrooms) must have a waterproof covering to resist condensation.

Types of wall coverings

Standard papers are the least expensive and one of the more fragile coverings. This is true both when hanging them and afterwards. They are not cleanable, but they can give a delicate atmosphere to bedrooms and spare rooms.

Heavy duty papers are made in several layers, sometimes embossed (textured), and are more durable.

Washables (often called 'vinyl-coated' wallpapers; not to be confused with paper-backed vinyls) are heavy duty papers that have been coated with a clear water-resistant surface that can be wiped (but not scrubbed) clean. This is also useful when hanging them, as paste can be easily removed from the surface without marking. Once hung, these papers are quite difficult to remove.

Very heavy papers are available either with wood chips for maximum disguise of surface faults or deeply embossed patterns that imitate tiles, rough plaster, pebbledash, etc. These papers are usually painted after hang-

ing and are very hard wearing. They are excellent for areas that may get damaged as they can be re-painted and even filled to look as good as new. A word of warning, however: once painted, they are very difficult to remove.

Other varieties of wallpaper include *ready-pasted papers* (adhesive applied during manufacture) that only require dipping in water before hanging, *dry-strip papers* that can be removed by pulling them off without soaking and scraping, and *flocked papers* that have patterns of raised velvet-like pile, usually in

Left *A tiny attic room is given style by an all-over treatment of standard wallpaper. Painting the beams instead of papering them helps to set off the pattern.*

Left *Here is the effect of using a painted heavy paper below to take the hard wear and standard wallpaper above, separated by a wood moulding.*

Right *Suede is a luxury wall covering that needs very careful hanging and should only be used where there will be little chance of it being touched.*

traditional designs. Flocks are difficult to hang because the pile is easily marked by adhesive or pressure.

Vinyl wall coverings are medium to heavy weight and consist of a layer of vinyl (on which the pattern is printed) over a paper backing. Vinyls are hard wearing and can be scrubbed, so they are perfect for kitchens, bathrooms, hallways, childrens' rooms, etc. Their patterns and colours are similar to wallpapers, though they are also available in plain colours with textured surfaces to sim-

ulate fabrics, cork or even tiles. There are flock vinyls and also metallic finish vinyls, and many are ready-pasted.

Although they are usually more expensive than paper, vinyls are probably the most practical (and easiest to hang) wall coverings as they don't tear easily and may be washed clean. However, the fact that they are water-proof means you have to use an adhesive containing a fungicide to prevent mould growth underneath them. Also, any overlapping of vinyl over vinyl requires a special glue.

Painting heavyweight paper (here, below the dado rail) with oil-based paint makes it highly durable.

Reflective finishes like this metal foil wall covering help to create a feeling of space.

The instructions on the rolls will usually specify what type to use.

Fabrics have long been used, but pasting them to walls is a difficult task and the results can be disappointing. However, most fabrics are available trimmed and mounted on paper backing, and may be hung as wallpaper, though some require special adhesives and techniques do vary. Hessian, silk, linen, woven grasses, felt, wool yarns and real cork fall into this category. Bear in mind that natural materials are affected by sunlight and colours can fade unevenly. Also, these materials are much more expensive than paper or plastics, and more easily spoiled during hanging, so gain experience with other types before attempting them.

Glass fibre in random weave is a very strong covering that can be used to hide and reinforce cracked walls.

Wood veneer on a heavy canvas backing can be used to achieve a panelled room effect.

Deep relief panels of a putty-like compound on a very heavy paper backing are made to simulate fabric, stone, brick, tiles and fielded wood panelling.

Metal foils are available in a variety of striking designs and colours. Unlike the vinyl metallics, however, they need careful handling, damage easily, are not washable, and show every slight defect in the surface beneath.

Borders are decorative strips that may be used to separate different wall coverings or finish edges in partially papered rooms i.e. to create the effect of a picture rail, frieze, cornice or dado.

Estimating for Wall Coverings

Before shopping for wall coverings, estimate how much you will need. It is important to buy enough, as most coverings are made in batches and colour matching is only certain between rolls bearing the same batch number. Estimating is made complicated by the fact that lengths and widths of rolls vary. Therefore, you must take the measurements of your room with you and calculate the number of rolls for each wall covering you consider. Dealers will advise you how much to allow for pattern matching with different designs, and usually will estimate for you. It is wise not to skimp as there is always the possibility of a length being spoiled during hanging.

Measure the length of the walls (including doors and windows) and add them together. If you divide by the width of a particular roll, this will tell you the number of lengths (called drops) you need. Measure the height of the ceiling and allow at least 100mm for trimming (or, in the case of repeat patterns, the distance between repeats) and calculate how many drops can be cut from a roll. Divide this number into the number of drops you need and this gives the number of rolls to buy.

For ceilings, decide which direction the lengths will be hung. Then measure how long the lengths will be and add the extra for trimming and pattern matching. Measure the ceiling the other way to calculate how many widths and estimate as for walls.

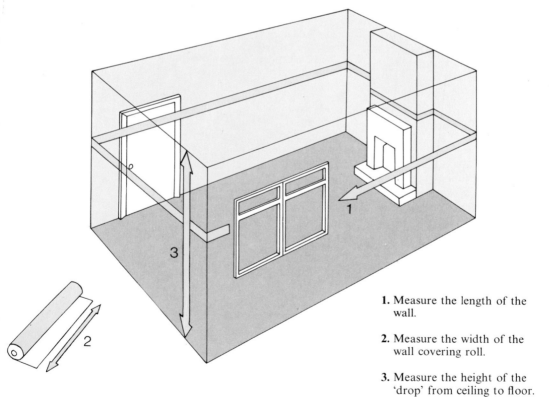

1. Measure the length of the wall.

2. Measure the width of the wall covering roll.

3. Measure the height of the 'drop' from ceiling to floor.

51

Preparing Walls and Ceilings

Begin by removing as much furniture as possible from the room and covering the floor (and remaining furniture) with dust sheets. Then take down all pictures, mirrors and lamps; in fact, anything fixed to the walls. This does not include light switches or wall or ceiling light fixtures.

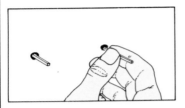

Mark each fixing hole with a matchstick to make it possible to find it later.

Now you need to assess the condition of the surfaces you intend decorating. How much preparation is required depends partly on the wall covering you've chosen. Glossy finishes (especially metallic foil), thin papers and geometric designs show unevenness more than heavy papers and embossed, large patterns.

Removing old wall coverings

As a general rule, old wall coverings should be removed, but if they are sound and firmly stuck to the wall, you can leave them on. However, you can't paper over washable papers, vinyl, or metallic or flocked papers.

If the previous one is a *vinyl wallpaper*, simply grasp a corner and peel it off, leaving the backing paper on the wall. This should then be sized after making any repairs to the plaster. Be sure the backing of the old vinyl is adhering well to the wall; otherwise, remove it.

You have a choice of methods of stripping wallpapers, but the idea is the same—to use water to dissolve the old adhesive.

Soak and scrape method: Score the surface of the paper with a stiff wire brush. This is particularly important with washable (i.e. water resistant) and overpainted papers. Next, fill a bucket with warm water and add a little vinegar (this reduces the surface tension of the water and helps it to penetrate the paper). Using a pasting brush, soak the paper as much as you can.

Work on a large area so that you can periodically re-soak the unfinished areas while you're scraping off. Use a stiff scraping knife, being careful not to dig into the plaster. Keep re-soaking until the paper scrapes off easily, leaving little residue. After stripping, wash off any traces of old paste with clean water.

For stubborn papers, try one of the *chemical wallpaper stripping products*. These cling to the surface and allow more time for the adhesive to soften. Don't confuse these with chemical paint stripper; they are water-based and don't create fumes. However, for papers that have been painted several times you can use a *chemical paint stripper*. Chose one that specifically states that it is designed to strip paper (not only paint), and follow the manufacturers' instructions. Paint stripper burns skin, so be sure to wear rubber gloves and also to protect any paintwork that may get splashed. This is a very messy and unpleasant method because of the fumes and should only be considered as a last resort. After stripping, wash down with water to remove all traces of adhesive.

Steam wallpaper strippers are an easier way of removing old wallpapers and are widely available from hire shops. They consist of a pad (rather like a large steam iron) that you hold against the wall with one hand, while scraping the adjacent area with the other. This becomes a continuous operation, and while it takes approximately the same amount of time as soaking and scraping, it involves much less effort and mess. Remember to wash the walls with water afterwards.

Painted walls and ceilings

Provided the paint is sound, painted walls and ceilings should only need washing and, if it is gloss, rubbing down with fine abrasive paper to 'key' the adhesive. If the paint is flaking, scrape off all loose areas, rub down with fine abrasive paper, and apply a coat of primer/sealer to bind the surface. Powdery paint could be distemper or whitewash. If it comes off during washing, remove as much as possible and, when dry, apply a coat of oil based primer/sealer.

New plaster and cement rendering

These need several weeks to dry before decorating. Seal plaster with primer/sealer and cement with masonry sealer before making surface repairs. After sizing, lining paper should be put up unless the covering you are using is very heavy.

Surface repairs

Filling cracks and dents is done with a flexible filling knife and filler as described in the *Tools and Materials* section of this chapter. Don't be tempted to skip this stage.

Making surface repairs

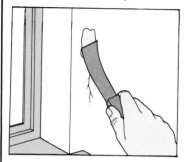

Scoop some filler on to the end of the knife and press the blade flat over the fault, sliding away to leave the filler in the hole. You may need several attempts to ensure the filler is pushed right to the bottom without air being trapped underneath. (If the filler bulges out of the hole, there's an air bubble under it.)

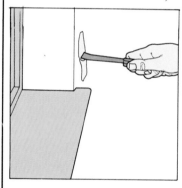

When you've applied enough to fill the hole, hold the knife almost vertically and scrape across the top to remove the excess. Professionals try to clean all the surplus away (including the ridges around the edges), leaving the repair flush. It's worth the extra time spent on the wet filler as rubbing down afterwards is messy, time consuming and hard work.

Large, deep holes should be filled in layers not more than 3mm thick. These dry quickly enough that you can apply a layer every so often while dealing with the small repairs.

This helps with faults that are wider than the filling knife as the surface can be built up gradually around the edges, reducing the area to be scraped off flush. Remember to clean the surplus from around the edges each time you fill.

Very large areas of damaged plaster should be repaired with plaster or one of the DIY plastering systems that is applied by brush. These are used in layers up to 3mm thick and take 24 hours to dry between coats, so, if the fault is deeper than this, use ordinary filler to build up the surface until only a 'skim coat' is needed.

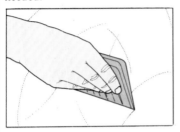

Keep working the surface (re-wetting if necessary) until you're satisfied with the finish.

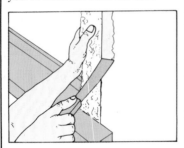

To get a neat edge on outside corners, hold a polythene wrapped piece of wood against one side and flush with the edge. Then fill as if it were a crack. Carefully slide the wood away as the filler sets.

Tips

Use a damp sponge to remove the last traces of wet filler from around the repairs.

Size

Surfaces must be smooth, clean, dry and even before putting up wall coverings. Also, you will have to remove excess absorbency that could allow the paste to soak in and cause peeling.

This is done with 'size', and the type of size you should use depends on the type of adhesive you are going to use.

The way to find out which type of size you need is to choose your wall covering first. Then buy the type of adhesive recommended by the manufacturer. The instructions on the adhesive will recommend the type of size to be used. The most common size is a solution of the wallpaper paste and water, but it isn't suitable for all adhesives, so follow the manufacturers' instructions.

If surfaces have been treated for dampness (e.g. with waterproof paints or foil vapour barriers) be sure to read the instructions on these products. They often specify that only heavy duty adhesives containing fungicide should be used over them.

Size is applied by simply brushing on with a pasting brush or large paint brush. Coat evenly and brush out thoroughly to avoid lumps. The important thing is to follow the instructions concerning drying time. The size must be dry before applying the wall covering. Hanging the paper too soon (or leaving sizing out altogether) is a common cause of problems later. Using size correctly prevents the surface absorbing the adhesive too quickly and allows more time to reposition the wall covering.

Lining paper

Lining paper can be used to prepare walls and ceilings either for wall coverings or for painting, and you should use the correct paper for the job. Standard lining paper is used with wall coverings and a non-absorbent finish paper for painting, although it is possible to paint over standard paper.

Overall, lining a room has three advantages: it improves the final result; it is an easier surface on which to hang wall coverings; and it gives you the chance to make a few mistakes without spoiling the job. Having worked your way around the room once, you will know the likely trouble spots.

The purpose of lining paper is to provide a surface that is consistent in texture and has a uniform colour. This can be especially important when there is discoloured plaster and filler on the walls.

Lining paper comes in several weights, the heaviest giving the most improvement to flaws in the surface. However, cracks should still be filled to give as smooth a surface as possible.

Medium weight lining paper is the easiest wall covering to hang and, as such, is the best introduction to basic wallpapering for beginners.

Before starting, choose the type of wall covering you will apply over the lining paper, as you must use a size and adhesive that is suitable for the top covering—not just the lining paper. For instance, if the top covering is going to be a washable paper, the manufacturer will specify a heavy duty paste containing fungicide.

Lining paper on walls

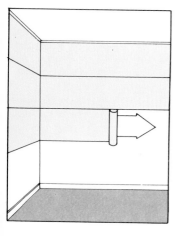

Lining paper is usually hung at right angles to the top wall covering, i.e. horizontally on walls, to avoid any chance of the joins between strips of lining paper falling in the same place as the joins in the top covering.

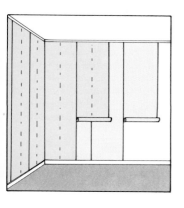

If you are wallpapering for the first time, it is easier to hang paper vertically on walls. But you must plan the joins carefully not to coincide with the top covering by starting in a different part of the room.

Lining paper on ceilings

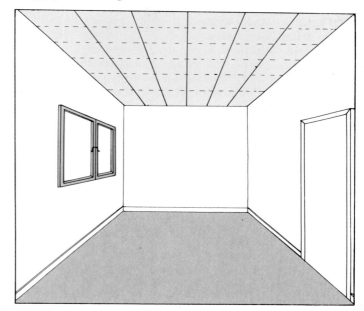

Ceilings should be decorated (whether painted or papered) first, to stop drips and splashes from spoiling finished work on the walls.

As ceilings are slightly more difficult than walls, you may choose to paint the ceiling and confine your first project to the walls. Alternatively, you can line the ceiling and walls and then decide whether to paint or paper the ceiling.

The correct starting point for the finished wall covering on ceilings is parallel to the window side of the room, working strip by strip toward the door.

You should put up the lining paper at right angles to this, but, if it would mean very long lengths (in a long narrow room for instance), put it up in the same direction. Remember to ensure the joins don't coincide with the top covering by starting in a different place. If the ceiling is to be painted after lining, hang the paper in the correct direction as this is the top covering.

Lining paper is hung by the same method as wallpaper (see next section).

Use the right paste and size for the top wall covering, not just the lining paper.

If you haven't hung wallpaper before, try starting with a medium grade lining paper to get some practice and improve the final result.

Papering Ceilings

Begin by assembling the tools, materials, and steps and ladders you will need: pasting table, pasting brush, seam roller, hanging brush, adhesive (correctly mixed), plumb line, chalk line, shears, damp cloth or sponge and clean water to rinse it in, sharp knife, steel straight edge, measuring tape, pencil, and an apron or clean dry cloth is useful for wiping your hands and the shears while hanging.

Now is the time to unwrap all the rolls of wallpaper to check for colour matching and faults.

Where to begin

Set up your working platform at the window end of the room. Working from the source of light towards the entrance of a room minimizes the appearance of the joins between strips.

Measure the width of the roll of paper and mark the ceiling either side at a distance 10mm less than this from the end wall. Fix one end of a chalk line with a nail or drawing pin to one of the marks and hold the line taut against the other mark. Then pull the line straight down with your other hand and let it snap back against the ceiling. (See illustration on page 45.) It should leave a distinct straight line of chalk that will

be the guide for the first length of paper. Remove the line and the nail.

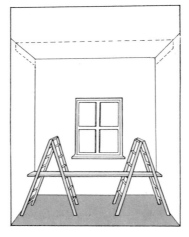

Measure the distance across the ceiling, adding approximately 100mm at each end to be trimmed off once the strip is up. This is the length of the first strip of wallpaper. If the room is regularly shaped, you should cut the remaining lengths at the same time to speed the work. Be sure to allow enough extra length on each piece for matching if there is a pattern on the paper. Also, if the pattern is large, take the time to measure the first length on the face of the paper to make sure the design will be well placed on the ceiling.

Pasting and folding

Lay the first length face down, on the pasting table, overlapping the far edge of the table by 10mm or so. Hold the end down with one hand or put something on it to keep it from rolling up.

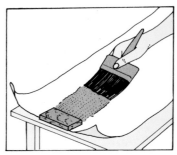

Apply a brushful of paste down the centre of the paper to make it lie flat, and then brush it evenly up to and over the edge of the overhang, always from the centre outwards. It is important to coat all of the paper, as dry spots will show later as bubbles, and areas too heavily coated will cause a bulge.

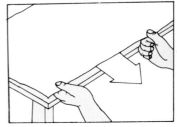

When the far side is well pasted, slide the paper to the near side of the table, overlapping as before, and repeat. Be careful not to allow any paste to stray on to the table as it will mar the face of the paper.

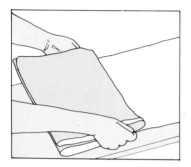

When the paper on the table is evenly and thoroughly covered, fold over approximately 30cm from the end (paste to paste) and lift this on to the next 30cm, continuing to the unpasted area.

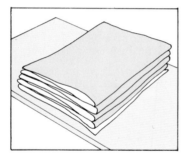

Paste and fold the remainder of the length in the same way. Try to keep the folds even as it makes the length easier to handle.

The instructions supplied with the adhesive or wallpaper will state whether the paper must be left for a few minutes after pasting, but it is important not to allow it to become tacky or it will then be difficult to slide the paper into position. Once you know how much time it takes to hang one length, you can work out a routine so that one length is always pasted and ready to be hung.

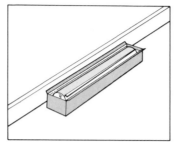

Ready pasted papers should be cut to length and soaked in the tray supplied with them for the length of time recommended in the instructions. Then, instead of folding, you can leave it rolled up to be unrolled a little at a time, as you put it up.

Hanging the paper

Have the hanging brush and shears ready to hand but be careful of placing shears in a front pocket as they can be dangerous when you are climbing on and off the platform.

The platform should be directly under the chalk line on the ceiling to hang the first two lengths. Then it should be moved after each length. This way you are always directly under the important edge of the paper, i.e. the side that is being aligned with the previous length.

Place a roll of paper or a cardboard tube under the

pasted and folded length and hold all the folds except the top one with your thumb. This must be held near the ceiling with one hand while positioning and smoothing each fold in turn with the other.

Open the top fold and carefully align the edge with the chalk mark, leaving the 100mm overlap at the wall, and smooth with the hanging brush from the middle outwards to remove bubbles. If you need to slide the paper, do it with the flat of your hand (not just fingertips) to avoid tearing it.

When the first fold is properly positioned and smooth, release the next fold from under your thumb and move along to put it in place and smooth with the brush as before.

It is especially important to keep the edge of the first length straight on the chalk mark. Curves in the edges will become worse with each length afterwards.

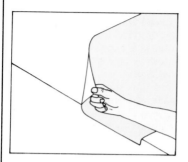

Try not to pull on one side or the other as this may stretch the paper out of true; slide it and, if necessary, peel off a little and replace in the correct position.

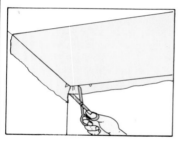

When the first length is in position, make a small cut at each of the corners where the paper overlaps the two walls.

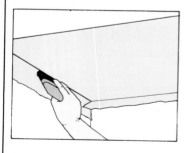

Use the brush to press the 10mm overlap into the corner along one side of the length. Then brush the overlap at each end into the corner.

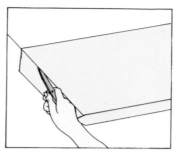

Use the rounded tips of the blades of the shears to gently crease the paper into the corner.

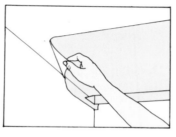

Then peel back enough of the paper to allow you to cut along about 10mm from the crease mark. If the walls aren't going to be papered, cut along the crease mark to leave the paper neatly finished up to the wall. Brush the paper back into place.

Paper the remainder of the ceiling in the same way, each length butting up to the previous one, not overlapping.

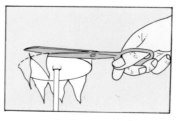

When you come to a light fitting, pierce the paper with the

shears and make cuts outward so the paper can be creased around the base of the fitting. Peel back each piece and trim along the crease as before.

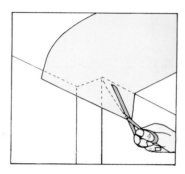

When the end or side of a length falls at the corner of an alcove, hang the paper up to the obstruction and make a diagonal cut up to the corner as shown.

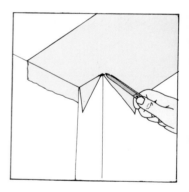

Then crease and trim each edge separately.

The last length probably won't be full width. If the strip of ceiling remaining to be papered is much narrower than the width of the paper, it should be cut to manageable size before pasting and hanging.

58

Papering Walls

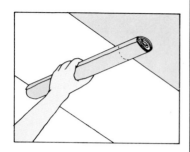

Hold a rolled up length of paper between the wall and edge of the previous length at the widest point, and allow approximately 25mm extra for trimming.

Lightweight papers can be cut loosely folded, but heavier ones may need to be laid out and cut down the full length.

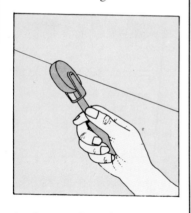

As the paste is setting go over the joins with a seam roller to make sure they are firmly stuck. Embossed papers can be dented by a seam roller; use the hanging brush instead.

Any air bubbles that do not seem to be disappearing as the paper dries should be pierced with a pin and the area brushed down. Be careful that paste doesn't come out of the pin hole and get picked up by the brush.

Where to begin

Deciding where to start papering the walls of a room depends partly on the pattern (if any) on the chosen paper.

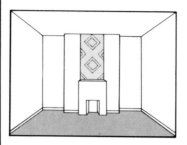

A large, bold motif or a geometric pattern should be centred at the focal point of the room. This may be the chimney breast or the centre of the most important wall, for instance. Also, there should be a complete pattern or motif near the top of the wall. Once the first length is hung, work outward from both sides.

If your paper has a *small pattern* or is *plain* simply hang the first length on the most important wall and follow the rule of working from the source of the light toward the door.

As it will almost certainly be impossible to match the pattern

on the last length, arrange to finish in the least important corner of the room (a doorway near the corner of two walls, perhaps).

Using the plumb line

Start by striking a chalk line as on the ceiling, except this time you must use a plumb line to make it vertical. Don't trust the side of a window or door frame to be straight enough.

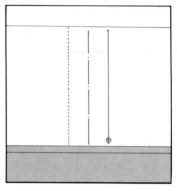

Near the top of the wall, measure the centre of the area where you will hang the first length. Then mark the wall to one side half the width of your paper. Tie the plumb line (rubbed with chalk) to a nail driven at this mark. Make sure the nail is long enough to allow the plumb bob to swing without touching the wall.

When the bob is hanging motionless, hold the line at the bottom taut against the wall with one hand and pull the middle of the line away from the wall with the other. Then let it snap back into place, leaving a straight, vertical line of chalk on the wall. This is the mark to guide the edge of the first length.

Pasting and Folding

Cut the first length (allowing 50mm extra top and bottom) to position the pattern as you want, and lay it face down on the pasting table overlapping the far edge by 10mm or so. Hold down the end with one hand or place something on it to keep it from rolling up.

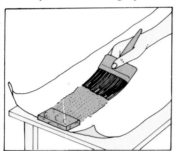

Apply a brushful of paste down the centre to hold it flat and brush the paste out and over the far edge. Slide the paper over the near side of the table and paste that side. Make sure the edges are well covered. Wipe off any paste that gets on to the table to prevent it from spoiling the face of the paper.

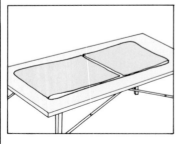

When you have pasted as much of the length as you can, fold the end (paste to paste) over to the centre of the length and slide the remainder of the paper on to the table and paste as before.

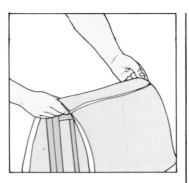

If the instructions supplied with the paper or adhesive state that the paper should be left for a few minutes after pasting, fold the other end over to the centre and hang the length over a chair. Once the first length is hung, you may paste two lengths and then hang one and paste one alternately, so there is always one length pasted and waiting.

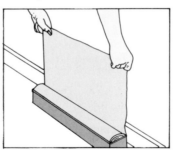

For *ready pasted papers*, soak the length in the tray for the length of time stated in the instructions. Then place the tray on the floor where the length will be hung and simply lift the paper out by the top edge. Allow the rest of the length to unroll in the trough so that any excess water can drain back into the trough. Hang the paper in position and smooth out on the wall.

Hanging the paper

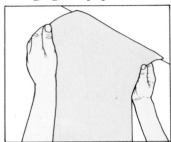

Open the top half of the folded first length and hold it up in line with the chalk mark. Overlap the ceiling by approximately 50mm.

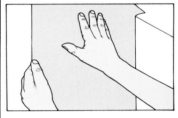

Put one hand in the middle near the top of the paper and slide the length into position. Remember to use the flat of your hand, not just fingertips.

Use the hanging brush down the middle and toward the edge and adjust the paper, if necessary, to keep it to the line. Once you are satisfied with the positioning, smooth the paper to the wall with the brush, always working from the middle toward the edges.

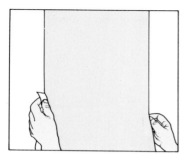

Unfold the bottom half and continue. Beware of paste squeezing out from under the edge and being picked up by the brush. Wipe the brush frequently on your apron or a cloth.

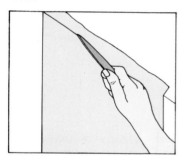

Once the whole length is firmly smoothed to the wall, use the round tip of the shears to crease gently into the corner along the top.

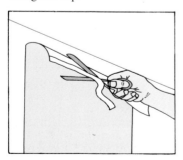

Peel back the top, cut carefully along the crease and brush it

back into place to finish neatly to the ceiling. Repeat at the bottom. Wipe off any excess paste immediately from the ceiling and skirting board.

If the ceiling has paper that isn't water resistant (washable), be careful not to let the pasted side of the wallpaper touch it. Leave a small overlap and don't push it into the corner until you are going to trim it. That way you can hold the end of the paper away from the ceiling while creasing it.

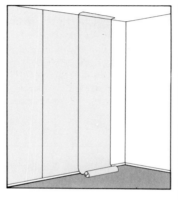

Measure the next length by putting the roll on the floor. Hold the end of the paper up to the wall until there is enough overlap at the top and, if necessary, the pattern matches the first length. If the next possible pattern match means having an overlap at the top of approximately half a length, this is called a 'half drop and repeat' pattern, and you should use two rolls of paper, cutting a length from each one alternately. Otherwise there will be too much waste. If you wish, you may cut all the lengths for the room before beginning to paste and hang them.

Coping with Obstructions

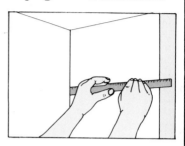

Inside corners: Measure the distance between the edge of the last full width and the corner at the widest point. Allow an extra 25mm and cut a length to this width.

Paste and hang the piece with the overlap going around the corner, being sure to brush the paper well into the corner.

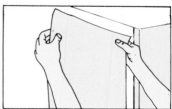

Hold the length of paper you cut off the last piece up to the corner, as shown, and mark the wall 5mm further away from the corner at the top and bottom of the wall. If the piece you cut off is too narrow, use a full width piece.

Using the plumb line as before, mark the wall with a chalk line using the mark that is furthest from the corner as a guide. Paste and hang this length to the chalk line, with the other edge overlapping the first length. Now you can continue hanging, knowing the new lengths will be straight and vertical.

Outside corners: You should not fold a length around an outside corner as walls are seldom vertical or straight.

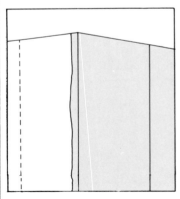

Follow the same procedure as for internal corners, trimming a length to overlap the corner by 25mm. Plumb a new line on the adjacent wall so the second part overlaps the first, as near the corner as possible.

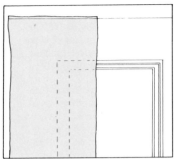

Door and window frames: Hang the top portion of the length as usual and let the paper fall over the frame.

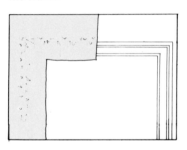

Cut around the frame leaving at least 50mm too much paper overlapping. Then press the paper gently onto the top corner of the frame and dent it slightly.

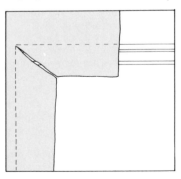

Make a diagonal cut to the mark made by the corner.

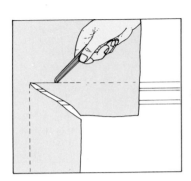

Now you can brush the top edge into the corner on the top of the frame and crease it with the shears.

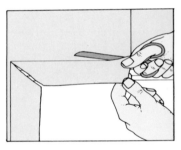

Peel the edge away and be careful not to tear the paper at the corner. Trim along the crease.

Hang the rest of the length along the edge all the way down, and push the paper onto the bottom corner of the frame (if it is a window frame). Make a diagonal cut as you did for the top corner and brush down, crease, and trim the edge down the side of the frame (all the way to the skirting board if it is a door frame).

Light switches: Begin as usual, allowing the paper to hang over the switch.

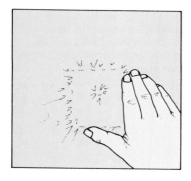

When enough of the length is smoothed to hold it to the wall, press the paper gently onto the switch, peel it back and pierce the centre with the shears.

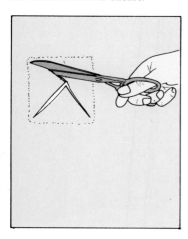

Make a diagonal cut to each corner of the indent on the

paper if the switch cover is square, or several cuts if it is round.

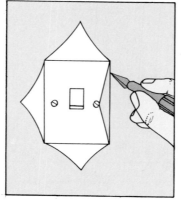

Crease each flap against the edge of the switch cover and trim with a sharp knife.
  Be careful cutting the paper as it tears easily when damp, and wipe any paste from the knife after each cut.

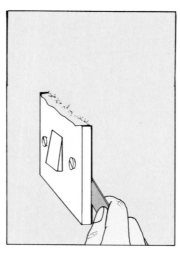

If you first turn off the electricity at the main switch, you can cut each flap a little too long, loosen the bolts

holding the switch cover, and push the edges under it. Don't leave more than 3mm of paper underneath the switch cover. *Don't do this without first turning off the electricity.*

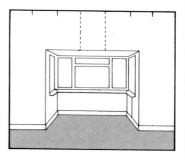

Bay windows and reveals: Using a pencil and a roll of paper as a guide to the width of each strip, mark out where lengths will fall on a wall that has a bay window or window reveal (recessed into the wall). There must be a length either side of the recess that can be folded around the corner. Usually the solution is to centre a length over the reveal and work outwards to either side.

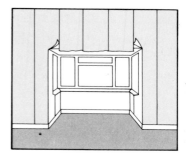

Paper the wall as shown, leaving the short lengths untrimmed. Then paper the ceiling of the bay allowing 25mm overlap up the wall under the short lengths.

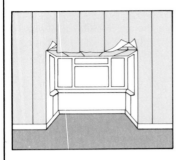

Brush them down (applying fresh paste if it has dried in the meantime) and trim off to the corner.

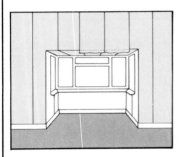

You can use a straight edge and pencil to lightly mark a straight line and then cut with shears.

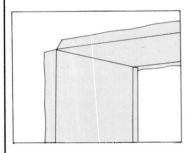

Shallow reveals may be papered inside first, with a small overlap onto the wall around the edges. Then paper the wall as usual, trimming the lengths up to the corners.

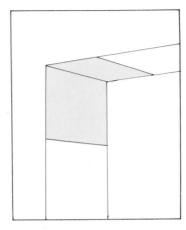

For a *very shallow reveal* (say 150mm deep), you may be able to fold the lengths from the wall into it. In this case, cut and paste a small piece of paper into the top corners, as shown.

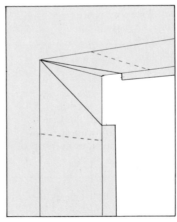

This will make sure there isn't a small area of bare wall left at the corners.

Radiators: If you don't want to remove them or swivel them out of the way, paste a full length of paper only half way from the top.

Hang this length as far as pasted and, with the bottom folded face to face, push the paper down behind the radiator as far as the brackets.

Crease the paper on the brackets and pull the paper out again.

Make a cut from the bottom up to each crease and a diagonal cut to each corner as shown.

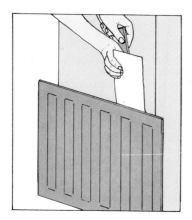

Then, holding the bottom of the length up to the wall, paste the remainder and brush it down behind the radiator. A cloth wrapped around a piece of wood or wire may help to smooth down the paper where you can't reach it.

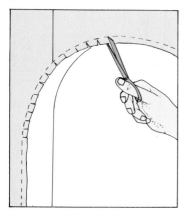

Arches: Paper the wall first, allowing 25mm overlap at the edges of the arch, and make cuts in from the edge of the overlap every 25mm or so, as shown. Fold these flaps around the corner and smooth them down well. Trim off any edges that overlap to keep the edge neat.

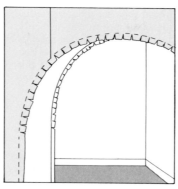

If the arch is a *doorway*, paper the other wall, if desired.

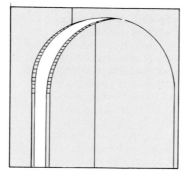

If the arch is a *recess*, paper the back wall area, keeping the pattern matching the lengths above, and allowing a 10mm overlap at the sides and top of the arch.

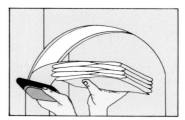

Finish with a strip of paper around the inside. Cut the strip carefully as it won't be possible to trim it once hung.

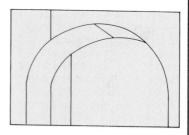

If the pattern would look wrong upside down, use two strips joined at the top. Overlap the ends of the two strips 25mm or so, and use a steel rule and sharp knife to cut through both layers at once. Remove the offcuts and smooth down the ends to finish neatly.

Stairwells and high walls: Pay particular attention to the safety of your working platforms. Take up stair carpets.

Remove hand rails that are fitted to side walls, if possible. If the rail is touching the wall you can trim the paper above and below as separate lengths, but ensure they are lined up. Very long lengths of lightweight paper may tear under their own weight when being hung, so choose a heavy paper or vinyl covering, or get a helper to support the folded length while you hang from the top. On side walls of stair wells, hang the longest length first to a plumbed chalk line.

Hanging Other Wall Coverings

Vinyls are hung in the same way as paper. They are easier in that they don't tear and paste can be wiped off without marring the face. Care must be taken to push them well into corners and around edges as they are less supple than paper and can tend to spring back.

Remember that vinyls need specific adhesives for hanging and also a special glue to stick overlaps. This must be used with care to prevent it touching the surface where it would show.

Paper backed fabrics such as hessian, felt, wool strand, silk, woven grasses, and suede need very careful hanging as the surfaces are spoiled by adhesive or even by water marks. If in doubt, try a small area before deciding. Adhesives and techniques vary and each manufacturer supplies instructions for joins, overlaps etc. Remember that sunlight affects these materials. Also, use them only where there is little likelihood of their being touched.

Un-backed fabrics can be applied to walls using techniques that fall outside the scope of this book. These include stapling to wooden battens or one of the track systems made for the purpose.

Metal foils are also very delicate, both during and after hanging. Adhesive (usually two coats) must be applied to the wall, not the foil. A short pile roller is used as brush marks would show in the surface. Also, the bristles of a hanging brush would dent the surface, so it must be smoothed with a soft felt or smooth rubber roller. There must be no lumps in the adhesive and, of course, the surface beneath must be absolutely smooth. Lengths should be butt joined and unsightly overlaps may be cut through using a steel straight edge and sharp knife as described earlier.

Apart from tearing, the biggest problem with foil is that it creases. Practise on a small area free of awkward corners before attempting a room. Metal foils can be very effectively used as features on panels (perhaps with borders) or one wall to create a feeling of space. Buy pre-trimmed foil as it is time-consuming cutting selvedges, and joins are more difficult.

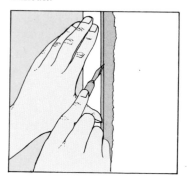

Selvedges may be trimmed before hanging or by cutting through both layers of an overlap, but this is a long job.

A note of warning—metal foils conduct electricity, so switch off at the main switch before trimming around light fittings, switches, and sockets. *Don't remove switch covers and insert foil under them.*

Wood veneer is available on a heavy backing of canvas, either pre-finished or ready to be sealed. As you would imagine, it is much less pliable than paper, often coming in panels, rather than rolls, and sometimes numbered to match the grain of adjacent lengths. As joins will show and overlapping is impossible, it is best to use it on plain walls without many awkward corners or obstructions.

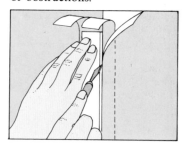

It can be folded around corners and butt joined to the next length by cutting through both at once.

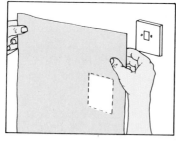

Lengths must be offered up to the wall repeatedly and

66

trimmed to final shape and size before hanging. This includes switches and wall sockets, etc.

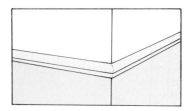

If you decide to partially cover a wall with one of these, a border of wood moulding may be used to finish the edge.

Cork is made in rolls on a paper backing, pre-finished and washable. It is not much more difficult to hang than a heavy paper or vinyl, but, to look effective, joins must be as unobtrusive as possible and, of

course, they can be no overlaps. Be sure to buy pre-trimmed.

Glass fibre is useful for badly cracked walls as it helps hold the surface together. Use the paste specified by the manufacturer. Trimming can only be done when the material is dry, i.e. before it contacts the adhesive, and each join must be cut through both layers.

After marking the wall where the joins will be, paste the wall

leaving 25mm free of paste down each side.

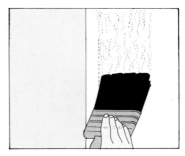

Hang the first length and paste the wall where the second length will be.

Overlap the next length by 25mm and cut through both layers.

Remove the offcuts and smooth down with a roller.

SPECIAL EFFECTS

Left *Pages of magazines or newspapers can be hung in the same way as wallpaper.*

Below left *The success of this tiny bathroom is due to the attention paid to detail. Not only has the wallpaper been used on the shelves and cupboard door, but notice how the border at the top and bottom has been matched with the paint used on the ceiling, mirror frame and woodwork.*

Below *Here are two striking patterns of vinyl wall covering with the joins hidden by borders. Smaller borders have been used to finish the edges of the doors and the bottom of the wall.*

Left Using the same wall coverings on doors and other flat surfaces is an inexpensive way of adding a designer touch.

Borders may be used to divide walls and ceilings and create the effect of cornices, picture rails and dadoes. The main thing to remember is that they must be hung straight as any inaccuracy will spoil the effect. You should always snap a chalk line for each length of border. This includes horizontal and vertical. It is best to ask a helper to hold the other end of the line as you won't want to drive nails into the newly papered walls.

lining paper or newspaper and place the border, face down, as shown. Brush on the paste, allowing it to overlap onto the paper beneath. Take care not to move the strip.

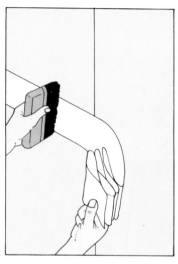

Hang the borders as for wallpaper, but place them in position carefully to avoid marring the wall covering with paste.

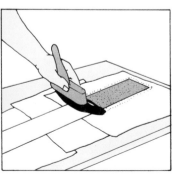

When pasting narrow strips, cover the pasting table with

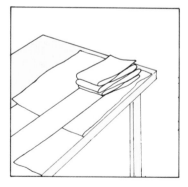

When you have pasted as much of the strip as you can, fold it as you would for a ceiling and place it down on a different part of the table, as shown. This way the paste won't spoil the face of the strip. Of course, you must cover the table with fresh paper for each strip you paste.

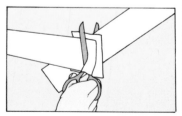

Where two strips meet, join them this way. Placing a sheet of paper between, overlap the ends and cut through both strips at once with the shears, as shown. Remove the offcuts and smooth down the ends.

TOP TEN TIPS

1. Always choose the type of wall covering you will use *before* preparing the room and buying the adhesive or size. There may be specific instructions on the wall covering stating which adhesives and sizes must be used for lining paper or surface preparation.

2. Always check the batch numbers (if any) on the rolls are the same before you unwrap them. Then, on the table, roll quickly through each one to make sure there are no faults.

3. Follow the manufacturers' instructions regarding mixing of adhesives. When mixing cold water paste, always add the powder slowly to the correct amount of clean water, stirring constantly. This avoids lumps in the paste that would show in the finished job.

4. A string tied across the paste bucket makes a convenient place to rest the brush when it's not being used. You can also use the string to wipe any excess paste off the brush.

5. If you're a beginner, try hanging a medium-weight lining paper before attempting the final covering. This will give you a 'practice run' and also improve the finished job.

6. Plan the whole job first. Never let the joins in the top wall covering coincide with the joins in the lining paper or any old wall covering beneath.

7. Keep paste off the table by overlapping the wall covering 10mm on one side and then the other. Be sure the edges are well pasted. Brush outwards. When pasting narrow strips or borders, cover the table with clean lining paper. Place the strip on a clean piece each time you paste and change the lining paper when it's used up.
Use a roll of the wall covering (or lining paper) and a pencil to mark the wall or ceiling where the widths will be.
When lining the room first, use a different coloured pencil to mark where the widths of lining paper will be.

Below A cool and light bedroom with colour co-ordinated paper and fabrics.

8. Wallpaper should be left to soften for a few minutes after pasting. When pasting lengths of paper, paste two at the start. Then, hang the first drop and, before hanging the second, paste the third one. That way, there is always one length waiting while you're hanging the previous one.

9. Save some of the leftover wall covering to use for repairs later.

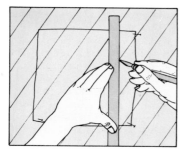

Place a piece of paper over the damaged area (making sure to match any pattern) and secure it down in position with pins. Cut through both layers with a sharp knife and metal rule. Cut a shape that will show the edges least.

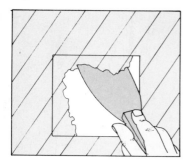

Remove the patch and carefully scrape away the area of damaged paper inside the cut lines.

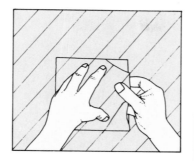

Paste the new patch and place it on the repair carefully to avoid squeezing paste out at the edges.

10. Here's a way to repair light and medium weight papers.

From a spare piece, tear out a piece large enough to cover the damage. Make it irregularly shaped and feather the edges so they are as thin as possible. Place the piece over the damage so that the pattern matches and see that the edges are as hidden as possible. Keep tearing the edges until you're satisfied with the match. Then paste the patch and put it on. Line it up without sliding it and be careful not to let paste from the edges smear the paper.

STRIP IT

CONTENTS

Introduction

This chapter tells, clearly and simply, how to strip and re-finish furniture, floors and woodwork in your home. If you have a particular project in mind, you will find all the necessary information—materials and tools needed, tips, etc.—on a few pages in the appropriate section. If you're wondering whether it would be a good idea to introduce the natural wood look into your home, there are plenty of illustrations to set you thinking and to show what can be achieved.

Why strip? It is the warm, natural look of wood that has made stripping popular, but there are practical advantages too! Modern wood finishes are easy to care for; if they get the odd knock, it doesn't show as with painted surfaces. At most, all a natural finish needs is an occasional coat of wax—much easier than re-painting—and it is just as easy to keep clean as paint. Wood looks better and more comfortable with normal wear and improves with age.

A natural wood finish is certainly the least expensive flooring and one of the best-looking. Stripping is cheap, although you have to be prepared to devote a lot of time to it, and you have the satisfaction of knowing that the results are uniquely yours.

What to strip. Floors are a most rewarding project because of the impact a new floor has on a room. It doesn't matter whether the old floor is parquet or pine boards, a polished wooden floor has a character distinct from any other.

Cupboards, shelves and fireplaces in older houses are often original and of good workmanship. By stripping, you completely transform them, often drawing attention to features that would otherwise not be noticed.

Doors, window frames and other woodwork are obvious candidates for stripping. Of course, stripping all the woodwork in a room is an enormous undertaking, but if you tackle just parts of it—say a particular feature—you can draw attention to it and often tie the room and furniture together visually.

Finally, any wooden furniture can be

Above: *Stripping one feature of the woodwork can be as effective as stripping all of it.*

Right: *The stripped softwood floor matches the table top, and continuing the same floor through the next room creates a feeling of space.*

dramatically changed by stripping. By giving different pieces the same finish, you can combine the most unlikely periods and styles.

You can often find reasonably priced furniture in junk shops and at auction sales, but don't forget to look around your home and in your own attic first.

After stripping. You can change the colour of the wood by bleaching or staining it accordingly. Then you must give the surface protection from dirt and the drying effect of air. It is usual to seal the wood with a matt polyurethane sealer, followed by several coats of wax. For very hard wear, a surface film of polyurethane varnish or urea-formaldehyde is best. However, you will find details of more traditional finishes, and where to use them, later in the chapter.

FURNITURE AND WOODWORK

The most important point is to start small! If you strip and re-finish a small box or one chair, you will be in a position to know which method of stripping suits you, and how far your patience and enthusiasm will take you. As with all DIY projects, the time necessary to complete a job will probably be more than you imagine, so build your skill and confidence with care.

There are three main categories of furniture and woodwork: softwood, solid hardwood, and veneered hardwood.

Softwood. 'Country' furniture, as it is sometimes called, was usually made of pine or other softwood and was nearly always meant to be painted. This is why the pine chests and dressers, so popular today in stripped form, often have joints that can be seen.

Included in this category is nearly all the woodwork or joinery in houses, both old and new. Cupboards, skirtings, window-frames, doors, shutters, panelling, etc. are usually softwood.

Hardwood. Solid hardwoods such as mahogany, oak, walnut or beech have traditionally been considered superior to softwoods and worthy of a polished finish. This requires a more sophisticated construction to hide the joints. Most chairs are made of hardwood because of its strength and durability. A well-made piece of hardwood furniture will last indefinitely, given reasonable conditions and occasional attention. This is true for hardwood household joinery, although it is rarely found. You could find a mahogany mantelpiece or bannister under layers of paint.

Small boxes such as these can sometimes be found in junk shops, and make an ideal project for the beginner.

A plate glass screen replaces an unwanted door without lessening the natural effect of the woodwork.

This hardwood overmantel was discovered under layers of paint. Patience was required to bring out the detail.

Veneer. This is a thin layer of decorative wood which is glued to solid wood beneath. The technique of veneering allows you to have furniture with the outward appearance of beautiful woods, while the carcase of the piece is made from a timber that is stronger, more stable, and better suited for construction. Generally speaking, veneered furniture is the most delicate of the three types, and the most difficult to repair.

Marquetry (inlay) is a form of veneering that consists of a pattern of pieces of veneer inlaid in the surface of solid wood or veneer. It isn't normal to find veneer on old woodwork, but test in an inconspicuous place.

Having chosen the piece you intend stripping, you may first want to identify the type of wood from which it is made. Use the identification guide (pages 78–79). If the furniture has a natural finish, you will be able to see at a glance, but if it is painted look carefully for a bit of bare wood to see what is underneath. A gentle scrape with a penknife in an inconspicuous spot may help you to see what colour the wood will be when stripped.

Look for signs of woodworm (borer). This must be treated with a proprietary product as soon as possible to prevent it from spreading. Check also for any repairs that may be needed. Inspect painted articles for signs of badly-done repairs that may have been covered deliberately. The repairs described on the following pages will give you an idea of the defects to watch out for, and enable you to decide what you feel you can tackle.

Types of Wood

Here are illustrations of some of the most common woods found in furniture, floors, and woodwork in Europe and North America. Practices vary in different parts of the world according to availability and price, but the same general rules apply.

European Whitewood – is a softwood of the type that is popularly called 'pine'. It is used for all types of woodwork, furniture, and floorboards.

Douglas Fir – is similar to European Whitewood and is grown in North America, New Zealand and Europe.

European Oak – is a very hard and durable wood that has long been used for furniture, floors, and woodwork of every type. Although usually used in solid construction, it is sometimes found as veneer. It is also very weather resistant when used outside.

Softwoods have always been the least expensive wood for all household joinery. Included in this category are whitewood, spruce, Douglas fir or Oregon, European redwood, hemlock, and several species of pine, such as Eastern and Western white

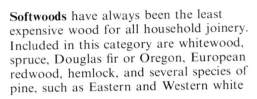

American White Oak – has similar properties to European oak and has been very popular for woodstrip and woodblock floors because of its colour and durability. One property of oak is that ferrous metals (iron or steel nails and screws) can discolour it. Always use brass or copper fixings.

Ash – is especially good for frame making due to its toughness.

Beech – is a fine textured and resilient wood that is popular for chairs, worktops, and desks, etc.

pine (North America), pitch pine, Scots pine, parana pine, and radiata pine (Australia and New Zealand). These are all fine textured, close-grained woods and don't need to have their grain filled to get a smooth finish on them.

Hardwoods are found either in solid construction or used as veneer. Although not all hardwoods are actually harder than softwoods (balsa wood is a hardwood!) the common hardwoods are generally more resistant to denting and scratching.

Western Red Cedar – is a softwood and is used for exterior claddings and joinery because of its resistance to weather. As with oak, you should use non-ferrous nails and screws.

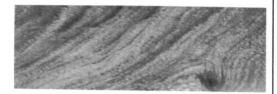

Walnut – is most distinctive as veneer as it can have a very wild and decorative grain (burr walnut), but is also used for legs and frames in solid form. Usually finished medium brown.

Mahogany – is a beautiful wood that has long been a favourite with cabinet makers and joiners for its colour and also because of the smooth finish it gives.

Rosewood – is usually a veneer with some solid pieces although it has sometimes been used to make solid tables or underframes.

Yew – is most often seen as a veneer. Although it is technically a softwood, it is hard and durable.

Teak – is the most durable wood known. It contains a natural oil that resists parasites and fungi. It is most suited to an oil finish. In fact, to apply any seal or varnish, it is necessary to scrub the natural oil off the surface with white spirit.

Damage and Repairs

There are many simple repairs you may have to make. The most common faults are loose joints, splits and warping. Dealing with these usually involves the use of glue and you must take care not to get this on to the bare surface of the wood. In particular, make sure no glue is rubbed into the grain, for it can show through later as a patch under the finish. Carrying out these repairs *before* you strip the wood helps to protect it from the glue and makes it possible to wipe off the excess while it is still wet.

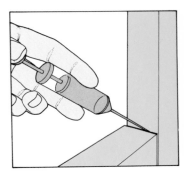

Loose joints

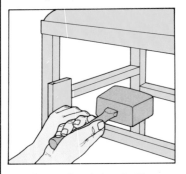

To dismantle a joint, hold one part of it firmly and tap the other part with a mallet. Use a block of wood to protect the piece you are striking. Do not bend the joint too far out of alignment or you may break it.

The original hide glue used in furniture making softens when warmed and moistened. For a stubborn joint, try placing a damp cloth over it and warming it gently with a domestic iron.

Any proprietary wood glue will do when you come to re-make the joint, but badly fitting, wobbly joints need a gap-filling (non-shrinking) glue to help keep them tight. A glue that is transparent when set is an advantage, and of course you should follow the manufacturers' instructions.

Modern glues are almost impossible to remove once set, so be sure to get the alignment of the joint right the first time. You won't be able to dismantle it again. A 'dry run', re-assembling the parts without glue, should ensure all goes smoothly, although it may be a little more difficult to slide the parts together once the glue has been applied.

If the loose joint cannot be taken apart, perhaps because it would mean dismantling many other joints, try opening it as much as possible and working a gap-filling glue as far into it as you can. Sometimes a large hypodermic syringe can be useful for this. Be sure to clamp the parts securely until the glue has set.

Masking tape applied along the line where the parts meet will keep the squeezed-out glue from marring the surface. Once the joint is clamped, and the excess glue squeezed out, peel off the tape. Don't wait until the glue hardens.

Splits

Legs and posts should have glue thoroughly worked into any splits, and then be clamped tightly.

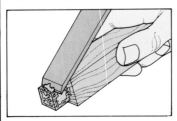

Scrape the old glue off the parts of the joint.

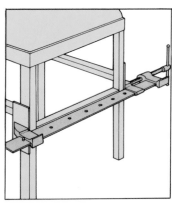

Clamp the parts together until the glue has set.

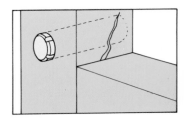

A dowel inserted through the split will greatly increase the strength of the repair, but be sure to make the hole where it won't be seen.

Panels split when the wood shrinks (wood shrinks in width, not in length). The most likely place is where two pieces are joined edge to edge. In such cases the edges are straight and the gap fairly constant.

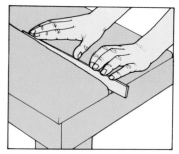

The best remedy is to shape a thin piece of matching wood to fill the gap, glue and tap it into position. This piece should be slightly wedge-shaped so that it fits tighter as it is pushed deeper into the split, and it should stand proud of the surface. The excess can be pared with a chisel or planed once the glue has set, taking care not to damage the surrounding wood. Finally, finish with fine abrasive paper wrapped around a block to leave the repair smooth.

Warping

Warped wood can sometimes be straightened, but there is no guarantee of success. Wood shrinks and swells in width and thickness according to its moisture content, but different sides of the same piece shrink or swell to a greater or lesser extent. The result is bending

and twisting of the wood.

None of these remedies should be tried until the wood has had time (several weeks) to become accustomed to the conditions in which it will live—and then they should be used gently. Drastic measures are to be avoided, and they probably won't produce a lasting cure anyway.

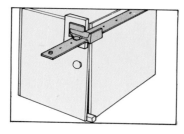

If cupboard doors are twisted, try clamping them closed with a small block of wood holding one corner slightly open, twisting the door in the opposite direction to the warp. So, if the top corner does not close properly, clamp it closed and place the block to prevent the bottom corner closing. Inspect the door after a few days to see whether the remedy is working. If not, leave it clamped for longer.

For solid (i.e. not veneered) panels or table tops that are warped, try slightly moistening the concave side with a damp cloth and a warm iron. On no account should moisture be used on veneer as it could loosen it or, worse, swell it.

Sometimes panels are finished on one side only. This means that the unfinished side will respond much more quickly to changes in humidity so strip and leave to dry before trying to straighten.

Other problems

Blisters in veneer (or edges that have lifted) are simple to repair.

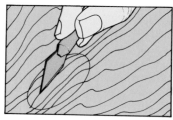

Use a sharp knife and a straight edge to cut through the blister in one stroke, starting just before the blister and continuing, along the grain, just past it. With a penknife, gently scrape out any debris under the veneer and work glue underneath as far as possible.

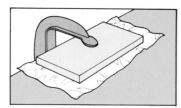

Use either a clamp or a heavy weight to press a flat piece of wood firmly on top of the repair. Place a sheet of polythene between the repair and the piece of wood to prevent them sticking together. Leave for 24 hours and then rub down with fine abrasive paper wrapped around a block, being very careful to rub with the grain and not to sand through the veneer.

Knots. Pine furniture may contain knots that have become loose. Glue back into position exactly level with the surface as they are very hard to smooth down afterwards.

81

Stripping Paint and Varnish

There are several methods of removing paint and varnish from wood. In general it is best to adopt the least drastic method that will be effective. For instance, it is better to use a chemical stripper that can be cleaned off with white spirit rather than water, since it is never a good idea to soak wood with water. However, if the article is so large that you would have to use vast quantities of liquid, or if you elect to use the newer forms of chemical stripper such as the paste or blanket methods then it will have to be water. This choice applies to solid wood—never use water on veneered surfaces!

Whichever method you select, remember to protect everything except whatever you're stripping. This includes your hands and clothes. Paint stripper burns skin and should be immediately washed off with cold water if contacted. Make sure you work in a well ventilated area because the fumes from the stripper can be overpowering. To guard against drips and splashes, place the article (if it's movable) on many layers of newspapers or put newspapers all around it. You should remove metal fittings.

The other point to remember is to proceed slowly on one area or surface at a time. There is nothing more frustrating than rushing from one patch to another, never quite finishing properly.

Tools and materials: Enough stripper for the area you are working on (see manufacturers' instructions); various metal scraping knives; coarse wire wool; an old paint brush; a metal container (not plastic) to scrape the paint into; lots of newspapers; rubber gloves; white spirit; clean rags; a container of clean water in case of accidents; scrubbing brush; trowel (for paste method); plastic spatula (for blanket method); thick working gloves (for blowtorch or hot air methods).

82

Liquid and jellied chemical strippers

Choose one that is soluble in both water and white spirit to give you the choice when cleaning it off. Wipe the surface to be stripped with white spirit to remove any wax.

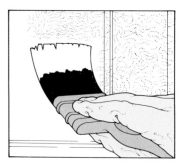

Brush the stripper on quite thickly and allow it to remain until the paint begins to crinkle. If there are many layers of paint, it will take some time for the stripper to penetrate.

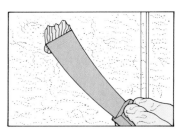

Push some of the paint aside with a scraper to see if the bare wood has been reached. If you can see the wood, or if the stripper seems to have stopped working, gently scrape off the mixture of paint and stripper into the metal container. Re-apply stripper to areas of paint that remain—don't be tempted to dig at stubborn areas with the scraper as you will damage the wood.

When all the surface layers of paint are gone, dip a piece of wire wool in stripper and rub the surface with it to remove the last traces. As each piece of wire wool becomes clogged with paint, put it into the container with the scrapings and start another piece.

When all the paint or varnish is removed, the surface must be cleaned thoroughly to remove all traces of the stripper which would otherwise dissolve the new finish. If you are using water, a scrubbing brush is useful for getting into grooves and corners. Remember that water will raise the grain of the wood and mean more sanding smooth later. [Don't use water on veneer.] The alternative to water is white spirit applied with wire wool and then with a cloth. Keep cleaning until you are certain all trace of the stripper is gone.

A new liquid stripper is becoming available (in some markets) that doesn't need to be washed, just peeled off.

Metal fittings, e.g. handles, hinges, etc., that you have removed can be stripped by leaving them in a glass jar of liquid stripper. When the paint has dissolved, rinse well and allow to dry.

Paste strippers

These are less messy than the liquids, especially on vertical and overhead surfaces. There are two types, both applied as a paste, but one combines with the paint and peels off with it. It is sometimes possible to re-use the paste, provided it has been kept moist. Their main disadvantage is that they must

be washed off with water and so can not be used on veneer. There can also be a tendency for paste strippers to darken wood, though this can be remedied by using a colour restorer.

First wipe the work with white spirit to remove any wax.

Trowel on the paste at least 3mm thick, working it well into crevices and corners and making sure there are no air bubbles under it. The paste must be kept moist while it works, so cover it with a sheet of polythene or give it an occasional spray of water. It may take from fifteen minutes to several hours for every layer of paint to be penetrated, so check for bare wood periodically by lifting a small area of the paste.

When you think it's ready, gently lift the paste and paint

(they will come off in pieces) or, if you're using the peelable type, peel the layer of paint and stripper away from the wood and place in the container. Keep re-applying moist paste as necessary to remove all the paint. To clean off, use water and a scrubbing brush or wire wool until you are certain all trace of the stripper is gone. Use plenty of clean water for a final rinse and allow to dry thoroughly.

Blanket method

This is a chemical stripping method that uses a paste on which you place a special fibrous blanket. This makes it possible to peel the blanket off together with the old paint. It is very useful for complex shapes and hard-to-reach places and is the least messy stripper to use. Against it, however, is the fact that it takes longer to work than the others and must be cleaned off afterwards with water; so it shouldn't be used on veneer or particularly good pieces of furniture.

Mix the powder with water according to the instructions, stir, and leave to stand for ten minutes.

Apply a thick layer of paste over an area that can be covered with the blanket (if

necessary, cut the blanket to suit the area you're stripping). Make sure the paste is worked well into corners, grooves, etc. Wet the blanket in soapy water, wring out, and apply it to the pasted surface (it should cling without being supported).

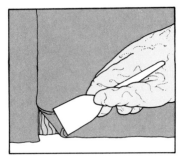

Leave it for two hours and then, using the plastic spatula, peel back a small part of the blanket to see if bare wood is showing underneath. If it isn't, cover again with the blanket and leave for another hour. Keep testing occasionally until every layer of paint is penetrated, showing the wood beneath.

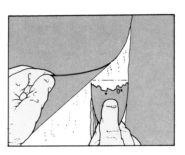

Wearing the gloves, peel the blanket away with one hand and lift off the paint with the spatula, keeping paste, paint and blanket together as much as possible. Wash the blanket well in hot soapy water, after

removing as much of the paint residue as you can. Leave the blanket in the water, ready for the next use. Re-apply fresh paste to any areas of paint remaining, using the blanket only if it seems it will be necessary to leave it some hours.

When all the paint is gone, remove any paste from the wood by scrubbing with a solution of warm water and a little vinegar. Sponge off, using single strokes and a warm water and vinegar solution. Finally, wipe all the wood with a cloth and neat vinegar. Allow to dry.

Blowtorches and hot air paint strippers

Heat is an effective way of softening paint, but great care must be taken not to scorch the wood as burns are very difficult to remove. However, if you are careful, this can be an inexpensive way to strip a large area. Remember not to use heat directly on glass, such as windows.

Always work with the grain of the wood, not across it, and try not to dig into the surface. With a little practice, you will be able to use the torch or blower while lifting off with the scraper in a continuous operation. The paint is soft

Stripping Clear Finishes

when hot, but it cools quickly to hard again, so it is important to remove each area of paint as soon as it is ready. Be sure to wear a thick glove on the hand holding the scraper and take care not to drop hot scrapings on your arm or foot as they can burn. Put out any paint that catches fire and keep an eye on the heat when you get near the ceiling. When you have removed as much paint as possible with the scraper, use liquid stripper and wire wool to strip the last layer.

Caustic dipping

A commercial process, not suitable for do-it-yourself use. It should only be considered as a last resort as there can be warping and loosening of joints. Caustic removes all the natural oils from wood and leaves it looking bleached out and slightly greyish. It is necessary to neutralise the caustic after dipping and some companies do this but, if there is any doubt, rinse the article with a solution of vinegar and water and finally with clean water. When dry, some of the colour can be put back with a proprietary colour restorer.

Tips

After caustic dipping, hose down large articles in the garden or yard.

Don't use water on veneer.

Don't dig at stubborn areas with a scraper—you'll damage the wood. Apply more stripper.

First you must find out what finish you are trying to remove. Begin by rubbing an area with a cloth dipped in white spirit to dissolve any wax on the surface. Keep rubbing until the cloth remains clean. If you seem to be getting down to bare wood and still removing something, then you are dealing with a *wax* or *oil finish*.

If the cloth and white spirit stop affecting the finish on your test area, dab on some methylated spirit and see if the surface becomes tacky. If it does then the finish is *French polish* (or some other *shellac-based polish*).

If your test area was not affected by methylated spirits, the finish is either *varnish* or *cellulose lacquer*.

Wax or Oil Finish: Scrub the wood with white spirit and fine wire wool until you are certain it is all removed. Wipe with a cloth and white spirit to check for any last traces—if the cloth is discoloured, something is still on the wood. If you have bought a piece of stripped pine furniture, it will probably have wax on it and this will need removing before staining or other finishing is possible.

French Polish (shellac): If your work piece is solid wood (not veneer) you can use methylated spirit and fine wire wool to remove the polish. Methylated spirit contains water and raises the grain of the wood, giving you extra work sanding it smooth later. If you do strip polish with methylated spirits, be careful not to soak any veneer, inlays or marquetry.

The alternative is to use a

white-spirit-soluble liquid paint stripper (buy one that states it will remove polish) and fine wire wool.

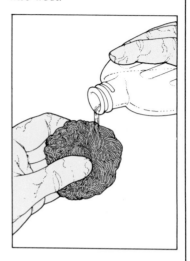

Apply the stripper to the wire wool and, when this becomes clogged with polish, put it into a metal container and start another.

Work quickly on veneer as the stripper could soften the glue that holds it down. As each small area is stripped, clean immediately with white spirit on a cloth. Don't leave the stripper on the wood as if you were stripping paint.

Varnish and Cellulose Lacquer: These should be stripped with a liquid stripper as for paint; but you shouldn't need as much stripper and it should take less time to work. Use a stripper that states it will remove cellulose lacquer. Clean with white spirit to remove all trace of stripper.

If the piece is veneered, try using wire wool as described above.

This old varnished scullery dresser was purchased at a very reasonable cost because of its rather lacklustre, dark appearance. After stripping and refinishing, while not perfect, it becomes an attractive addition to any kitchen. New fittings help to enhance its bright, fresh appearance. A piece of furniture this size takes some time to strip, so it would be best to house it in a garage or little used room until finished.

Sanding and Filling

Sanding

Now that the wood is bare, you can assess the condition of the surface. Check carefully for dents, scratches and burns.

Shallow scratches can be sanded out, but too much sanding in one place can leave a depression that will be noticeable later. While sanding, try to widen the area around a scratch to blend with the surface. Always sand in the direction of the grain—never across it.

An electric orbital (not a disc) sander is useful for large flat surfaces, but use a fine grit paper as there will be small circular scratches that will need sanding by hand in the direction of the grain. If possible, use these machines outside as they create a lot of dust, and wear goggles and face mask.

For flat surfaces, the sandpaper should be wrapped around a block of wood, or a cork or rubber sanding block.

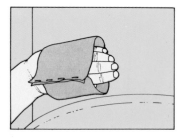

When dealing with large curves, you can staple the two ends of the paper together and put your hand through the middle, like a glove. For grooves and awkward shapes, wrap the paper around any object that will give you a useful shape. The important thing is to sand all the wood thoroughly. Be careful with veneer—it's possible to sand right through it, especially near the edges.

Dents can sometimes be pulled up again if you place a damp cloth over them and warm them with a domestic iron. Once again, this treatment is not suitable for veneer.

Burns must be sanded out until the charred colour is removed, and filled if necessary.

Filling

Before filling, decide whether you wish to change the colour of the wood (and perhaps test a small area) so you know what colour of filler to use. In general, fillers should be a little darker than the final colour of the wood as they won't absorb stain once they're dry.

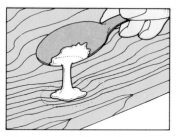

If the wood will not have heavy wear, a little *wax* (from a crayon or candle of a suitable colour) melted in a spoon and dripped into the fault will do. Let the wax cool and gently shave off the excess with a sharp blade.

If you intend to varnish the piece, you will need to seal all the wax repairs with a shellac polish first, as oil-based products will not adhere to the wax.

Alternatively, use a cigarette lighter to melt a *shellac stick* of an appropriate colour over the fault and, when it begins to harden, use a sharp blade to remove the excess. Rub smooth with fine wire wool.

For more durable fillers, use *proprietary stopper*. These come in various colours and shades that can be mixed together or with woodstains.

Apply the stopper with a flexible knife, leave until hard, then sand smooth. Try to keep the filler from spreading away from the dent. It tends to show in the grain of the surrounding wood if rubbed in when it's wet. It is better to overfill and sand off later than to spread it around.

Remember that you can't restore any surface to perfection, so it's worth considering how much filling your furniture really needs. A slight dent in the surface is preferable to a large expanse of filler.

Grain filler is used to fill the pores on open grain hardwoods such as mahogany, oak, ash and beech. The pores appear as tiny pinholes or as lines in the surface and they will show in the finish.

The easiest way to fill them is to use proprietary grain filler that is applied by brush or cloth. When partially dry, it is rubbed off across the grain, leaving the filler only in the grain and not on the surface. When completely dry, it should be sanded smooth. More than one application may be necessary.

Changing the Colour

Now that you have prepared the bare wood, you have the choice of staining it darker or bleaching it lighter. If the wood has accidental stains that still show after stripping and sanding, you can try a two-part wood bleach over the whole surface. This should remove the stains, but will lighten the wood as well. If desired, it can then be stained darker again.

Bleaching is best done with proprietary wood bleach systems and the manufacturers' instructions should be followed exactly. One point to remember is that all bleaches require the use of water, so you are advised not to use them on veneers.

Stains are available in three types—oil-, spirit-, and water-based. The easiest to use are oil-based as they do not raise the grain or affect veneer. Choose one that states it is diluted with white spirit and buy colours from one manufacturer to be sure you can mix them together to get the colour you want. Test on an inconspicuous part of the piece in strong daylight. Apply the stain with a soft lint-free cloth (or a brush can be used for large areas). Try not to flood the surface of the wood and keep working until each surface is evenly covered. Overlapping where stain has already penetrated will produce a dark line. You

Stripped and stained to resemble mahogany, this desk, shelf and window frame have been brought together to make an attractive work area.

Right: *Here is a selection from the extensive range of colours and natural wood shades widely available in stains and varnishes.*

should also watch out for areas of wood that are more absorbent than the rest, especially ends of pieces of wood (end grain) and edges near joints. Wiping with white spirit before staining will help to make the absorbency more constant. Subsequent coats of stain will darken the wood further, but as it is not removable, test an inconspicuous area beforehand. Stains work best with natural wood colours. Results may be disappointing with other colours such as green, blue, etc. because of the different areas of absorbency in the wood. For these colours, it is better to use coloured varnish.

Coloured varnish is available in various colours and natural wood shades as well as matt, satin, and gloss finish. There is the advantage of applying both colour and finish in one operation, but as the colour is on the surface, any chipping will show the bare wood colour beneath. In order to keep the colour even, it is best to apply a coat of clear varnish before the coloured one. This will keep areas of greater absorbency from showing darker.

Fuming is another way of darkening wood. It is suitable for hardwoods such as oak, mahogany and walnut. See page 102 for the technique.

Refinishing

The range of finishes for wood is extremely wide, but in choosing one, bear in mind the wear the surface will receive. For instance, coloured varnish on a door or door frame would soon be chipped, and French polish on a kitchen table would be spoiled with normal use. So, first decide whether the surface should be heat, water and alcohol proof.

Traditional oil, wax, and shellac-based polish finishes are marred or stained by hot plates, water and spilled drinks, and general hard wear. Therefore, table tops, work surfaces, banisters, doors, chairs, etc. are best finished with polyurethane sealer, polyurethane varnish, or two-part plastic resin finishes. These will stand up well and may be waxed to mellow their appearance. On the other hand, some furniture and many parts of woodwork receive very little wear and aren't threatened by heat or liquids. With these you have the choice of any finish.

Here is a list of finishing methods, starting with the two types that are easiest to apply and give the best results.

Sealers and polyurethane varnish

(hard wearing, heat and moisture proof)
A sealer differs from a varnish in that it is absorbed into the surface of the wood rather than forming a film on top of it.

However, for furniture (as opposed to floors) two coats of matt-finish varnish thinned 10% with white spirit is an effective sealer. It will protect the wood from liquids and dirt, while avoiding the slightly artificial look of several coats of gloss varnish. It is also easier to apply as it is brushed on thinly and each coat (including the final one) is lightly rubbed with fine wire wool to remove any runs or rough spots.

When the final coat is dry, you should apply several coats of wax polish to protect it. Maintenance is simply an occasional wipe and coat of polish.

Shellac-based polishes

(easy and quick to apply; neither hard wearing nor heat proof)
There are several of these, namely French polish, button polish, white sealer, etc. They are all easy to apply as wood sealers and have the advantage of drying very quickly.

Apply them by brush or cloth, thinning with methylated spirits if necessary. Rub down lightly with fine wire wool between coats. As they dry so quickly, there shouldn't be any waiting. Apply successive coats until the surface of the wood seems full and smooth. Allow the final coat to dry for a few hours and then apply several coats of wax polish.

This finish should not be confused with traditional French polishing.

Traditional wax finish

(hard work; neither hard wearing nor heat proof)
Melt equal quantities of shredded beeswax and turpentine in a tin placed in a dish of hot water. The vapour is inflammable so don't do this near a flame. Once melted, stir and allow to cool.

Apply a thin coat with a cloth, rubbing in a circular motion to work the wax well into the grain. Leave it for 24 hours to harden, and then polish vigorously. At least 5 coats will be necessary.

Modern wax finish

There are several proprietary wax polishes that are faster drying and more resilient than beeswax. These come with full instructions but remember that wax on bare wood is not a very practical finish. You can always seal first with shellac or polyurethane varnish.

Traditional oil finish

(*hard work; not heat proof*)
Mix equal parts of boiled and raw linseed oil and simmer for 15 minutes. Add $\frac{1}{8}$th part

turpentine, and allow to cool.

Rub the oil into the wood with 400 grit wet and dry paper, working with the grain. Wipe off the slurry that is produced with a cloth, rubbing across the grain, and leave to dry for 24 hours. Repeat until a shiny finish is produced.

Cloths used with this oil should be disposed of by burning immediately after use as there is a danger of spontaneous combustion.

Modern oil finish

(*easy; not heat proof*)
Teak oil or Danish oil do not produce the high gloss of the traditional oil finish, but they can be reapplied easily and can be buffed to a satin sheen.

Apply with brush or cloth and allow to dry. Read the

instructions on the tin as some products contain fungicide and are meant for outdoor use only.

Cloths should be disposed of by burning immediately after use as there is a danger of spontaneous combustion.

Polyurethane varnish

This is the most popular do-it-yourself finish. There are many brands on the market, usually available in gloss, satin and matt finishes.

Apply with a soft brush, the first coat thinned 10% with white spirit. For a smooth finish it is best to rub down with fine wire wool after each coat except the last; at least two coats will be necessary.

This finish can look artificial, but it's possible to use it as a sealer and mellow with wax.

FLOORS

Wooden floors are of two kinds. The most common are *floorboards* (usually softwood, but not always) that are nailed to timbers beneath. The other type is *hardwood block*, *strip* or *parquet*. These consist of pieces of hardwood that are glued to a smooth surface below. Some modern floors of this type use veneered plywood, rather than solid wood;

these are not suitable for stripping. It is only in preparation that the two types are treated differently.

Sanding and sealing of floors must be done in one operation, so you must arrange to have all the materials beforehand and allow plenty of time without traffic in the room. The room should be emptied of all furnishings.

The size of the room will determine the amount of time required, but it is important not to mark the floor once it has been sanded, and also to apply the coats of sealer in quick succession—i.e. as soon as the previous coat is dry, but before it sets hard.

If circumstances make it necessary to leave the job for a day between coats, it will be necessary to rub the sealed floor with wire wool to 'key' the next coat. If there is to be a planned stop overnight, it would be better to stop after the sanding and apply the first coat of sealer the next day.

Drying time may vary between products, so plan your schedule according to the manufacturers' recommendations.

Parquet – hardwood blocks laid, in this instance, in a herringbone pattern.

Floorboards – the softwood planks in this children's room are in excellent condition.

Sanding and Staining Floors

Materials: Belt floor sander; rotary disc floor sander for the edges and corners; vacuum cleaner; paint brush (preferably a little narrower than the floorboards); wood stain (optional); proprietary floor seal; fine wire wool; rubber gloves; rags; electric floor polisher (optional); goggles to protect your eyes; face mask to avoid inhaling dust particles.

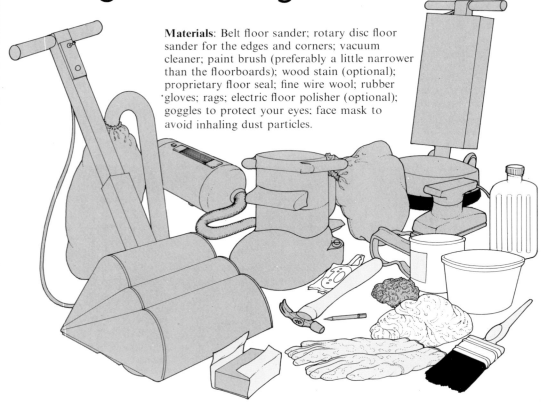

Preparation

Floorboards. Pull out all carpet tacks and nail down loose boards.

Woodblock and parquet. Pull out all carpet tacks and check for loose pieces.

Clean any dust and debris out of the holes until the loose pieces fit flush with the others.

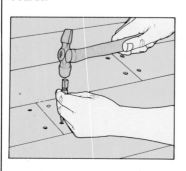

Using a nail punch, drive all nail heads down at least 3mm below the surface. Be sure not to miss any as they could damage the sanding machine.

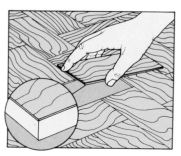

Pull up and check a piece of your parquet floor to make sure it's solid wood. Veneered plywood (as illustrated above) is not suitable for sanding.

Glue down any loose pieces with contact adhesive. If there is a large build up of wax on the floor, remove most of it with wire wool and white spirit.

The two types of sander you need are widely available for hire, and should come with plenty of replacement sanding belts and discs on a 'pay for what you use' basis. If possible, hire a sander of the vacuum type which cleans up most of the dust created by the sanding. There is more of this than you probably imagine. It is advisable to completely close the room to contain the dust.

Commence work with the belt sander, using a medium grit belt. Remember that if you are sanding softwood floorboards you will be removing more wood from the surface than if the floor is hardwood block or parquet.

Tilt the machine back before switching on—**'never allow the sander to run on the spot'** as it will sand a deep furrow into the floor.

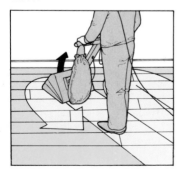

Once the machine is running, lower the belt gently as you

move off diagonally across the floor. At the end of the strip, tilt the machine back before you stop and turn around for the next strip.

The speed you move across the floor determines the depth of cut, so proceed smoothly and steadily, sanding as much of the floor as possible with the large sander. Remove only as much wood as necessary.

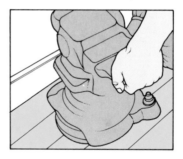

Next, use a medium grit disc on the rotary sander to sand the edges and places where the belt sander wouldn't reach. The last corners can be rubbed down by hand with sandpaper wrapped around a block, rubbing with the grain.

Tips

Always wear goggles and face mask.

Don't wear loose clothing or ties.

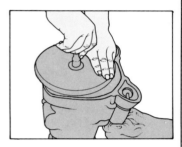

Change the disc on the rotary sander to fine grit and go around all the edges and corners again. This is to smooth the surface of the wood, so try to work in the direction of the grain (except on parquet). Be sure to cover all the areas you previously sanded with the rotary sander. Doing the edges at this stage means there will be less walking on the main part of the floor after its final sanding.

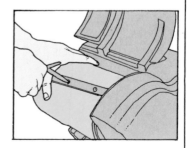

Now, change the belt on the large sander to fine grit and smooth the main part of the

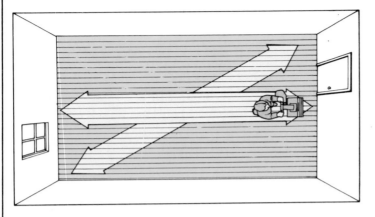

Apply the stain evenly with a lint-free cloth. Rubber gloves will keep the stain from your fingers. Do a small area at a time, working continuously in one direction. Dealing with the entire length of one or two boards at once is a good idea. Try not to overlap areas already stained or there will be a dark edge. Allow to dry thoroughly before applying seal.

floor. This time, work along the length of the boards—i.e. with the grain—not diagonally as before.

Vacuum the entire room thoroughly to remove all dust—the worst enemy of a good finish is wood dust, so take the sanders out of the room and don't forget to clean the tops of skirting boards etc. A cloth dampened with white spirit will pick up the last traces from the floor.

Staining
If you want to stain the wood darker, now is the time to do it.

These pieces of softwood (of the type usually found as floorboards), show how stain or coloured varnish can subdue or bring out the grain. Test a small area first.

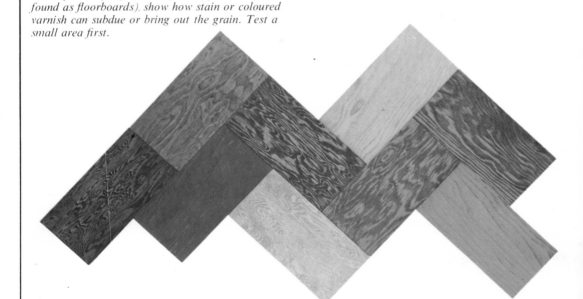

Sealing Floors

Following sanding (and any staining) a floor is completely 'bare' and must be sealed. The purpose of sealer is to soak into the wood and so prevent liquids and dirt from being absorbed or moisture from evaporating.

Sealer should not be confused with varnish, which is a finish (similar to paint) and not practical for floors as it will eventually crack and chip. The floor will then need re-sanding and refinishing. It is better to use a proprietary floor seal, such as urea-formaldehyde. This is not as brittle and needs only an occasional coat of wax for protection.

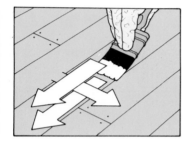

Floorboards. Brush the sealer on liberally, working along one or two boards, first with the grain, then across it to spread it evenly, and finally lightly with the grain again to minimize brush marks.

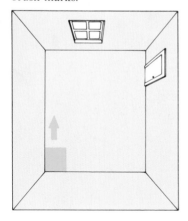

Parquet. Start in the furthest corner from the door and work quickly. Work in sections of about 1 metre square, and try to finish each strip before the seal dries.

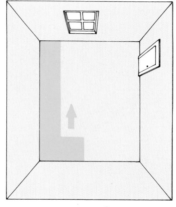

As one strip is finished, go back to the other end of it to start the next strip. That way the seal will have as little time as possible to dry along the edge and cause a visible overlap with the next strip.

As the seal dries, you will be able to see where the wood is still absorbent. When the first coat is dry, but before it hardens (see the manufacturers' instructions), apply the second coat. For parquet and woodblock floors, divide the area into different strips from the first coat to keep the overlaps from building up.

When this coat is dry, judge whether the wood is well sealed or requires further coats. Hardwood parquet, block and strip floors will be less absorbent than softwood floorboards and so will require fewer coats. Two coats should be enough for hardwood.

When the final coat is dry, feel around the surface for any rough patches where the grain of the wood may feel 'furry'. Rub these with fine wire wool to smooth them before the seal sets hard. Remove the dust immediately, and leave the seal to harden.

Furniture or traffic will mark the floor during this time. The manufacturers' instructions will state how long it must be left.

Polishing

After it has fully cured (hardened), the surface must be protected with several coats of silicone wax polish.

Many types of floor polish are available, including glossy, matt and non-slip. The more coats, the better the finish and protection, so don't skimp.

Apply the polish according to the instructions. An electric floor polisher is useful for this first polishing, though it's up to you to decide whether to hire or buy one.

Maintenance

The floor is now protected against spills and scuffing, and should need only a quick buff with a cloth (or electric polisher) to keep the shine in the most used areas.

Stubborn stains will come off if you wipe them with white spirit or one of the cleaner/polishes that are available.

SPECIAL EFFECTS

Furniture, floors and woodwork can be personalized still further with wood stain or paint applied either freehand or by stencilling. The traditional paint used was buttermilk with pigment added to produce soft earth colours. This effect can easily be achieved today with modern emulsion or acrylic paints, but remember that, on wood, soft colours look best. **Paint** is easier to use than stain as it is applied after the wood has been sealed and mistakes are easily wiped off while wet.

The best way to begin is to buy ready-cut stencil plates from craft and art shops. You should also use the brushes made for the purpose. These are round with the bristles trimmed flat and are held vertically to stipple the paint through the plate. This helps prevent the paint from creeping under the edges of the plate and spoiling the design. The best paints to use are artists' acrylic-based colours, sold in tubes by art shops. They have the advantage of being quick drying and having a consistency that covers well in one coat.

On floors or other places likely to receive hard wear, the finished stencil should have seal or varnish applied over it to protect it. **Stains** must be used on bare wood and the result is permanent. Also they can only be used to darken, not lighten, a surface. However, if the design isn't too ambitious, delicate effects that are very hard wearing can be created.

Interest is added to this stripped pine corner display cabinet by painting the inside with matt finish oil-based paint.

Before laying, pieces of this beautiful oak floor were stained black to achieve this pattern. This was a demanding task as any mistakes made with stain are permanent.

Discreet touches of colour enhance the design of this unusual bedside cupboard.

How to Stencil

Stencilling with paint
Wood must be sealed beforehand, but remove any wax with white spirit.

Tools and materials: Stencil plate; stencil brushes; tubes of acrylic paint; masking tape; a board or something to use as a 'dabbing board' or palette; newspapers; a piece of chalk; cloth to wipe up excess or spilled paint.

Stencilling with stains
As this must be done on the bare wood, take every precaution against getting stain where it's not wanted. If you're working on the floor, protect it with dust sheets (not newspapers) to avoid marks caused by walking on it.

Setting out the design and fixing the stencil plates is the same as for paint.

Use a cloth to apply the stain, rather than a brush. The danger is that the stain will creep under the edges of the plate as it is absorbed into the wood.

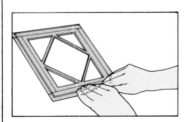

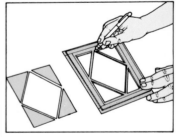

Measure and lay out the design, lightly marking with chalk the positions in which you will place the plate. Tape the plate into position and ensure it is flat against the surface.

Squeeze some paint on to the palette and dab the brush in it; then, dab it on newspaper until it leaves an even circle of paint. This is the correct amount of paint to hold in the brush.

With the same dabbing motion, apply the paint through the holes in the plate. Repeat with any other holes and other colours needed to complete the part of the design covered by the plate in this position. Use a different brush for each colour. Remove the plate very carefully to avoid smudging the design, and wipe it clean before re-positioning it.

It may help to trace the outline of the design with a felt tip pen in a suitable colour before staining. This also helps to give more definition to the edges.

After staining, the wood must be finished as described earlier. If you are using varnish or seal, use a minimum of brushing—the solvent may smear the stain.

Ready cut stencil plates in a wide range of designs are available from art shops.

TOP TEN TIPS

1 Start small! Try stripping a small box or chair before tackling a large project.

2 Repair the furniture before stripping it rather than afterwards. That way you'll have a better idea of how the repair will look when it's refinished, and also the glue and dirty hand marks won't be absorbed by the bare wood.

Drawers that don't close properly are a common problem and the fault is usually worn runners. You must either add just enough wood to the runners (or the bottom of the drawer) for it to close straight and sit squarely in its opening, or replace the runners with new ones.

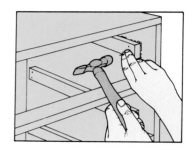

To replace runners, mark a straight line where they should be and glue and pin new strips. Make sure the edges of the drawer that sit on the runners are straight as they may be worn too.

Metal plates and *angle brackets* that can be used to strengthen furniture and woodwork are widely available.

This corner bracket for table legs takes some effort to fit, but is very strong. It uses a bolt screwed diagonally into the leg and a plate which is fixed to the underframe of the table. A nut then pulls the bolt (and the leg) tightly into the corner of the underframe.

Fuming
Fuming is a traditional way of darkening hardwoods such as oak, mahogany and walnut. In a suitable, well ventilated work area, such as outdoors or in a garage, where the flooring material will not be damaged, make a tent with a sheet of polythene. Stand the piece to be treated inside the tent with an open dish of .880 ammonia (specially formulated for this purpose and available from some paint suppliers and chemists). Place weights around the edges to make the tent as airtight as possible and leave it for an hour or so. To check for colour change, rub an unseen area with a cloth dipped in linseed oil. The longer the wood is fumed, the darker it will be. Warning – ammonia fumes are poisonous, so take care not to inhale them.

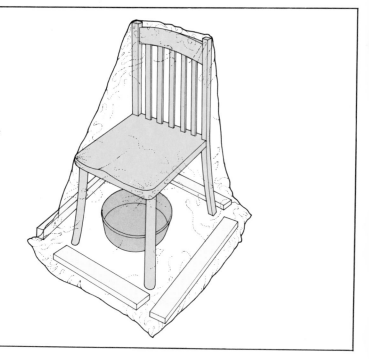

Loose or creaking stair treads can be cured by fixing metal shelf brackets underneath to stop the movement—providing the underside of the stairs is accessible.

3 Metal fittings should be removed before you strip any wood. Handles, catches and locks that are broken will need to be replaced. When shopping for new ones, take an old fitting with you so you can get one of the correct size. In the case of handles, make sure the new ones will cover the fixing holes of the old, but don't fit them until the job is complete.

4 Try to use the least drastic method for stripping wood. Liquid and jellied strippers (especially those that wash off with white spirit rather than water) are less hard on wood than the caustic pastes that must be removed with water. *Never* use water on veneer.

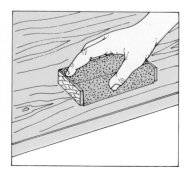

5 A good finish depends on the smoothness of the wood. Sand all surfaces with fine grade abrasive paper in the direction of the grain. When sanding veneer, be careful not to sand through it, especially along edges.

6 Use a dry paintbrush (or a brush attachment on a vacuum cleaner) to remove all dust from the grain of the wood after sanding. Then use a cloth dampened with white spirit to pick up any last traces before applying the finish.

7 Furniture that is sold already stripped will probably have wax on it. Before refinishing, you will have to remove the wax with white spirit and fine wire wool.

8 Always test the colour of stain or finish on an unseen part of the wood.

9 To prevent stain from appearing darker where the wood is more absorbent, wipe the surface with white spirit and then with a dry cloth just before applying the stain.

10 Hard finishes such as polyurethane varnish, sealer, and French polish take several days to cure (harden) after they dry. Don't put objects on shelves, window sills, and floors too soon or the finish will be marked.

Safety Tips

Protect everything (including your skin) from contact with chemical strippers. Wear rubber gloves and old clothes and, if possible, do the job outside.

Stripping products are poisonous. Read all safety warnings about first aid *before* it becomes necessary to take action.

Never store chemicals in bottles or jars that could be mistaken by children for soft drinks etc. Always label clearly and store away from children and animals.

Some chemical strippers can dissolve plastic buckets etc. Always use a metal container for disposing of the residue.

Rags used to apply oil to wood are a serious fire risk. Always dispose of them immediately after use by burning.

Shellac polishes can burn at very low temperatures. Store them in small, airtight containers and don't use them near naked lights.

Always wear goggles and a mask when using mechanical sanders.

Don't wear loose clothing or ties while using power tools.

TILE IT

CONTENTS

Introduction

The use of clay tiles to protect and decorate walls and floors is as old as brick making and pottery, and certainly precedes the invention of paint and even paper.

The advantage of being able to manufacture and decorate each small piece separately before applying it eliminates problems in construction (such as expansion) and offers many possibilities for design.

Today, most decorating materials are available in tile form. As well as the vast ranges of ceramic tiles, there are mirrored glass, cork, plastics, aluminium, stainless steel, vinyl, rubber and carpet.

Tiling techniques are the same for all materials except for the methods of cutting them and adhesives for fixing them. Tiles are easier to handle than sheet materials, and actually fixing them to walls and floors is simple. The one problem is that the first tile determines the position of every other. This is where do-it-yourself tiling jobs can be spoiled before they begin. The secret is to plan the entire job before fixing that first tile. This is called 'setting out'.

The main area of the wall or floor is called the 'field' and is always tiled first with whole, uncut tiles. This leaves the spaces around the edges, called the 'border', to be tiled seperately, each tile being cut to fit. A well-done job has a balanced appearance, as though the tiles fell into place quite naturally and without effort. However, this is the result of spending as much time setting out the job as in fixing the tiles.

This chapter will help you to do a good job. It will also help you to choose the right tile for the project you have in mind, and there are lots of colour photographs to set you thinking about that next project.

Above *Antique tiles are often to be found in second-hand shops and on market stalls. They can be attractively used either in sets, or by matching-up a number of odd tiles by colour, design, size, etc.*

Left *Large unglazed quarry tiles are a perfect foil for the renovated cafe table which serves as a home office area in this country style kitchen.*

Above *A combination of ceramic and cork tiles make this bathroom very easy to keep clean. The cork tiles have been finished with polyurethane, but areas likely to get very wet have been tiled with a ceramic tile. The cork has been extended to cover all other shelves, ledges, etc. so giving a 'total look'.*

Left *The pale green of the stained glass has been echoed in the tiles in this tiny bathroom. To avoid a feeling of claustrophobia, all paintwork, fittings, towels, etc. have been kept either white or pale pink.*

TOOLS AND MATERIALS

Here is a list of the tools and materials you will find mentioned later in the chapter.

Spirit level: An accurate level is a must for planning the layout (setting out) tiles on walls and determining the slope of floors.

Chalk line is a reel of non-stretch string that is used to make straight lines on walls, floors and ceilings.

To 'snap' a chalk line, fasten one end to a nail (or get a helper to hold it) on one mark, and hold it taut to the second mark. Then pull the line away from the surface and let it snap back. There will be a straight line of chalk between the two marks.

Plumb line is a string with a weight on the end that, hanging free, shows a true vertical. It can be rubbed with chalk and used as above.

Battens are lengths of softwood used in setting out wall and floor tiles. Choose straight ones

of about 50mm × 25mm (unless a specific size is stated).

Gauge stick is a setting out tool you make yourself. Lay out a row of tiles, being sure to space them as they will be when fixed. Simply butt self-spacing tiles together. Then place a batten next to the tiles and mark it at the corner of each tile. Use the gauge stick by placing it against the wall or floor to find the best position for the rows of tiles.

Scriber is used to set out floor tiles. It is easy to make yourself, as it is simply a batten approximately 1 metre long with a nail driven through both ends, so that the points protrude.

Tile cutters: There are several types of proprietary tile cutters. The most common resembles pliers with two 'wings' and also a wheel used to score the tile. The jaws are used to snap the tile on the line.

For cutting floor tiles, it's

best to hire a steel tile cutter. It'll cost more, but save on shattered tiles.

Adhesive spreaders are plastic or metal trowels with notches on the edge. They apply adhesive in even ridges and so help to avoid thick and thin patches. Often they're supplied free with the adhesive.

Float is a rectangular metal or wooden plate with a handle on the top. It is used for spreading screed or laying sand and cement mortar on floors.

Tile spike is a traditional tool for scoring the line where a tile is to be cut. This creates a weak point, making it possible to break the tile along the line.

Tile nibblers are pincers that are used to break off small pieces of tile, 'nibbling' away the waste on an awkward shape.

Tile breaking board: A flat piece of wood is helpful for snapping the tiles once they're scored.

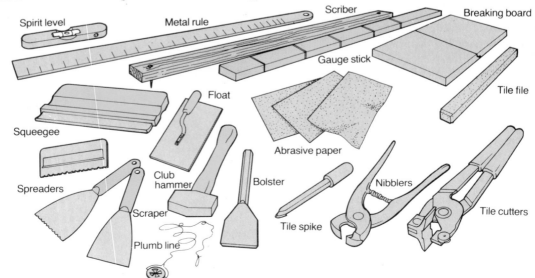

You can place matchsticks under the line at each edge, or for better results, fix a piece of bare wire across it. This supports the full width of the tile, giving a better chance of breaking it on the line.

Straight edge: A metal rule or straight strip of metal is necessary for guiding the tile spike (or cutter wheel) or the trimming knife.

Tile file: The best tool for smoothing the cut edges of ceramic tiles is a carborundum file, made of the same material as a knife sharpening stone. In fact, a stone can be used, although it's not as good for getting into small places.

Rubber squeegee: To spread grout over the tiles and into the joints, use a thin rubber wiper with a handle of the kind used to clean windows. It's quicker than a sponge.

Filling knife and scraper: These look similar, but have different functions. The scraper is stiff and is used to remove wallpaper and flaking paint. The filling knife is flexible and is used to apply filler to cracks and holes in walls and ceilings.

Bonding agent: When sealing cement floors or to help new cement to bond to old, you should use a polyvinyl acetate adhesive diluted with water.

Self-levelling compound screed is a water or resin based compound that is mixed to a creamy consistancy and poured over slightly uneven floors. It doesn't require skill in smoothing the surface because it finds its own level and flattens out.

Adhesives: Don't try using the wrong tile adhesive for the job. They are designed for specific purposes. The manufacturers always state which one to use for walls and which for floors. Also, you must use a flexible adhesive whenever tiling a surface that may have some movement, such as chipboard, hardboard or plywood sheets.

There are frost-proof adhesives for use outside and heat-resistant ones for work surfaces and fire places, and for surfaces that are often under water, such as shower floors, you must use a waterproof adhesive.

Contact adhesive: If the manufacturer recommends fixing cork tiles with contact adhesive, use a water-based (rather than solvent-based) one. These are much easier to apply and have no heavy, inflammable fumes.

Grout: As with adhesives, the material in the joints between the tiles must be flexible, frost-proof, heat-resistant, or waterproof as the situation demands. Also, on tiled work surfaces where food is prepared, use a non-toxic grout.

Filler for surface repairs comes in powder form to be mixed with water, or ready to use. Modern resin-based fillers are better than cellulose filler as they dry without shrinking, so cracks and holes can be filled flush.

Silicone caulk: Available in tubes and in various colours, this mastic makes a water-tight seal between bath tubs and basins and the tiles. It remains flexible enough to accommodate movement. It also provides a good way of sealing the join between floor tiles and wall tiles.

Chemical wallpaper stripper is a jelly-like product that clings to the surface of old wallpaper and can be used instead of water and vinegar when following the soak and scrape method. (See page 113.)

Types of Ceramic Tile

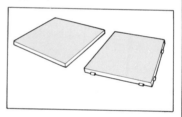

The *field tile* is used for the main part of the wall or floor. Some tiles have *spacer lugs* on the edges to be butted together. These are called self-spacing tiles.

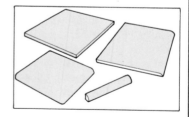

Universal tiles have two adjacent glazed edges for use on external corners. *Round-edge* (RE) tiles have one tapering edge and *double round-edge* (REX) tiles have two. *Quadrant tiles* are narrow round-edge tiles.

WALL TILES

Tiling a complete wall with mirror tiles has the effect of making the room seem twice the size.

Tiling a complete wall with mirror tiles has the effect of making the room seem twice the size.

Ceramic tiles for use on walls are available from many scources in vast ranges of colours, designs and sizes. Surfaces may be as smooth as glass or textured and matt. In fact the surface of glazed tiles is glass, making them a practical, hardwearing surface.

As well as different finishes, tiles may have different properties according to the use for which they're meant. Some tiles are heat-resistant while others are frost-proof.

Modern ceramic tiles have lugs on the edges to take the effort out of keeping them uniformly spaced. Square tiles with unfinished edges are called 'field tiles'. However, where tiles meet on external corners, there are special tiles that are used to finish the edges. The traditional tiles for this are called 'round-edge (RE), which has a rounded finished edge, and 'double round-edge' (REX) with two adjacent finished edges. These tiles are laid to cover the edges of the field tiles.

To finish the edge of field tiles on a flat surface, such as the top row of a half-tiled wall, there are 'quadrant tiles'. These are like a narrow strip of a round-edge tile. They can help give an authentic look to traditional patterns and antique tiles.

Another type of edge finishing tile is sometimes called a 'universal tile'. These usually have two glazed edges.

Mosaics are supplied in sheets of equally spaced pieces (known as chips), making them as easy to fix as tiles.

Just as there is a choice of types of tiles, so tile adhesives and grouts are also made for different purposes. See the 'Tools and Materials' pages to make sure you buy the right one for the job and always follow the manufacturers' instructions.

Plastic tiles are made from thin plastic sheet to imitate ceramic wall tiles. Although they aren't as strong as ceramic tiles, their surface is warmer and they are very easy to fix, usually with self-adhesive pads. Their main disadvantage is that they cannot withstand heat, so don't use them near cookers or fireplaces.

Cork, rubber, vinyl and carpet tiles may be used on walls, although cork is the most usual. The attraction of these materials, apart from their appearance, is that they are warm to the touch and also help to reduce noise by absorbing, rather than reflecting, it. The advantage of using them in tile form is that waste is kept to a minimum.

Cork is available in different qualities for floors and walls. The floor tiles are compressed to increase their density. Wall tiles come in different thicknesses and densities. Unfinished cork can be finished with two coats of clear polyurethane or (on walls) left natural.

Cork tiles are available in various natural shades and some tiles have a slight grain direction that can be used to create a pattern.

Metal tiles are fixed with pads in the same way as plastic ones. They are usually fixed butted together (without grouting) and provide a heat-resistant and washable surface, although splash marks must be cleaned off regularly.

The aluminium ones usually cut easily with scissors, but you may need tin snips for stainless steel tiles.

A major feature of metal tiles is that they can be bent around internal and external corners.

Mirror tiles are simply mirrored glass cut into tiles. The most important thing to remember is that the surface to which they are fixed must be absolutely flat and smooth. Any unevenness will cause a distorted reflection. One way to overcome this is by fixing plywood or chipboard to the wall.

As mirror tiles are butted together without grout, it's a good idea to lay them out first on a flat surface. They may not all be exactly square and there can be some variation in size.

With all tiles, the quality of the job is decided at the planning stage. It takes as long to find the best arrangement, both for working out a pattern and to give the overall job a professional symmetry, as to actually fix the tiles.

Preparing Walls

Plaster

New plaster needs at least one month to dry out before it can be tiled. Remove any little splashes (small bumps) of plaster and fill any cracks or dents. Then prime with a plaster primer or any universal primer to create a non-absorbent surface for the tile adhesive.

Filling cracks and dents

This is done with the flexible filling knife and filler described in 'Tools and Materials'.

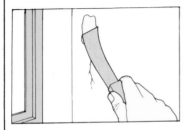

Scoop some filler on to the end of the knife and press the blade flat over the fault, sliding away to leave the filler in the hole. You may need several attempts to ensure the filler is pushed right to the bottom without air being trapped underneath (if the filler bulges out of the hole there's an air bubble under it).

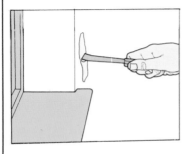

When you've applied enough to fill the hole, hold the knife almost vertically and scrape across the top to remove the excess.

Professionals try to clean all the surplus away (including the ridges around the edges) leaving the repair flush. It's worth the extra time spent on the wet filler as rubbing down afterwards is messy, time consuming and hard work.

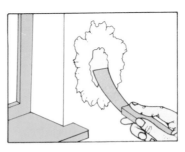

Large, deep holes should be filled in layers not more than 3mm thick. These dry quickly enough that you can apply a layer every so often while dealing with other small repairs.

Filling with thin layers helps with faults that are wider than the filling knife. The surface is built up gradually around the edges, reducing the area to be scraped off flush. Remember to clean the surplus from around the edges each time you fill.

Very large areas of damaged plaster should be repaired with plaster or one of the DIY plastering systems that is applied by brush. These are used in layers up to 3mm thick and take 24 hours to dry between coats so, if the fault is deeper than this, use ordinary filler to build up the surface until only a 'skim coat' is needed. Keep working the surface (re-wetting if necessary) until you're satisfied with the finish.

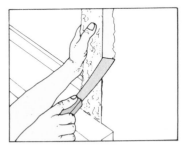

To get a neat edge on outside corners, hold a polythene-wrapped piece of wood against one side and flush with the edge. Fill the gap as if it were a crack. Then slide the wood away when the filler begins to set. Use a damp sponge to remove traces of wet filler.

Wallpaper

Wallpaper or other wall coverings cannot be tiled. It is necessary to strip off all layers of old paper to reveal the plaster. Do this either by the 'soak and scrape method' as described below, or use a steam stripper, widely available from hire shops and easy to use. (See page 52.)

Removing wallpaper

First, check whether the paper is of the 'peel off' variety by grasping a corner and pulling. Vinyl types are easily removed like this, but they leave their paper backing on the wall. This must be removed in the normal way.

To remove other wallpapers, begin by scoring the surface with a stiff wire brush. This is particularly important with washable (i.e. water-resistant) papers and those that have been painted over.

Next, fill a bucket with warm water and add a little vinegar (this reduces the surface tension and helps it to penetrate the paper). Using a large paint or pasting brush, soak the paper as much as possible.

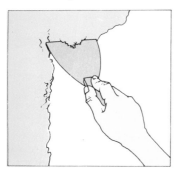

Use a stiff scraping knife to get under the paper, but be careful

not to dig into the surface of the plaster. Keep re-soaking until the paper comes off easily, leaving little residue. After stripping, wash off any traces of old adhesive with clean water.

For stubborn papers, try one of the *chemical wallpaper stripping products* instead of water and vinegar. These cling to the surface and allow more time for the adhesive to soften.

Painted walls

Gloss paint must be rubbed down with medium grade abrasive paper to key the adhesive. Matt finish paint needs to be washed and rinsed. Use a scraper to remove any loose paint and then fill as plaster. Remember to prime any bare areas or filler.

Old ceramic tiles

Existing tiles may be tiled over if they are firmly stuck and any cracks filled. If the old tiles are glazed, rub them down with a coarse grade silicon carbide paper to scratch the surface slightly. This will help 'key' the surface for the adhesive. Then wipe the surface with a cloth dampened with white spirit to remove any dust and old polish.

Brick or rough concrete

Uneven masonry walls will have to be plastered or rendered or lined with chipboard or plywood.

Wood

Timber is not a suitable surface for tiles because the boards move in relation to each other. On a smooth wood wall, you can fix sheets of thin hardboard as described in the 'Floors' section. However, if the wall

seems unstable, it's best to line it with plywood or chipboard sheets that are fixed to battens. Then it must be sealed with primer.

How to line walls

To make a smooth, stable surface for tiling, you can fix plywood or chipboard (particle board) sheets to battens.

Screw battens to the wall not more than 30cm apart. Fix the first one at the corner. Using the width of the sheets, calculate the other battens to be spaced equally, with a batten at the join with the next sheet. The last sheet on the wall will probably need to be cut to fit.

If there is a window or door, fix battens around the edges. Cut the sheets to fit the area to be tiled.

Use a long, straight piece of wood to keep the battens straight and parallel with each other. If necessary, use pieces of wood to space some battens away from the wall.

When all the battens are up, mark their positions on the sheets and screw the sheets to the battens. Prime the wood with an oil-based primer to create a non-absorbent surface and to prevent rust on the screw heads.

Fixing Wall Tiles

First, choose the most important wall or surface. Decide this according either to how prominently it is featured, or how many awkward corners and obstacles are on it. The tiles on any adjoining walls will have to follow suit.

On a plain wall without obstacles, the tiles should be fixed so that the cut border tiles are of equal size on each side and top and bottom. Also, the border tiles should not be less than half a tile width. If, when setting out, there are spaces at the ends of the vertical or horizontal rows that are narrower than this, reduce the number of whole tiles in the row by one.

It is difficult to cut thin strips (less than 25mm) of ceramic tiles and narrow 'L' shapes are fragile and unsightly. The final result will depend most on how carefully you can arrange to have the fewest problem border spaces to fill, and on placing them where they won't be noticed.

Having chosen your tiles, make a gauge stick of a convenient length for the job.

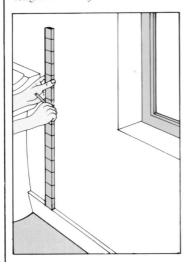

If you're tiling *floor to ceiling*, hold the stick vertically to find the best arrangement for the *horizontal rows*, marking the wall with a pencil where the joins will be. Use trial and error to balance the top and bottom rows of cut tiles equally.

If there is a sink or bath, it's better to have a row of whole tiles along the top of it. On the other hand, if there is a window, it is usually best to treat it as the focal point, and centre the rows of tiles on this.

When you think you've found the best arrangement, mark the wall where the bottom of the lowest row of whole tiles will be.

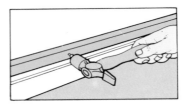

Cut a length of batten to fit the wall and drive nails into it every 30cm or so. Hold the batten on the mark and drive the first nail. Then, using the spirit level to get it perfectly horizontal, drive the remaining nails far enough into the wall to hold the batten firmly, but not all the way in. This makes it easier to remove the batten later.

Rest the gauge stick vertically on the batten at different points along the wall to see how doors, windows, sinks, etc. will be affected.

Now you should be able to decide which feature or obstacle is the most important and what compromise will be best for the others. If necessary move the batten.

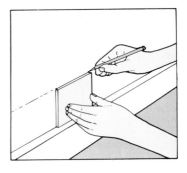

If you're *half-tiling*, and want to use a number of rows of whole tiles, use a tile and a pencil to mark the wall (or walls) along the skirting board. Cut a batten to fit the wall and drive nails into it every 30cm or so.

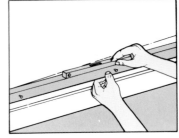

Hold the batten against the wall and use the spirit level to adjust it level with the lowest point of the line. This makes sure there will be no gap below the bottom row of tiles, although it may be necessary to cut some of them if the skirting board isn't level. Drive the nails into the wall far enough to hold the batten, but not fully home.

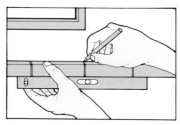

Now you can use the gauge stick to plan the *vertical rows*. Hold a spirit level and the gauge stick in one hand to keep it approximately level and mark the joins on the wall with a pencil.

Treat windows and other obstacles as for horizontal rows or allow equal size cut tiles at either side of the wall.

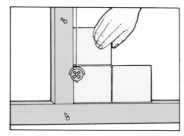

Once you are satisfied with the setting out of the vertical rows, nail a batten either at the central join or at the last row of full tiles on one side of the wall. Use the spirit level or a plumb line to make sure it's perfectly vertical.

It's a good idea to try holding a number of tiles without adhesive in the corner between the battens to make sure they are at right angles to each other.

Fixing ceramic wall tiles

Now you are ready to begin fixing the tiles. All the whole tiles will be fixed first. The cut tiles are left until the adhesive under the whole tiles has hardened.

Follow the manufacturers' instructions in mixing or stirring the adhesive and have the spreader, a damp sponge, and a supply of matchsticks (if the tiles don't have spacer lugs).

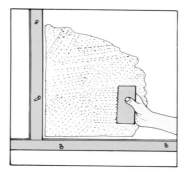

Begin by spreading approximately 1 square metre of adhesive where the battens meet. Make sure the wall is covered up to, but not touching, the battens.

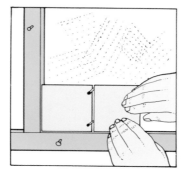

Starting with the bottom row, press the tiles, without sliding them, firmly into the adhesive. Push self spacing tiles together

so the lugs are touching. Insert matchsticks between tiles that have no lugs.

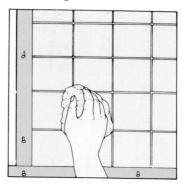

Continue tiling until the area of adhesive is covered. Wipe off any adhesive that squeezes on to the surface of the tiles with a damp sponge.

Then spread another area and continue along the bottom. After every three or four horizontal rows, hold a batten and spirit level along the top of the tiles to make sure they're horizontal.

When you come to a place where the bottom row of whole tiles will be higher, such as above a basin, bath, or window nail up a short batten (using the spirit level) to keep them from slipping down before the adhesive sets.

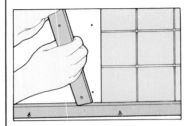

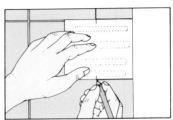

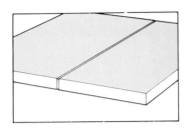

If the vertical batten is in the centre of the wall, remove it carefully to tile the rest of the wall.

Finish fixing all the whole tiles and then remove any adhesive from the space around the edges, which would interfere with fixing the cut tiles later.

Allow the adhesive to set before taking down the bottom battens.

How to cut tiles

Now you are ready to fill the remaining spaces. All the cut tiles are to be fixed so that the 'factory edge' is next to another tile, and the cut edge against an adjacent wall or fitting.

You will need: a tile spike and breaking board or a proprietary tile cutter, a metal straight edge, pencil or chinagraph pencil, tape measure, tile nibblers and tile file.

If you have a long row of straight cut tiles to fix, you can cut and fix one at a time, or cut all of them first and then fix them. If you do cut them all first, number the spaces on the wall and the back of each tile so you known which one fits where.

Here is a method of measuring that ensures the tile will fit even if the width at the top and bottom of the tile are different (against a sloping wall, for instance).

Hold a tile with it's face to the wall and mark the edge at the top and bottom where the uncut edge will be. Allow space for the join with the fixed tile and also for a small gap with the other wall.

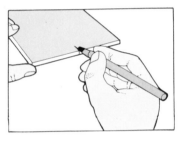

Looking at the edge of the tile, transfer these marks to the face side. If the tiles are glazed, use a chinagraph pencil to make the marks clear.

Place the tile on a piece of wood and use a straight edge and tile cutter to score a line across the face.

The depth of the scored line is not as important as how sharp the bottom is. It is better to make one confident, smooth cut than to scratch several times with too much force. You must score right around the edges of the tile to make sure there will be a clean break.

Place the tile on a breaking board with the line directly over the wire or ridge (or place a matchstick under the line at each edge) and snap it by pushing down on both sides equally.

Alternatively, you can use the edge of a table. Hold one side firmly and snap off the other side.

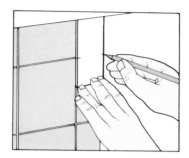

To measure the corner tile in the row, hold it up once for the width and cut, and then repeat the operation for the height.

The easiest way to measure an odd-shape cut is to make a paper template the same size as a tile, and make cuts in it so that each flap can be folded to the shape of the obstruction.

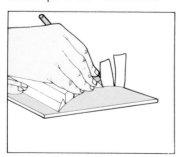

Place the template on the tile and mark and score the shape.

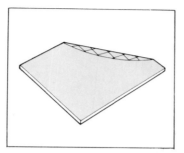

Score a line to remove as much of the waste as you can, and then score a grid of lines, being careful to keep them on the waste side of the line.

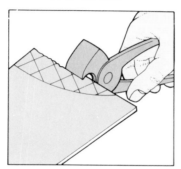

Use the tile nibblers to break off small pieces until the line is reached. Then, if necessary, smooth the cut edge with a file.

Where you must fit a tile around a pipe, mark where the

pipe will be on the tile by measuring from the adjacent tiles.

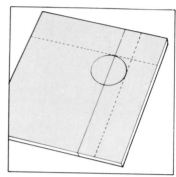

Score around the edge of a coin or other round object that is a little larger than the pipe, and also score a straight line across the tile through the circle.

Snap the tile along the straight line, and then nibble out the semi-circle on each piece.

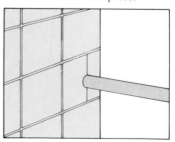

When the pieces are fixed, the join will hardly show.

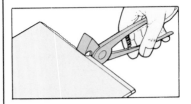

When you must cut a small strip from a tile (perhaps when trimming the bottom row of tiles), score it in the normal way, and use the nibblers rather than snapping it.

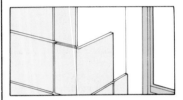

On the inside of a window reveal, fix whole tiles (either round edge or glazed edge) over the top of the tiles on the wall. Make sure the joins match the wall tiles and cut the end ones as necessary. Then fix cut tiles between the frame and the whole tiles.

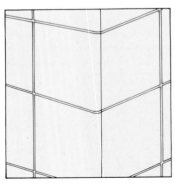

On outside corners, use the finished edge tiles on the more important surface to cover the edges of the tiles on the other.

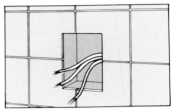

To tile round a light switch or power socket, first switch off the electricity at the mains. Then remove the cover and cut tiles to fit around the box. After replacing the cover, you can restore the electricity.

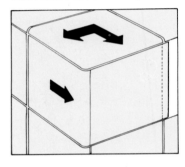

When you come to tile three surfaces (such as a boxed-in basin) use an REX or double finished edge tile on the top, overlapping the edges of the tiles on the sides. To keep the joins matching between the top and the sides, one of the tiles on the corner will have to be cut.

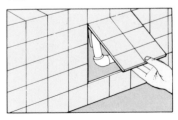

When tiling the panel at the side of a bathtub, remember to make a removable section for access to the plumbing. This can be held in place with a hinge and magnetic catches. Be sure to use flexible adhesive on panels and don't grout the joins at the edges.

Grouting

When all the tiles have been fixed, leave the adhesive to harden for the time recommended by the manufacturer (usually 24 hours). The next job is to fill the joins between the tiles with a suitable grout – see 'Tools and Materials'.

If you have tiled around a bath or sink, first use a silicone caulk between these and the tiles. Grout can become discoloured here and also the movement may cause it to crack. Allow the caulk to harden before grouting the wall.

Mix the grout, adding colour if desired, following the manufacturers' instructions. You will also need a rubber squeegee, a bucket of clean water, and a flat sponge.

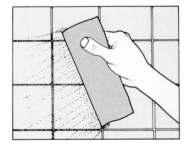

Spread the grout liberally over the joints, pushing it well in. Use the squeegee or sponge diagonally to move the excess along to the next area.

Use a flat sponge to wipe most of the grout from the face of the tiles before it sets. Rinse the sponge frequently in the clean water (rinsing under the tap can silt up the drain).

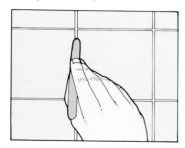

As the grout begins to harden, use a stick with a rounded tip along the joints to give a neat finish.

When the grout has set, remove the excess grout with a damp sponge, rinsed often in clean water. Then remove the last film of grout by polishing the tiles with a soft cloth.

Fixing mosaics

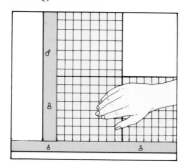

Set out the job in the same way as for normal ceramic tiles, treating each sheet as a whole tile. Set up vertical and horizontal battens. If there is a protective paper covering on the face of the sheets, leave it on until they're fixed and dry.

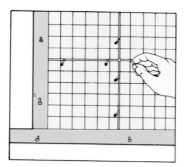

Fix 3 or 4 sheets at a time. Use a card or wood spacer to make the gaps between sheets the same as the gap between each tile on the sheet, unless the manufacturers' instructions say to butt them together.

If there are arrows on the back of the sheets, make sure they all point the same way. When all the whole sheets have been fixed, leave them to dry.

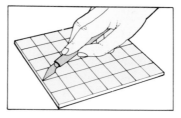

Cut off enough rows to more than fill the space.

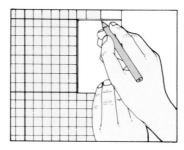

Place the partial sheet face to the wall and mark the edges.

Use the spacer card against the wall to make the correct gap between sheets.

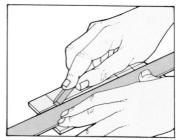

Place the sheet face up on a piece of wood and score the line across all the tiles.

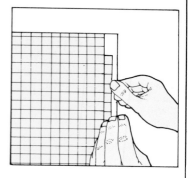

Cut the last row of tiles from the sheet and spread adhesive in the space to be filled. Fix the partial sheet.

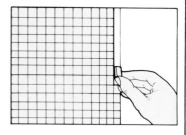

Break the individual tiles with the tile cutter, fixing each one as you go to prevent them getting mixed up.

Plastic tiles

Setting out is done as for ceramic tiles, but don't worry about intricate cutting as the plastic can be easily cut with scissors.

The back of each tile is hollow. It is fixed to the wall by placing self adhesive foam pads on the corners and, usually, one in the middle.

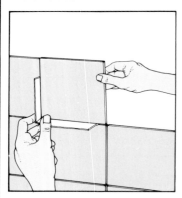

Peel the backing paper off the pads and press the tiles firmly in position, spacing with a card if necessary. The pads grip immediately, so you won't be able to adjust the tiles. Fix the whole tiles first, then fill in the borders.

Follow the manufacturers' instructions for grouting.

Metal foil tiles

These are fixed with pads in the same way as plastic tiles, except that the edges are butted close together.

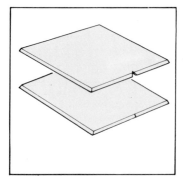

To bend them around corners, snip the bevelled or curved edges as far as the flat area for internal corners, or remove a wedge shaped piece for external corners. Start with a thin wedge and use trial and error to find the best shape.

Bend the tile to the required angle over a sharp edged piece of wood.

Mirror tiles

These are fixed either in the same way as plastic and metal tiles, or with a special adhesive specified by the manufacturer.

Mirror tiles are cut in the same way as ceramic wall tiles. Use a glass cutter to score the line and then snap it over a sharp edge. Intricate cuts are extremely difficult so it may be best to confine these tiles to an area without problems.

Cork tiles

Setting out for cork tiles is the same as for ceramic wall tiles. Cork is much easier to cut so awkward border tiles are less of a problem. Cork tiles are best set out with equal space borders (side to side and top to bottom) of not less than $\frac{1}{2}$ a tile width.

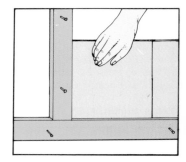

Fix a horizontal batten as for ceramic tiles. Then either fix a vertical batten at the centre join or use a chalked plumb line to snap a vertical line as described in 'Tools and Materials'.

For instructions for fixing cork (and other soft tiles) see the 'Floors' section.

SAFETY WARNING
Metal conducts electricity, so trim tiles around switch and socket covers. Don't remove the covers and insert tiles behind them.

Ceiling Tiles

Although any tiles can be used on the ceiling, expanded polystyrene tiles are more usual. Polystyrene tiles are the least expensive covering for a ceiling, apart from paint, and are available in a wide range of designs and patterns. There are also covings to be used around the edges of the ceiling to simulate plaster and tidy the joins between ceiling and walls.

Preparation is the same as for walls, but hairline cracks and small holes can be left. The main consideration is that the surface is sound and flat. Contours in the ceiling will cause the tiles to adopt crazy angles and look very untidy.

To avoid fire hazard, polystyrene tiles must be fixed with no air gaps behind them. Use the adhesive specified by the manufacturer and spread it over the whole tile. Don't use blobs of adhesive on each corner. Beware of using them on low ceilings over cookers or around metal chimneys that pass through the ceiling. Also you must not paint the tiles with oil-based paint; this also constitutes a fire risk. Only water-based emulsion paints are suitable.

middle spaces. As polystyrene tiles are not exactly regular, leave a tiny (1mm) gap between them.

To help keep the rows straight, stand back every so often and sight down the joins. Fix all the whole tiles.

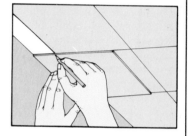

When only the border spaces remain, hold a tile upside down with its edge against the wall and mark the edges where it overlaps the last tile. Use a knife or a felt tip pen to nick the edge.

Place the tile face up on a piece of wood and use a metal straight edge and sharp knife to cut a line between the two marks. Make several passes with the blade at a low angle, as the beads of polystyrene sometimes tear out, leaving a ragged edge. A curved blade helps to make a cleaner cut.

You can use the methods described for measuring and cutting soft floor tiles (page 131) for any awkward edges.

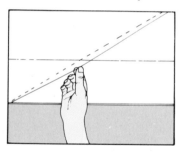

Set out the tiles to suit the most important wall or feature in the room in the same way as floor tiles. Snap the two chalk lines at right angles to each other.

Mix up the adhesive according to the manufacturers' instructions and spread it on the back of the first tile. To prevent it squeezing out

between the tiles, it's best not to brush it quite to the edges.

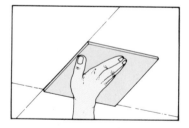

Place the tile in position where the chalk lines intersect and press it with the flat of your hand onto the ceiling to make sure it sticks all over. Don't use fingertips on polystyrene tiles or the surface may be dented.

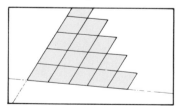

Work outward along the lines from the first tile, filling in the

FLOOR TILES

Ceramic floor tiles are the longest lasting floorcovering you can use. They are thicker than tiles made for walls, and also fired at so high a temperature (vitrified) that the particles of clay fuse together. This makes them almost unbreakable when laid, but it can also cause problems with cutting them to fit.

Traditional quarry tiles in natural earth colours are still available, but there are also huge ranges of designs and colours in modern, self-spacing versions. Most ranges of tiles include RE and REX tiles, and there are also covings that can be used, in place of skirting boards, around the edge of the tiled floor.

As floor tiles are much stronger than wall tiles, they are the best choice for work surfaces, hearths and window sills etc. Unglazed floor tiles will withstand the heat of a hot roasting pan without damage. However, if you use glazed tiles on a surface where food is prepared, make sure the glaze doesn't contain lead. Also, you must use heat-resistant adhesive and a non-toxic grout.

The first thing to consider is how much you can raise the level of your floor without causing too much other work. Doors can be taken off and trimmed quite easily, but check cupboard doors, too, and have a look at washing machines or dish washers that fit under the work surface.

There are two methods of laying ceramic floor tiles. You can use a thin layer (3 or 4mm) of adhesive or lay the tiles on a sand and cement screed at least 12mm thick. How to do this is described on the following pages.

If you are tiling an outside patio, path, or balcony, you may use either method, but be sure to use frost-proof tiles and adhesive.

Above *Provencal quarry tiles are very attractive, either inside or outside. These are unglazed, and being a non-porous tile should not stain easily. In a kitchen, however, it might be advisable to use a glazed version.*

Left *These glazed quarry tiles have been carried over the threshold to the patio, so pulling the two areas together and making both seem larger.*

Cork, vinyl, rubber and carpet floor tiles have the advantages of being comfortable and quiet to walk on and also easier to lay. However, they require a smooth and flat subfloor if they are to last well, so preparation is all important.

Cork floor tiles are compressed to increase their density. As with wall tiles, they are available with their surface already sealed by the manufacturer or left natural. In the case of floors, they must be sealed with at least two coats of polyurethane varnish or whatever the manufacturer recommends.

Vinyl coated tiles are one 'of the least expensive floor coverings and are much easier to use than in sheet form. Also, some tiles are self adhesive.

Solid vinyl tiles are expensive, but very hard wearing. They are available in wide ranges of colours and designs, some imitating marble, stone, wood etc.

Synthetic rubber tiles aren't cheap but they will last. They are very comfortable and quiet to walk on and the studded versions are popular for their 'high tech' look. However, colour ranges are limited when compared with ceramic and vinyl tiles.

Carpet tiles are sold in most qualities from inexpensive cords to heavy duty contract types and plush velvet piles. The advantage of tiles is minimum waste in fitting and also being able to replace a few worn tiles (or move them to a part of the floor that doesn't show) without replacing all of the carpeted area. Using different colours of carpet tiles to create patterns can give an attractive effect. Be sure to buy a few spare tiles of each colour to replace damaged or worn areas later.

Above *Cork floor tiles are one of the most economic floor coverings available. They are easy to lay and can be easily extended to cover adjacent areas like this seating unit.*

Left *Rubber flooring was originally developed for commercial purposes but is now available for domestic use. It is very hard-wearing whilst being soft on the feet.*

Preparing Floors

If the floor is affected by damp, you should get professional advice. It can be difficult to be certain of the exact causes and building practices vary in different areas. When obtaining advice, be sure to state your intended floor covering to ensure it will be compatible with the remedy proposed. If you do the work yourself, read all manufacturers' recommendations on the products used. All solid floors must have a damp proof membrane.

Preparing for ceramic floor tiles

Concrete floors that are smooth, dry and flat are suitable for all types of tile and methods of laying. If the floor is new, it should be left for 4 weeks before any tiles are laid.

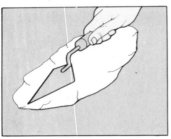

Any small holes or dips in the surface should be filled with a mix of 1 part cement to 3 parts sharp sand. Use a proprietary bonding agent (pva) in the mix, and brush the area to be filled with the bonding agent diluted with water immediately before filling.

Uneven concrete floors should be checked with a long batten

and spirit level to determine the difference in height between the highest and lowest point.

If this is not more than 12mm, you can use a self levelling screed compound.

Wire brush any dirt out of cracks and wash the entire floor with detergent and water to remove oil or grease.

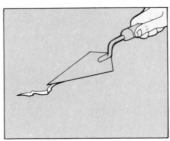

Fill all deep (10mm) cracks with 3 to 1 sand and cement morter, using a bonding agent, as above.

Mix up the self levelling compound according to the manufacturers' instructions. It should be a creamy consistency and have no lumps.

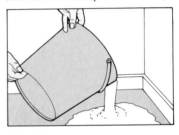

Starting in the furthest corner from the door, pour some on to the floor.

Spread it with a steel float to a depth of about 3mm. Don't worry about marks in the surface as these disappear as the compound levels itself.

Continue to pour and spread until you finish at the door.

Leave the compound to harden (see manufacturers' instructions). When the floor is hard enough to walk on, use a little water and the float to smooth any small bumps on the surface.

If the floor is too uneven to use a self levelling compound, the tiles will have to be laid on a *sand and cement screed* at least 12mm thick at the highest point of the floor. See the tile manufacturers' instructions concerning the minimum thickness.

You can choose to lay the screed first and leave it several weeks to harden before fixing the tiles with thin bed adhesive. However, tiles are best laid directly onto the new screed, so it is better to do the job all at once. (See page 128.)

The only preparation necessary before laying the screed is to give the floor a coat of proprietary sealer if the surface is dusty.

Old tiled floors may be tiled over, providing the tiles are securely fixed. Tap each one with a piece of wood to see if any sound 'hollow'. Any that

do need taking up and re-placing with adhesive, or the gap filled with sand and cement.

If you want to remove the old tiles, perhaps to keep the floor at the same level, use a bolster and club hammer at the base of each tile. Depending on how the tiles were fixed, you may have to use a self levelling screed on the floor beneath.

Wood Floors
Although concrete is the most suitable surface, you can use a special flexible adhesive to lay tiles on well prepared wood floors. The sand and cement screed method is not suitable.

Since you will need to line the floor with plywood or chipboard sheets, make sure that you won't need access to pipes or wiring under the floor. Also, as the tiled floor will be almost airtight, check that underfloor ventilation is adequate.

Parquet or wood block floors that are flat may be covered with 3mm thick hardboard instead.

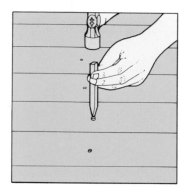

Drive the old nails below the surface and nail down loose boards.

Use plywood or chipboard at least 12mm thick. These are available in various sheet sizes, so work out the most economical ones to buy. Cut them to fit and put them in place.

Walk on the floor to check for movement. If necessary, insert packing underneath to level the edges where the sheets join.

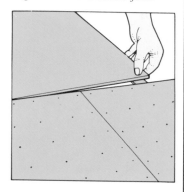

Drive nails every 10cm over the whole surface. Be sure to use nails of a length that won't go all the way through the floorboards beneath. They may penetrate pipes or wiring.

Once nailed down, the sheets must be sealed with two coats of oil based or water based primer.

Preparing for soft floor tiles
Follow the same procedure just described for each type of floor. The main consideration is the smoothness of the floor. Any small bumps or hollows will quickly show through the tiles and cause uneven wear.

If a sand and cement screed is necessary, it will have to be left approximately four weeks before being tiled.

Laying Floor Tiles

It is easier to set out floor tiles than wall tiles because you can dry lay them (ie: without adhesive). All floor tiles (except ceramic tiles being fixed on a fresh cement mortar screed) are laid from the centre of the room towards the edges. Therefore, the first job is to find the centre of the room.

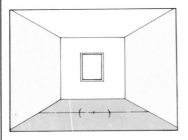

If the room is *square or rectangular*, measure two opposite walls and mark the centre of each. Then snap a chalk line between the two marks.

Measure and mark the centre of the chalk line and this is the centre of the room. Now you need a line at right angles to the first. Using a scriber (as described in 'Tools and Materials') place one nail on the centre mark and scratch a mark either side on the chalk line.

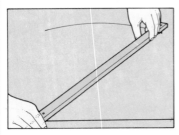

Place the nail on one of the scribed marks, and scribe an arc to both sides of the line.

Then repeat with the nail on the second mark.

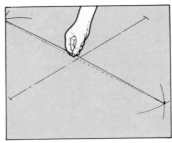

Snap a line between the points where the arcs intersect, and this line will be at right angles to the first line.

If the room is *not regular in shape*, it is usually best to set out the tiles parallel with the wall where the main entrance door is situated.

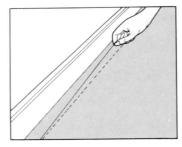

Measure 10cm from the wall at each side and snap a chalk line between the marks. Measure and mark the centre of the line.

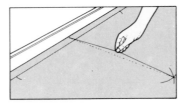

Use the scriber to mark the line either side of the centre and

then scribe arcs from each of these points. Snap a chalk line between the centre mark of the line and the point where the arcs intersect. The second line will be at right angles to the first. Extend across the floor.

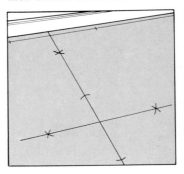

Measure the second line and mark its centre. Use the scriber as described above and snap a third line at right angles to the second one.

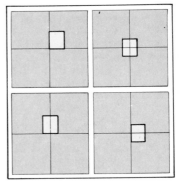

Once there are two central lines at right angles to each other, dry lay a row of tiles in both directions across the room. The first tile can be placed in any one of four positions where the lines intersect. Adjust the rows until there is at least $\frac{1}{2}$ a tile width left at the border on each side.

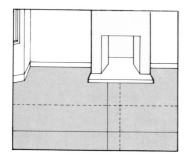

If the room has a major feature such as a fireplace or bay window, centre the tiles on it by snapping new chalk lines parallel to the old ones. Two features (on adjacent walls) are the most that can be treated this way. If in doubt as to what features to use, dry lay as many tiles as necessary to see which arrangement is best.

Laying ceramic tiles on thin bed adhesive

Set out the floor and dry lay the tiles as described above. Push the lugs of self spacing tiles together or, if there are no lugs, use a piece of cardboard or wood. The manufacturer of the tiles may recommend minimum joint gaps.

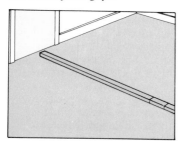

Fix a straight batten along the chalk line that is at right angles to the door and mark the position of the first (or central) tile.

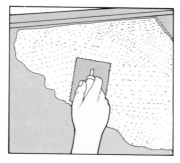

Spread about 1 square metre of adhesive with the notched trowel, making sure to get it up to the batten. Working on a small area makes sure the adhesive is wet enough when the tiles are laid. If you find that there is a skin forming on the surface, remove the adhesive and spread that area again.

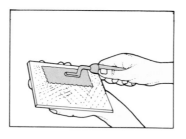

If the adhesive manufacturer recommends that the tiles (as well as the floor) should be 'buttered' with adhesive, follow the instructions as to thickness.

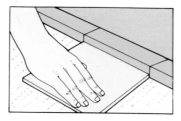

Lay the first tile at the mark and push each tile firmly into

the adhesive to create a good bond and eliminate air gaps.

If necessary, space the tiles with the same piece of cardboard or wood used when dry laying them.

Keep a close eye on the joins running at right angles to the batten to keep them straight.

Check every three or four rows with a batten for straightness, both along the edges and across the tops. Adjust, if necessary, before the adhesive has started to set.

Keep spreading areas of adhesive and laying tiles until all the whole tiles are laid, always working toward the door.

Remove adhesive from the edges of the floor where cut tiles will be laid.

Remove the batten carefully. Repeat on the other side of the room, working toward the door. Tile the rest of the floor.

When all the whole tiles are laid, leave the floor without walking on it for 24 hours (see manufacturers' instructions). If there must be some traffic (after several hours), place some sheets of plywood or similar to spread the load over a wide area.

Cutting ceramic floor tiles

You will need some type of heavy duty tile cutter for floor tiles. Hire shops usually have these and some tile stockists and contractors provide a cutting service. If you want to cut all the tiles before you start laying them, number each space and each tile on the back.

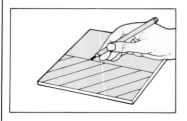

If you are taking the tiles away to be cut, mark the cutting lines with an indelible felt pen (or score with a spike on glazed tiles) and mark the waste side of the tile like this. Tiling

contractors use a circular saw with a thick blade that is cooled by water. They will need to cut on the waste side of the line, and pencil marks may get washed away.

Measure the tiles to be cut in the same way as wall tiles.

Grouting

Floor tiles are usually grouted with a mixture of cement and water. However, there are proprietary grouts and also coloured additives. Be sure to use a flexible grout on wooden subfloors. If you use these, follow the manufacturers' instructions for mixing. Otherwise, mix 1 part cement to 1 part water.

Pour some grout onto the tiles and use a rubber squeegee to push it well into the joints, pushing the excess to ungrouted areas. Work on an area you can reach without walking on the grout.

Wipe the surface of the tiles fairly clean with a damp

sponge. Don't worry about the thin film of grout that remains. This can be cleaned off later. Fill the joints with grout flush with the surface of the tiles, rather than using a rounded stick as with wall tiles.

Laying mosaics

This is best done on thin bed adhesive. It is possible to lay them on a sand and cement screed, but keeping them level is tricky. If your floor requires a screed, it's best to let it harden and use a self levelling compound if necessary. After a few weeks you can lay the mosaics with adhesive.

Set out and dry lay the sheets in the same way as floor tiles. Use a spacer of wood or card to make the gaps between the sheets the same as the gap between the individual chips.

Follow the same procedure as for ceramic floor tiles, and see the 'Mosaics' section of 'Tiling Walls' for methods of measuring the border sheets.

Cement mortar screed

To lay a level screed, you must work in bays formed by battens laid across the width of the room. Each bay must be set out, levelled, and filled with mortar. Then the mortar is tamped down, levelled off and the tiles are laid before moving to the next bay.

Begin by dry laying the tiles as for the adhesive method. As it won't be possible to use battens at right angles, you will have to keep the rows straight by eye. To help, you can stretch a string down the length of the room tied to nails driven into the skirting boards a few centimetres from the floor.

When you have found the best arrangement, mark the floor at the last row of full tiles at the furthest end of the room from the door and check that the line is square with the room. This will be the line of the first bay. Mark the skirting board at each end of the line to make it easy to position the first batten.

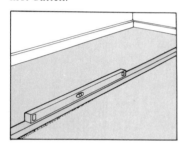

Use a long batten and spirit level to find the highest point on the floor. The screed will be 12mm thick (the thickness of the battens) at this point. The rest of the screed will be made level with this.

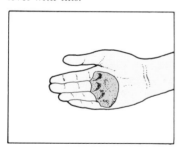

Prepare the mortar to the ratio of 3 parts sharp, washed sand to 1 part cement, mixing these thoroughly before adding water. Then mix only enough water to make the mortar hold its shape when squeezed in the hand; no more. This is called the semi dry method.

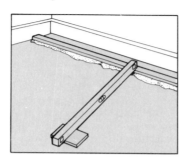

Place a piece of wood (or any object) 12mm thick on the highest part of the floor and lay the first batten of the bay on a layer of mortar. Use a batten and spirit level to level one end of the batten forming the bay to the highest point. Tamp the batten down or place more mortar under it to adjust it.

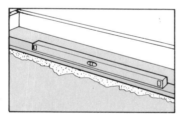

Then use the spirit level along the length of the batten to make it level with itself. Check that it is still on the line.

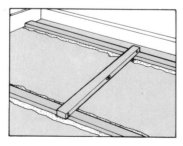

Next, lay the second batten on mortar parallel with the first, at a distance that you can reach

over easily, say 1 metre. Use the spirit level to make the second batten exactly level with the first along the entire length.

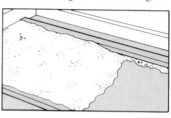

Shovel mortar into the bay, spreading it out with a float until the bay is filled above the level of the battens. Be careful not to knock the battens out of position.

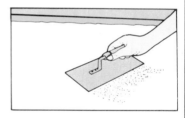

Tamp the mortar all over with the float, moving mortar from high spots to fill depressions. Keep adding and tamping until all the mortar is equally compressed.

Use a straight batten to scrape the top of the mortar level with the battens. If necessary, tamp and scrape again until the entire bay is level.

To help the tiles adhere to the screed, mix up a 'slurry' of 1 part cement to 1 part water and pour enough to cover the surface of the bay. Spread it over the screed with the float.

Lay the tiles, using a spacer card if necessary, starting with the back row. Tamp each one with the handle of the trowel to settle it firmly in the mortar.

Use a timber straight edge to beat down all the tiles in the bay and then use the spirit level to check the tiles are flat.

When all the whole tiles are laid and levelled, you may cut the border tiles and lay them immediately. Otherwise you must use the trowel to remove a little mortar from the surface around the edges and cut and fix them later with thin bed adhesive. Be sure to leave enough depth for the edge tiles.

Lift the first batten carefully out of the mortar and place it in front of the second one to form the next bay. Repeat the levelling procedure and continue until the floor is finished.

Leave the floor without walking on it for 12 hours and then, when the border tiles are laid, grout all the tiles in the same way as for the adhesive method.

Cork, vinyl, rubber and carpet tiles

Set out the floor as for ceramic tiles, and fix a batten.

Use the adhesive recommended by the manufacturer. Cork tiles are usually fixed with a contact adhesive, and carpet, rubber and vinyl are usually fixed with a latex based flooring adhesive (unless they are self adhesive).

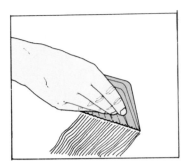

If you are using *flooring adhesive*, use a notched spreader to cover an area you can reach and begin laying the tiles immediately.

If you are using contact adhesive, spread an area you can reach and also coat the backs of enough tiles to cover the area, being careful not to let adhesive go over the edges. You will then have to follow the adhesive manufacturers' instructions about how long to wait before laying them.

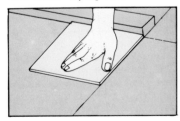

If the tiles are *self adhesive*, simply pull off the protective backing and stick them down.

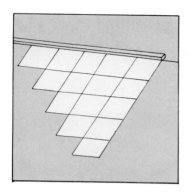

through the bottom tile along
the edge of the top tile.

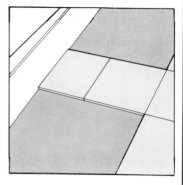

Lay the central tile first, and
work outwards in both
directions, filling in the middle
spaces as you go.

As you can walk on the
newly laid tiles, it's possible to
fill in the spaces around the
edges immediately.

To position each tile, hold it
above the floor with two edges
against the battens (or the
edges of previously laid tiles).
This is especially important
when using contact adhesive, as
it may not be possible to adjust
the tile once it's laid. Press each
tile down firmly all over and
use a damp cloth to wipe away
any adhesive that is squeezed
up between the edges.

With these soft tiles, it is best
to leave the last row of whole
tiles until cutting the border
tiles.

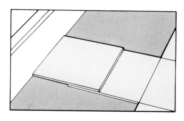

Dry lay a whole tile in the
border space tight against the
edge of an already fixed tile.
This is the tile to be cut. Then
place another whole tile on top
with its edge touching the
skirting board.

Use a sharp knife (with
replaceable blades) to cut

Simply reverse the position of
the whole tile and the cut tile.

For fitting tiles around
irregular shapes, follow the
methods described for ceramic
wall tiles, e.g. paper template
etc. Cork, vinyl and rubber can
be marked with a pencil, but a
piece of chalk is best for carpet.

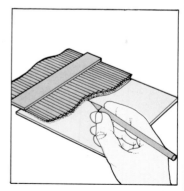

For rubber, vinyl and cork tiles,
an adjustable shape tracing
template can help when fitting
around architraves and intricate
shapes. A light placed directly
above makes transferring the
shape to the tile easier, simply
trace the outline of the shadow.

131

SPECIAL EFFECTS

When laying tiles most of us don't think beyond a straight-forward covering of a single area with a chosen type of tile. Before making a final decision, consider if there are any individual touches that would set your job apart from others. Sometimes a clever use of contrasting or toning colours, or the introduction of some random tiles will put the designer stamp on it. Left-over tiles can be used for small areas such as table tops, decorative inserts in plasterwork, window ledges, etc, and so help to give a 'total' look to a room.

Above *Plain white and plain blue 100cm tiles completely cover this tiny modern bathroom. The blue abstract design on the cupboard door adds interest without interfering with the simplistic design.*

Right *A collection of antique tiles of different designs have been laid on this kitchen work top. If you decide to do this it is important to have a theme of one sort or another. It could be a question of colour, or subject perhaps, but there needs to be something to link that particular collection of odd tiles.*

Top left *A tessellated pattern of brown and white provencal tiles provides a softer line for this bedroom and adds some interest.*

Top right *Black and white vinyl tiles laid alternately in groups of four make this cheap form of floor covering look much more important. The fact that they have been laid diagonally across the room also helps.*

Left *Vinyl tiles come in many different colours, textures and patterns. Those covering the floor in this bathroom have been continued up the side of the bath, to match the decorative border design of the ceramic wall tiles. The border helps visually reduce the height of the room.*

TOP TEN TIPS

1. Estimating the number of tiles you need is quite simple. Because there are so many different sizes and shapes of tiles, it's best to calculate the area you're going to cover in square metres.

Tiles are usually sold in packs that state the area covered by each pack. This is usually 1–2 square metres for floor tiles and perhaps 2/3 square metre for wall tiles.

It's important to remember that you will need extra tiles to allow for breakages and other accidents during laying, so estimate generously. Also, it's always a good idea to have a few spares in case some are damaged in use. There can be colour variation in different batches of tiles, so it may not be possible to find matching ones later.

To find the area of a *floor*, simply multiply the length in metres by the width in metres. The result is the area in square metres.

If the room is irregular, find the area of alcoves and window bays separately. Then add these to the area of the main part of the floor.

In the same way, you can subtract the area of chimney breasts or cupboards where tiles won't be needed.

Finding the area of *walls* is done in the same way. Multiply the length of each wall by the height, and then subtract the areas of doors or windows. Once again, it is better to over estimate slightly.

Then, if you're estimating for *ceramic tiles* you must calculate the number of finished edge tiles to buy (either RE and REX or glazed edge universal).

As you may not know the size of the tiles you will choose, make a rough sketch showing the window or external corners where the edges need finishing. Write the length of these edges on the sketch.

When buying the tiles, substitute the finished edge tiles for field tiles. In other words, if you need 30 RE tiles for an external corner of two walls, buy 30 fewer field tiles than your original estimate.

Remember to allow extra finished edge tiles as well as field tiles.

The packaging of *adhesive* and *grout* always states the approximate area covered by the contents.

2. Resist the urge to begin fixing tiles as soon as you start work. Remember that the result depends most on the planning, so take your time setting out the job and the rest of the work will follow easily.

3. Here's how to remove and replace a damaged ceramic wall or floor tile.

Use a hammer to crack the tile into small pieces, starting from the centre and working outwards. Use only as much force as necessary. Chip out the pieces carefully with a narrow cold chisel and club hammer. Be careful not to damage the edge of the adjacent tiles.

When all the pieces are removed, chip away any adhesive and scrape away grout from the edges of the space. Vacuum out the dust and grit.

Dry lay the new tile to be sure it fits and that there is room beneath it for the adhesive.

Fix the tile and allow it to set before grouting.

4. To remove and replace a cork, rubber or vinyl tile, use an old wood chisel and a hammer.

Pierce the tile in the centre and work outwards, being careful not to lift the edges of adjacent tiles. Use a stiff scraping knife to remove the old adhesive, and vacuum the space well to be sure it's clean and free of debris. Now lay the new tile.

Apply the correct adhesive and bend the tile as you fit it into the space. It helps to warm vinyl tiles for a few minutes to make them more pliable.

Then press down firmly, from the centre toward the edges, to remove air bubbles.

5. To drill holes in ceramic tiles for fixing towel rails etc., you should use a slow speed electric drill and a masonry drill bit. Mark the position of the hole with a felt tip pen, and stick clear adhesive tape over the mark. This helps keep the drill bit from slipping off the mark as the hole is being started.

Use the drill at the lowest speed and apply only gentle pressure.

If you insert a plastic plug into the hole to take a screw, push the head of the plug completely through the tile, into the wall. That way there is no chance of cracking the tile when the screw is tightened.

134

6. Be sure to use the right tile and adhesive for the job. Wall tiles for walls and floor tiles for floors and work surfaces or anywhere strength may be needed.

Use heat resistant tiles, adhesive and grout on fireplaces and kitchen work surfaces. Also, on surfaces where food is prepared, make sure the tiles have a non lead glaze and that the grout is non toxic and non stain. Special kitchen work surface grout is available.

Use frost proof tiles, adhesive and grout on exterior walls, patios, steps etc.

Use water proof adhesive and grout on areas that are often wet, such as shower cubicle walls and floors.

Finally, for any surface that is slightly flexible, such as chipboard (particle board) lined walls, plywood panels or hardboard covered wood floors, you must always use a flexible wall or floor tile adhesive.

7. If the grout on wall tiles becomes stained, it may be possible to clean it by rubbing it gently with a pencil eraser.

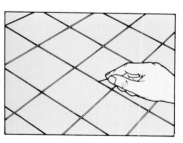

If the grout is too discoloured to be cleaned, use a nail to scrape out the old grout. Be careful not to damage the edges of the tiles.

Use a brush or vacuum

cleaner to remove the dust and then regrout the tiles.

8. Where the edges of tiles meet a bath tub, sink or work surface, use silicone caulk instead of grout. This will remain flexible to absorb movement and resist staining. Make sure the gap to be filled is clean, dry and free of grease.

Apply the caulk direct from the nozzle of the tube, working in this direction.

Then smooth with a wet finger and remove any excess immediately with a damp cloth.

9. To fit quadrant tiles around a bath or basin, always work toward the centre of each wall from the ends.

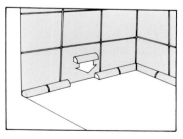

Fix the mitred tile in the corner and the round edge tile at the

other end of the row. Then fix whole plain tiles until there is a gap left in the middle. Cut a plain tile to fit, leaving the correct gap either side.

10. When the tiling is finished, follow the manufacturers' instructions concerning sealing and maintenance.

Cork floor tiles must be sealed with polyurethane varnish unless they are ready sealed by the manufacturer.

Unglazed ceramic floor tiles and vinyl tiles must be sealed with the correct proprietary sealants recommended by the manufacturer.

Although rubber floor tiles are not usually sealed, some have a protective layer of wax that must be removed with a cloth dampened with white spirit (mineral spirits).

Safety Tips

When cutting tiles with a spike or trimming knife, make sure the tile is well supported and that all parts of your body are out of the way.

Wear gloves or use barrier cream to protect the skin of hands when working with cement, adhesives and grout.

Keep sharp tools, adhesives, grout and all products away from children and pets.

Don't wear a tie or loose clothing when using power tools.

SHELVE IT

CONTENTS

Introduction

A shelf is any horizontal surface that can be used to store or display an object. This deceptively simple statement ignores the hundreds of ways that have been developed for making and supporting shelves.

Although there seems to be an infinite variety of shelves, for the purpose of this book they are divided into three categories: wall-mounted shelves, built-in shelves and free-standing shelves. Any of these can be single shelves or 'shelf units' (shelves that are assembled with sides or struts, making a box shape).

If you are thinking of buying or making shelves, there are (apart from price) only three considerations. The shelves must be a size and strength that will support the load placed on them. They must be of a type of construction that can be used in your chosen situation. Lastly, the overall design must

Right. *Deep, built-in shelves fill an alcove and adjustable shelving allows objects of a similar size to be grouped together.*

Centre right, below. *A high-tech shelf system designed for use in warehouses. Combined with plain wooden shelves, this makes a stylish bookshelf.*

Far right, below. *Built-in wooden shelving. Simple to construct and very useful in family rooms.*

Centre right, above. *Track shelving used to advantage in a tiny office. The shelves have been "wrapped" in plastic, as has the work-surface.*

Far right, above. *The supports for these dark green shelves have been painted white and are made of architrave off-cuts. The shelves are removable for easy window cleaning.*

create an effect that pleases you and is sympathetic to the style of the rest of the room.

This chapter shows you how to choose suitable shelves for different purposes and places, and helps you decide whether to make them yourself or buy them. The photographs will give you an idea of some of the effects that are possible, and perhaps spark off an idea that will solve a storage problem or finish a difficult corner or alcove.

Plan your project thoroughly, no matter how simple it seems. Always make a sketch of your design (to see that it will actually fit together) and show details of fixings. Then, try to imagine the various stages of assembly. This can save a lot of redesign during building when you may find yourself going about it the hard way.

WALL-MOUNTED SHELVES

Fixing shelves to one wall (as opposed to spanning between two) is one of the easiest and most versatile methods. The only requirement is a reasonably flat wall that is sound enough to take the load. With all the variations on this theme, the strength of the brackets, track systems, cantilever fixtures etc., is usually far greater than you're ever likely to need. The weak link is nearly always the wall fixing. However, any wall of brick or building block is quite strong enough for most purposes, and partition (hollow) walls are fine, provided the fixings are screwed to the vertical timbers inside them.

The most basic support is the **simple bracket** that is fixed below the shelf. Traditional ones were made of wood, brass, cast iron, or wrought iron scrollwork, and there are many beautiful examples for sale in antique shops. In fact, these have become so popular that reproductions are being manufactured. Modern designs, made of pressed steel, are the cheapest ready-made shelf support available.

A popular extension of the bracket idea is the **track system.** This consists of vertical metal (or, less often, wood) strips fixed to the wall. Adjustable brackets are attached to the strips by means of holes, slots, or some can slide to any position and be locked in place.

Further refinements that attach to the vertical tracks include light fittings with concealed wiring, bookends, partitions, and cabinet brackets to allow cupboards, desks and drawer units to be mounted as well as shelves. You can also use these systems to completely fit out the interior of cupboards and wardrobes, as there are clothes rail fittings, too.

Some manufacturers make only tracks and brackets, while others offer shelves, and furniture, too. As the different brands are not interchangeable, it's a good idea to collect as many catalogues as possible before buying. You may want to extend your system later on.

Above left. *Simple black brackets with veneered blockboard shelves provide storage space in a kitchen too small for cupboards.*

Left. *These commercially produced shelves are cheap and easy to fix.*

Above. *A single shelf running round the kitchen above the work surface. Fixed with cantilever brackets and tiled to match.*

Left. *Keep a look out for lovely old shelf brackets like this one. They can often be found in second-hand shops. Modern reproductions are also available, but will cost a lot more.*

Shelf support brackets, whether single or mounted on tracks, are the easiest solution to DIY shelves. By buying ready-finished shelves in standard sizes, or having them cut to length by the supplier, you can put up a roomful of shelves in a day with no woodworking at all.

Cantilever fittings make it possible to fit shelves without any visible means of support. They are metal rods that are set into walls and into holes in the back edge of the shelf.

Shelf units (i.e. more than one shelf attached to uprights) and cupboards can be mounted directly to walls by fixing small metal angle brackets or a wood batten at the bottom to support the weight. Then the top of the unit is fastened to the wall to prevent it leaning outward. Small, unobtrusive metal plates are usually sufficient for this.

Finally, there are some shelves that are designed to be hung on wires or ropes attached to the wall or ceiling.

Right. *Glass shelves on tracks, fitted in front of this bathroom window, make a perfect place for plants. The edge of the glass shelves should be ground.*

Top left. *A simple opening bridged by glass shelves and a collection of bottles is an attractive feature in this room. In this instance the shelves are not fixed to allow for easy cleaning, but this would not always be safe.*

Top right. *Unusual wall-mounted fittings support generous-sized kitchen shelving. The supports must be securely attached to a very solid wall as they may be expected to carry heavy items such as crockery.*

Left. *A system that completely covers two walls of this room and provides different width shelves for various purposes. A perfect solution for a small family room or bedsittingroom.*

Fixing wall-mounted shelves

The first concern when fixing shelves to walls is the type and condition of the wall. Strong fixings in masonry walls are easily made with screws and plugs or, for unusually heavy loads, expansion bolts. The main thing to remember is that plaster isn't strong, and so all holes must be drilled deep enough so that the plugs can be pushed through the plaster and into the wall itself.

Hollow partition walls can be awkward, as strong fixings can only be made to the vertical timbers (studs) inside them. The studs are usually not more than 600mm apart, equally spaced in the wall, but may not be in the places you want the brackets or tracks. You should be able to find the studs by knocking on the wall, moving from side to side. The spaces between studs should sound hollow and the studs, solid. This method works easily with modern plasterboard, but some old lathe and plaster walls can disguise the sound very effectively.

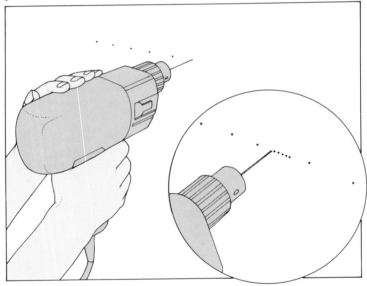

In this case, you will have to find the studs by drilling tiny holes about 25mm apart until you come to solid wood. Do this along the line of the proposed shelf, so you won't need to fill and redecorate the wall.

Find the edges of the stud by drilling more holes close together and marking the first hole either side that just misses it. Repeat the process about 600mm to one side of the first one, and then measure the distance from the centre of one stud to the next. Hopefully, the other studs will be the same distance apart.

Using Shelf Brackets

For small shelves, it's easiest to screw the brackets to the shelf and then hold it up to the wall.

Use a spirit level on the shelf or have someone stand back and tell you when it's straight. Then mark the positions of the screw holes with a pencil or bradawl.

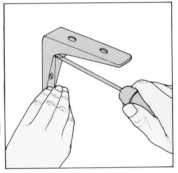

For long shelves, or where the brackets must be located on studs, it's easier to put the brackets on the wall first.

Fix one bracket at the correct height and then hold another against the wall, with the shelf resting on both.

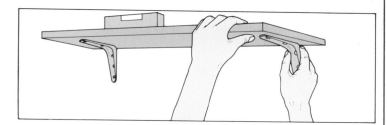

If the shelf sags, hold it on its edge to set the level of the second bracket. Once the two end brackets are fixed, find the height of any middle brackets the same way. This ensures the shelf will be straight.

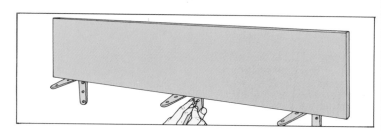

Lay the first shelf on the brackets and measure for any shelves above or below. Put up all the remaining brackets before fixing the shelves to them.

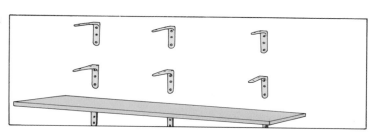

Place the top shelf in position and hang a plumb line (or a string with a weight) over the side. Line up each subsequent shelf with the string and fix to the brackets.

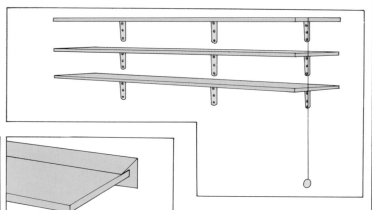

You can make your own wooden brackets and use plugs to hide the screw heads.

Here's a novel bracket made to take standard chipboard shelving. The shelf is inserted,

covering the wall fixings, and it will support quite a heavy load without sagging.

Putting up Track Systems

Track systems are fixed in much the same way as single brackets. If necessary, cut the uprights to length with a hacksaw, but be sure to have the uncut ends at the top when putting them up.

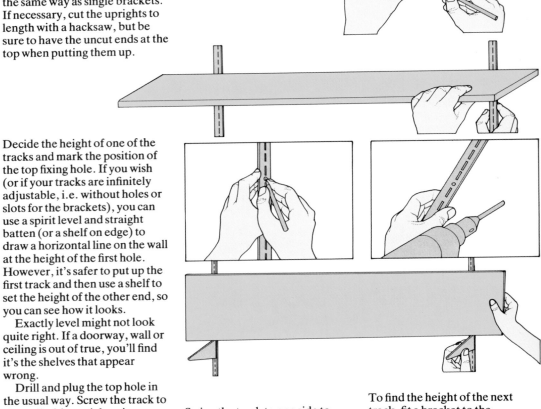

Decide the height of one of the tracks and mark the position of the top fixing hole. If you wish (or if your tracks are infinitely adjustable, i.e. without holes or slots for the brackets), you can use a spirit level and straight batten (or a shelf on edge) to draw a horizontal line on the wall at the height of the first hole. However, it's safer to put up the first track and then use a shelf to set the height of the other end, so you can see how it looks.

Exactly level might not look quite right. If a doorway, wall or ceiling is out of true, you'll find it's the shelves that appear wrong.

Drill and plug the top hole in the usual way. Screw the track to the wall without tightening, so the track is free to swing to a vertical position. Mark all the remaining fixing holes.

Swing the track to one side to drill and plug the other holes, and then screw it tightly to the wall.

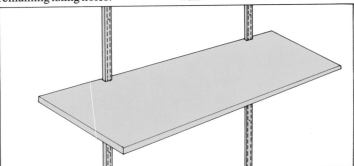

To find the height of the next track, fit a bracket to the corresponding holes or slots in two tracks and place a shelf on edge over the brackets. Then use a spirit level or let a helper tell you when it looks horizontal. If you have trouble deciding, put up more brackets and loose shelves until it's right.

When the tracks and brackets are up, fix the shelves in position using a plumb line, as for single brackets.

If you want the back edges of the shelves to touch the wall, you can cut notches in the back edge around the tracks.

Fixing shelf units to walls

Small shelf units, such as spice racks and what-nots can be fixed with small brass mirror plates arranged to be as unobtrusive as possible.

Larger units such as bookshelves, corner cupboards, etc., need support at the bottom, as well.

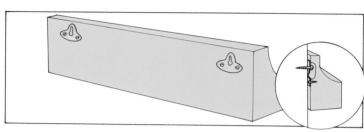

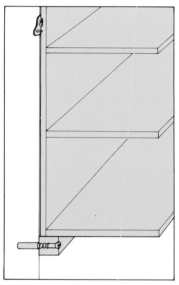

The strongest support is a batten, screwed to the wall underneath. Pins, driven through the bottom into the batten, will prevent it slipping off, and the plates at the top stop it leaning away from the wall.

A less visible method, although not quite as strong, is to fix thin brackets to the wall. The important thing is that the shelf must rest right in the corner of the bracket – any gap will allow the bracket to bend under load.

By using several brackets, any but the heaviest loads can be supported.

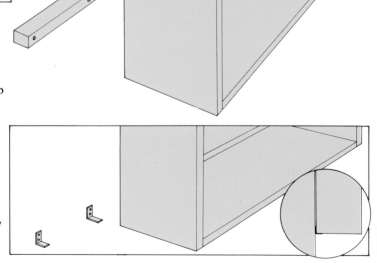

BUILT-IN SHELVES

Visually, built-in shelves offer attractive, simple lines that blend with the room and become part of it. The practical advantage is that all the available space is used and the awkward places between walls and shelf units and dust traps are kept to a minimum.

While there are many examples of ready-made 'built-in' kitchen units and bedroom cupboards on the market, shelves don't lend themselves so readily to mass-produced designs that can be truly described as built-in. There are free-standing shelf units that are made in several widths and are meant to be combined to fill various heights and widths of wall space. However, built-in shelves mean some work shaping them to fit the space.

From a construction point of view, 'built-in' means using the walls as a part of the structure. While this is the best method to

use in some cases, quite often it is easier to make a complete structure without using the walls, place it in position, and then disguise the joins between shelf unit and walls to make it look built-in. The advantage of this approach is that the shelves and uprights can be made straight and square instead of having to be shaped to the walls, floor and ceiling. Also, if only two or three shelves are permanently fixed to the uprights, the other shelves can rest on adjustable supports.

Another approach for the built-in look is to build the necessary upright supports to look like walls, rather than thin panels like the shelves, effectively adding walls that the shelves can be built-in to.

A work surface can be thought of as a large shelf, and can be used as a desk, table or kitchen counter top. Once in place, it can be the basis for smaller shelves, above and below.

Above. *Alcoves fitted with built-in shelving from floor to ceiling provide perfect storage for a large collection of books and small mementoes.*

Right. *The uprights for these shelves have been made of plasterboard and decorated to be part of the structure of the room. Shelves have been fixed at a*

variety of heights to allow for display of different sized books and objects.

Above left. *A very simple way to fit shelves in an alcove. Painting them the same colour as the walls has made them much more interesting.*

Above right. *This alcove was formed when cupboards were being fitted. The interior has been decorated and independently lit to provide display for a collection of wooden toys.*

Right. *Close-up of the strips which can be used to give variation in height of the individual shelves, enabling you to tailor the system for your specific needs.*

Top right. *These painted wooden shelves have a back to keep them rigid and form useful storage for a child of any age.*

Above left. *The uprights in these shelves have been drilled at regular intervals so that the owner has complete adjustability. The shelves are glass, but the method works very well with other types of shelf.*

Left. *The simple brass rod and fittings which hold these shelves can be bought in any hardware shop. They are available in brass and chrome and in a variety of sizes. Experiment with the placing of the rod to gain as much support and the best visual effect. It would not be advisable to span too large an alcove in this way.*

Fixing built-in shelves

The least expensive method of making shelves is to rest them on wood battens that are fixed to the walls of an alcove. Alcoves seem to offer an almost ready-made site for shelves. After all, there is a wall at the back and at each side to hold the supports. However, this method is not quite as simple as it looks: if the walls aren't straight or square with each other, each shelf must be shaped to fit the space it will occupy. Also, if the walls are very uneven, the supports won't fit flat against them. However, if the shelves are for books or will be well-filled, there will be very little of the shelves showing.

So, if the side walls are fairly flat and you don't mind the shelves not quite touching the back wall, it is only necessary to make the front edges of the shelves even with each other and the corner of the chimney breast. Otherwise, you can scribe each shelf into the alcove as described in the Tools and Techniques section.

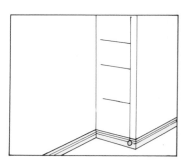

Mark the wall for the position of the front edge of each shelf by using a plumb line.

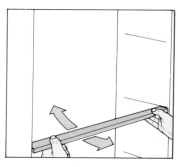

Measure the height of the alcove from the top of the skirting board and mark the approximate position of the shelves. It is usual for the spaces between the shelves to be larger at the bottom and reduce towards the top, but decide according to what you intend putting on the shelves.

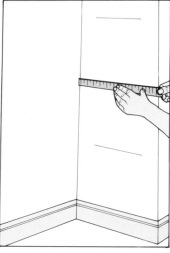

The front edges of the shelves should be slightly recessed into the alcove, and in line with each other. Measure the depth of the alcove at each mark, and make sure your shelves will fit into the narrowest part without sticking out. If necessary, you can cut all the shelves to the depth of the narrowest one; or, if this would mean some of them being too far from the back wall, use wider shelves and scribe the back of the protruding ones.

Then cut a piece of batten to length and get a helper to hold it across the alcove as if it were the front edge of a shelf (or you can use a small piece of wood to wedge it into place). Stand back and look at it from different angles, adjusting the batten until it looks straight. Mark the other wall, and use a plumb line on that side to mark the position of the shelf fronts.

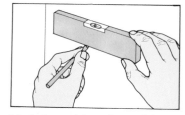

Mark the position of one of the shelves on one wall, using a spirit level to make sure the line is horizontal.

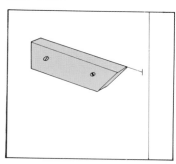

Cut a batten support to length and fix it so the top edge aligns with the mark. To be unobtrusive, the batten supports should be slightly recessed behind the front edge of the shelf, and the appearance will be further improved if you chamfer or round the front of the batten.

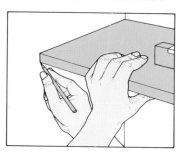

Cut a shelf to length and hold one end on the fixed support with a level resting on the top. Adjust the free end up and down until it is level, and draw a line on the wall along the bottom of the shelf, also marking the position of the front edge.

Then measure the length of the batten support for that side and fix it to the wall with the top edge aligned with the pencil mark. Place the shelf in position and check whether it is sitting properly on both supports.

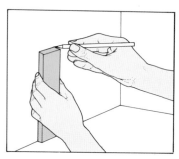

Now cut a piece of batten (or use a measuring tape) to set the height of the next shelf. Mark the wall at the top of the batten at each corner, and fix the next support in position. Then cut and hold the next shelf in position and proceed as with the first shelf.

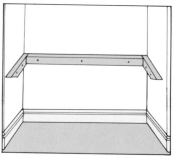

To prevent shelves sagging
An easy and effective way to keep thin shelves from sagging under heavy loads, is to fix a batten to the wall along the back edge. Cut these to fit and fix them flush with the top edge of the side battens.

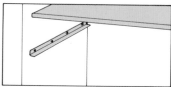

Instead of using battens, another method is to screw lengths of

thin metal angle (instead of battens) to the walls. The shelves can set on the flanges and be fixed from underneath. Be sure to make the shelves a loose fit so there's room for the thickness of the angle between the edge of the shelf and the wall.

Alcove shelf supports
Here's an alternative method for alcove supports. It looks best with glass shelves, but it would work with wood or man-made boards.

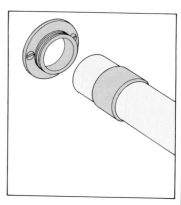

Buy wardrobe hanging rail (tube) and enough socket end fittings to make two supports for each shelf. These are available from DIY shops in chrome or brass finish and several sizes – 18mm or 25mm diameter is about right.

Measure the positions of the shelves as described above, and screw one end fitting to the wall. The tubes should be placed about ¼ of the shelf width from the edges. Then cut the tube to a length that allows you to insert one end into the fitting with the other fitting in place. Be careful that, once in position, the tube cannot slide far enough to come out of either socket.

Built-in units

Sometimes an easier method is to make a shelf unit with two sides and all shelves the same size. This should be made small enough to fit into the alcove at the narrowest and shallowest point. This reduces the amount of scribing to shape you have to do. It's only necessary to screw the bottom, middle and top shelves to the uprights; the others can rest on bookcase strips or adjustable shelf supports.

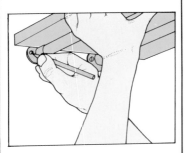

Hold it in position to mark the holes for the other end. Drill and plug the holes and then screw the second fitting to the wall with the tube in place.

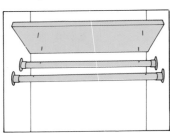

Repeat for the second tube, but place the shelf in position to mark the final holes. This will ensure the shelf rests along the full length of both tubes.

If the shelves are wood or man-made board, you can prevent then slipping off the tubes by driving 4 small nails into the bottom of the shelf and clipping the heads off. These can sit in holes drilled in the tubes.

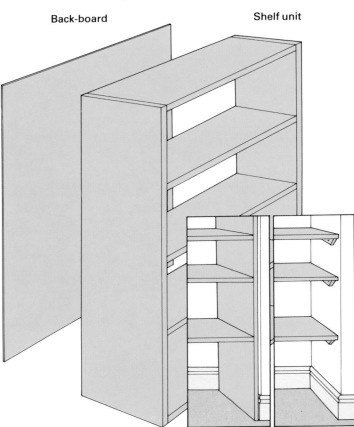

Back-board   Shelf unit

If the shelves don't fit against the back wall very well, you can put a panel of thin plywood, chipboard (particle board), or hardboard onto the back of the unit. You can, of course, decorate the face of the back panel before fixing it to the shelves, and still have the effect of seeing the wall between the shelves.

Corners
If you are building shelves into a corner, you again have to choose between using batten supports on the wall or making a second upright. In this case, the two-sided shelf unit is more desirable, as it will be difficult to make the shelves meet the wall as perfectly as they will fit the upright.

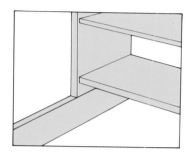

One way to deal with the skirting board, is to let the upright sit on top of it, but this may look awkward. It also makes the addition of a trim to the front of the upright difficult.

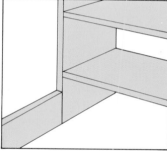

Another way is to cut the required length of skirting board away with a tenon saw. If the wall isn't straight and vertical (and what wall is?) then there may still be a difficult front edge to trim.

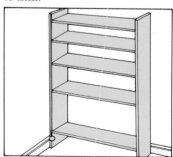

The best solution is to place the unit in position as close as possible to the wall and use a plumb line or level to make sure the uprights are vertical.

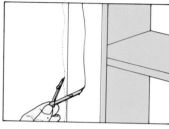

Then, any gap, however awkward, can be bridged by scribing a trimming piece to the wall.

Additional support
If the shelves are not going to be adjustable, you can put partitions in between them. These can be placed at random, or arranged to accommodate particular items, such as hi-fi, etc. If you place them in line with each other, use wire shelf supports to hold them in place.

This method makes a very strong unit, as the load on each shelf is shared with all those below.

A plinth under the bottom shelf, or feet beneath the bottom partitions, will allow you to make thin, long shelves to carry very heavy loads.

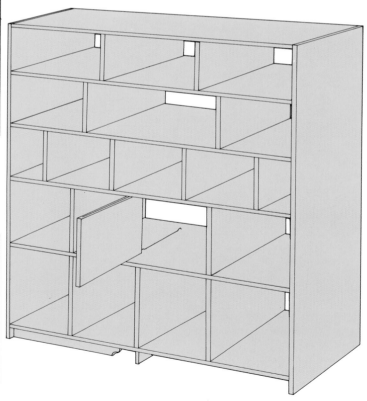

FREE-STANDING SHELVES

Free-standing shelves are any that you would consider as separate pieces of furniture – shelves that you could move from one room or house to the next, even though there may be some fixings to the walls or ceiling.

Apart from making them yourself, there are hundreds of manufactured pieces and systems. In general, this type of shelving is more expensive than the DIY types (some are very expensive). However, pieces of furniture that you can keep for years are a sort of investment. This is true of good quality systems that can be added to gradually, as you can afford them. Also, some systems cost very little more than DIY shelves, and the amount of work required to assemble a ready-made, free-standing set of shelves is considerably less.

One of the most popular systems consists of *upright metal or wood ladders* that carry shelves (as well as desks, cupboards and drawer units) between them.

Cubes that stack up are a versatile system. Most of these incorporate a means of fixing the cubes together and they can sometimes be wall-mounted. Also you can mix DIY shelves with them to make desks and extra shelves.

Poles or posts of wood or metal are made with adjustable feet at both ends. They are placed vertically between the floor and ceiling and the feet are screwed out until the post is effectively held by the pressure. Four of these then carry adjustable shelves between them. Pairs of posts can be added to extend the system sideways.

There are systems of *tubes* or *struts* that are held together with corner fittings. These build into frames that support shelves, and there are systems of flat panels that clip together into cubes. These offer some possibility for varying the overall size. You can have the glass cut to your size, but be sure to ask for the edges to be ground and polished.

Top far left. *Designed for shop-window display, a unit like this can easily be used in a home setting.*

Bottom far left. *Used as a room divider, this unit is given added permanency by the addition of a wooden strip where it meets the ceiling.*

Above left. *Another free-standing unit used as a room divider. This one is slightly raised off the floor and attached to the ceiling beam.*

Left. *A cube system, of which there are a number available, can be built into whatever shape you want without any DIY skills. A variation in the components purchased gives each arrangement individuality.*

Above. *This system relies upon the four uprights being adjusted between the floor and ceiling correctly before the shelves are added. Follow the instructions carefully.*

Designing a free-standing unit

Designing and making your own free-standing shelf units is not very different from built-in ones, apart from the lateral support needed to prevent them from leaning side to side. A quick look at the ready-made systems will show you the various devices that can provide this support. Otherwise, you can use the same sort of support as for a built-in or wall-mounted unit. Any ceiling or wall fixing (such as mirror plates) will prevent the top of the unit moving sideways in relation to the bottom.

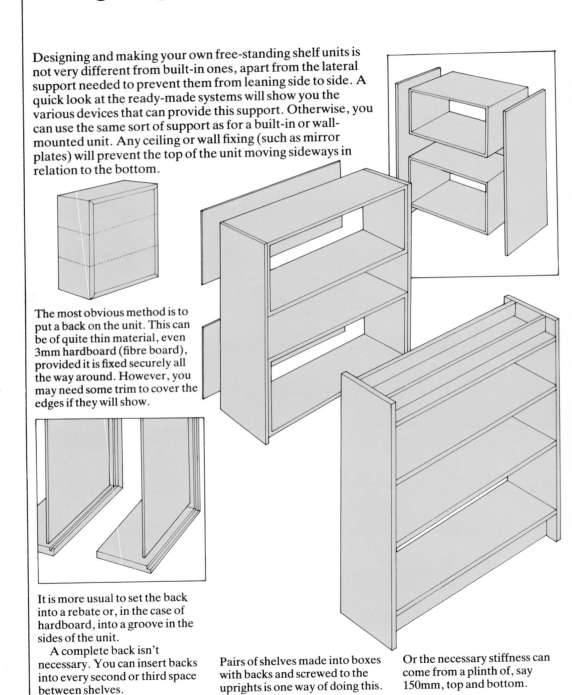

The most obvious method is to put a back on the unit. This can be of quite thin material, even 3mm hardboard (fibre board), provided it is fixed securely all the way around. However, you may need some trim to cover the edges if they will show.

It is more usual to set the back into a rebate or, in the case of hardboard, into a groove in the sides of the unit.

A complete back isn't necessary. You can insert backs into every second or third space between shelves.

Pairs of shelves made into boxes with backs and screwed to the uprights is one way of doing this.

Or the necessary stiffness can come from a plinth of, say, 150mm, top and bottom.

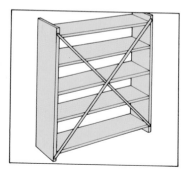

Diagonal braces are an often used method. These can be wooden struts, wire, metal rod or wood dowel.

No matter which of these methods you choose, remember that the stability depends on the overall height in relation to the length and width of the bottom. A tall, shallow bookshelf, no matter how rigid, will not stand alone safely.

One way around this, without fixing to the ceiling or wall, is to add a unit at right angles to the first.

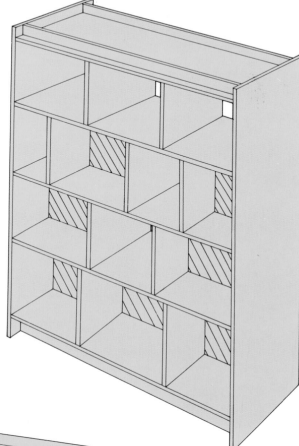

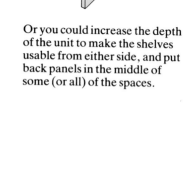

Or you could increase the depth of the unit to make the shelves usable from either side, and put back panels in the middle of some (or all) of the spaces.

Materials

The most widely used materials for shelves are solid wood, chipboard (particle board), blockboard, plywood and medium density fibreboard (MDF). These are all readily available and some can be bought partly or fully finished as shelves. If you want to do all the cutting to size yourself, timber merchants and large DIY chainstores are the cheapest place to buy them. However, many smaller DIY stores offer a cut to size service, and the effort saved is well worth the difference in price. Before placing your order, be sure to ask whether the cuts will be clean, straight and square; unfortunately, some cutting services are meant only to make pieces small enough to fit into your car.

Wood is the traditional material but, although it's the stiffest and strongest, it does have some drawbacks. It is expensive in comparison with the others, and is difficult to obtain in widths greater than about 250mm. Since wide pieces tend to warp or split more than narrow ones, it's usual to join narrower pieces edge to edge. A sufficiently strong joint can be made with ordinary woodworking glue and clamping until set, but the edges must be perfectly straight to make a close fit.

The growth rings in the wood should face opposite directions to minimize warping.

If you want wood shelves for a wall-mounted track system or brackets, you can use narrow widths as slats.

It's also worthwhile looking at ready-made wood shelves, available in standard lengths. Some are fully finished and others ready to finish as you choose.

If you're making a shelf unit or built-in shelves, the structure will help to hold the wood straight.

Chipboard (particle board) is the most popular material for shelves, probably because it is the least expensive, and comes in shelf size widths (as well as large sheets) with many different coverings.

Because of its lack of stiffness, chipboard needs support at closer intervals than other shelf materials.

The finishes available are real wood veneers, decorative PVC coatings, and melamine (usually limited to white, cream and imitation woodgrain) which is a very hardwearing, easy to clean surface.

You can buy chipboard in different widths with all the surface covered except the ends. After cutting to length, these are finished with matching iron-on strip.

Blockboard is made of a core of softwood battens held together by one or two layers of veneer on each face. Used with the core in the direction of the shelf's length, it is stiffer than chipboard. But as it is sold mainly in sheets, all the edges need finishing and there are sometimes gaps between the battens that can be awkward when fixing into the edges.

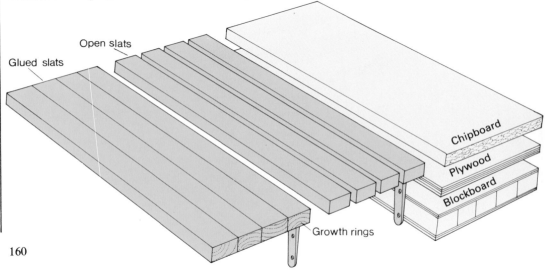

Open slats

Glued slats

Chipboard

Plywood

Blockboard

Growth rings

Different facings include many wood veneers and also plastic laminates.

Plywood is strong and more uniform than blockboard, but not quite as stiff. Again, it is sold in sheets rather than shelf widths and comes plain or with veneer or plastic laminate faces.

Medium density fibreboard (MDF) is sold in sheets and is probably the best material if you're going to paint the shelves. It has a very smooth surface that is without grain and is comparable to chipboard in strength and stiffness, although a little heavier. It is inexpensive, cuts very cleanly, can be shaped in any direction and doesn't have to be covered on the edges.

Hardboard is not exactly a shelving material, but it's used for backs of shelf units and cabinets. It is actually high density fibreboard and the most used thicknesses are 3mm and (less often) 6mm. It usually has one smooth face and one rough. The smooth side is suitable for painting, but you can also buy hardboard with a white enamel or melamine surface that matches white melamine covered chipboard. Used together, it is possible to make a shelf unit that requires no finishing at all.

Glass can be bought in sheets, but it makes sense to buy it cut to size from a glazier or DIY store.

Glass shelves need to have their edges ground smooth and polished, and your supplier will be able to advise on the best thickness and type of glass to use. This will depend on the size of the shelves, the method used to support them and what you intend to put on them. Plate glass 6mm thick is suitable for shelves up to 1m long which will carry light loads.

SUPPORTS

As well as strength, shelves must have enough stiffness not to sag under load. All materials (except glass) will bend a great deal before there's any chance of breaking. Remember that the shelf is likely to be supporting the load for a long time.

As a rough guide, these distances between supports would be suitable for bookshelves. As books (and records) are probably the heaviest item, lighter loads won't need so many. If you're using brackets, you can always add extra ones if you find the shelves tend to sag. For shelf units and built-in shelves, it's better to have too much support, rather than too little. Also, you can double the distances between supports by fixing wood battens either to the shelves to stiffen them, or on the wall behind.

Material	Distance Between Supports
12mm chipboard	300mm
15mm chipboard	400mm
18mm chipboard 15mm chipboard 18mm MDF	500mm
18mm plywood 18mm blockboard 25mm MDF 18mm wood (finished about 15mm)	700mm
25mm wood (finished about 21mm)	900mm

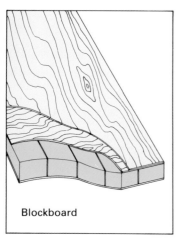

Blockboard

Fittings

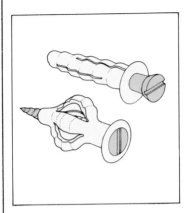

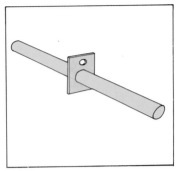

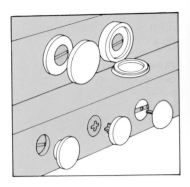

Fixing to brick, stone or building block walls is done with **plastic plugs** inserted into drilled holes. Screws then expand the plug as they're driven. The manufacturer will state the correct size of masonry drill bit and choice of screw sizes for the plugs. The larger the screw, the stronger the fixing.

There are special plugs for light-weight cellular block (breeze block) walls.

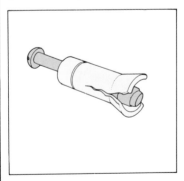

While plastic plugs and screws should be strong enough for almost any purpose you can also use **expansion bolts**, which are very strong. As they are available with hooks, they can be used for the type of shelves that hang on ropes or wires.

Cantilever brackets are high tensile steel rods that are set into holes in masonry walls. There is a plate in the middle to take a screw and plug, and then the rest of the rod goes into the hole in the back edge of the shelf. These brackets are invisible when the shelf is up.

For fixing the tops of shelf units to walls, there are **mirror plates** and **cabinet hangers**, and **metal angle brackets** can be used to support the bottom of all but the heaviest ones.

Metal angle of various widths (usually aluminium) is sold in lengths and can be used instead of wood battens to support shelves. Thin ones look best with glass shelves.

Screw caps of plastic are made to fit cross-headed screws, and some also fit different sizes of countersunk holes. These are very useful for white melamine covered chipboard, as there is no way to refinish the holes made for fixings, and the rim around the edge of the caps hides any chipped edges around the hole.

Knock-down fittings are popular for fixing man-made boards together. To join two panels, simply screw one half of the fitting to each, and then bolt the two halves together. You need to design the shelves carefully to keep these fittings unobtrusive.

Screws should be woodscrews except, when fixing into chipboard, a different thread is needed.

Adjustable Shelf Supports

There are many ready-made lightweight shelf supports. Some are simply buttons with pins that are hammered into holes in the sides of the unit, while others have plastic studs that push into sockets inserted into the sides. You can also use short pieces of dowel (round hardwood) in snug fitting holes. There are metal supports for glass shelves.

A neat, invisible support is made of wire, the two ends fitting into holes in the side. A groove is made in the ends of the shelves from the back but not quite to the front. The shelves slide into the unit from the front, obscuring the wires.

All of these (apart from the wires) require one support at each corner of the shelf. You can put them in one place only, or drill four rows of holes in the sides to enable the supports and shelves to be raised or lowered.

Another way is to use bookcase strips. These are fixed to the sides and have metal clips that fit into slots. Four strips are needed.

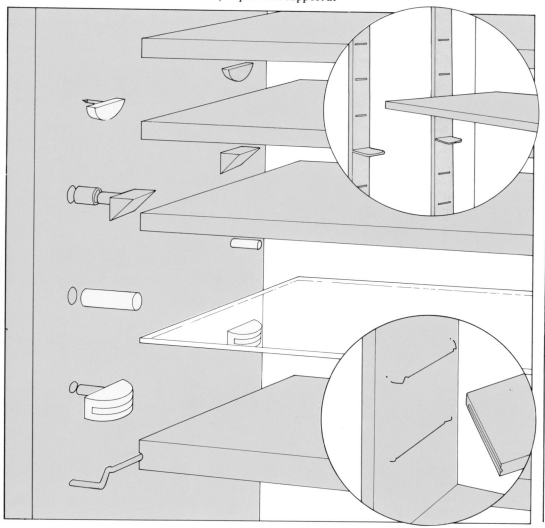

Tools and techniques

The first job you will come to is **cutting** the shelves to size. Any sharp hand-saw or power-saw will do. The important thing is to cut clean and straight. In the case of melamine and veneer, you must first score a line right through the decorative surface to prevent it breaking out. This is also the best way to cut wood cleanly.

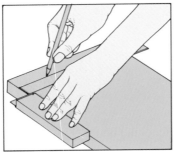

Use a setsquare or metal straightedge and a sharp knife to score a line all the way around the piece. But if only one side is to be seen, then you needn't worry about the other. Saw on the waste side, as near to the line as possible without chipping the edge you want to keep.

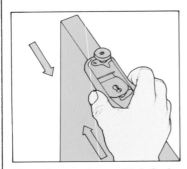

Plane the cut edge until it is flush with the scored line, always planing from the corner toward the middle. If you plane right across, the far edge will break out.

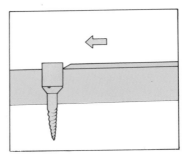

Boring neat holes can be a problem. Counterboring bits are available that cut holes exactly the size of screw heads. For wood, you can also get matched plug cutters that enable you to fill the hole with a plug of the same wood. Simply glue in the plug (be sure the grain is in the same direction as the surrounding wood) and pare the surface flush with a chisel when set.

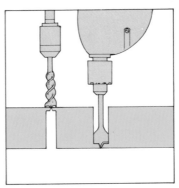

Large holes are best made with a brace and bit or a flat bit and power drill, working from each side toward the middle. As soon as the point comes through, turn the piece over.

Scribing is the technique of shaping panels so that they fit perfectly within the space, such as an alcove.

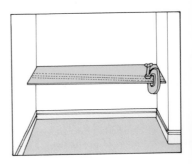

Cut a piece of thin scrap plywood or cardboard a little smaller than the space. You will need some ingenuity to find a way of holding it securely in place, with the front edge straight across the alcove. Battens slightly too long, wedged at the right height, are one way.

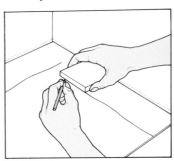

Using a pencil and small square piece of wood, trace a line around the three walls.

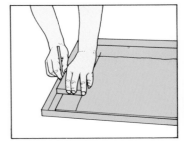

Then, place the template on the shelf material with the front edges flush, and transfer the lines onto the shelf. These are the lines to cut.

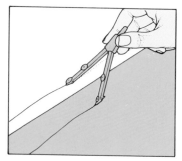

To scribe the back edge of a shelf to the wall, place it in position as near to the wall as possible, and set a pair of compasses to the width of the widest gap. Holding the compasses always at the same angle against the wall, mark the top of the shelf. Cutting this line will enable the shelf to touch the wall all along the edge.

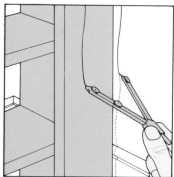

Use the same technique to scribe a wood trim for the side of a shelf unit. Temporarily fix the trim to the edge, keeping it straight with the upright, not the wall. Then set the compasses to the distance you want the trim to move toward the wall. Check that this is not smaller than the widest gap.

Edging with veneer or plastic is best done with the iron-on strip sold for the purpose.

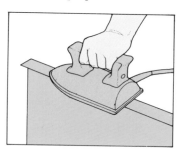

Simply cut off a piece a little too long and press it firmly over the edge with a medium hot iron. The adhesive melts quickly so there's no need to continue heating it for longer than 2 or 3 seconds. The important thing is to press it firmly. Allow it to cool.

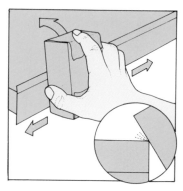

Then use a sanding block and medium to fine abrasive paper to weaken the edging, rubbing along the corner and bending it over. As you rub, gradually change the angle of the block until you're almost (but not quite) rubbing the face of the shelf. Repeat for the other edge.

Finally, use the sanding block or a fine file in this direction to trim the corners to a bevel.

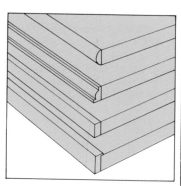

Using hardwood mouldings as **lippings** for blockboard, veneered chipboard or plywood makes a good-looking and more durable edge than iron-on strip. Mouldings are available in many shapes and some are made exactly the right width for man-made boards. Fix them with glue and small panel pins, setting the heads below the surface and filling with proprietary wood filler of an appropriate colour.

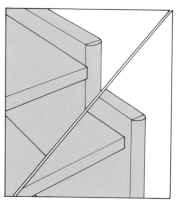

If you use shaped lippings, be careful when designing your shelves that the front edges don't meet like this, leaving a difficult mitre joint. It's easier to recess one panel behind the edge of the other.

TOP TEN TIPS

1. Consider getting all the pieces for your design cut to size by the supplier. Most of the hard work in making shelves is in the cutting, especially if you don't have room to support and manoeuvre large sheets.

2. If you plan to redecorate a hollow partition wall on which you will need fixings, find the studs beforehand and mark the positions on the skirting board.

Plan any redecoration to fit in with assembling built-in shelves. Painting or papering around shelves is messy and time-consuming.

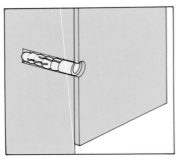

3. To make fixings to ceramic tiled walls, drill the holes very slowly with a masonry bit and make sure the plugs are inserted past the tile into the wall. That way, the expanding plug won't crack the tile when you tighten the screw.

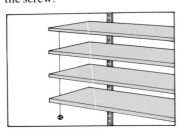

4. Line up the ends of shelves on track systems or brackets by

fixing the top one first and then dropping a plumb line (or a weight on a string) down one side. Place each subsequent shelf just touching the string before fixing.

5. When putting shelf units next to a wall, make sure the front edge is carrying most of the weight. Fitted carpets usually rise next to the skirting board causing the unit to lean outward.

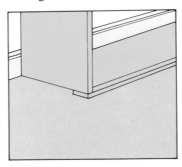

If the bottom is smooth, add a strip of wood to the underside at the front.

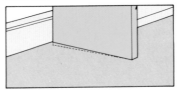

If it rests on uprights, you can cut away the back corners, or add adjustable feet to the front.

6. Self-adhesive rubber or foam pads will help keep glass shelves from slipping.

7. When fixing wood to the wall with plastic plugs, it's not necessary to drill all the holes in the wood first and them mark the wall. Drill through the wood and into the wall.

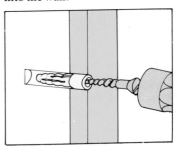

Insert a plug and tap it in flush. Then, insert a screw (without turning it) into the end of the plug and tap them into the hole. When the plug is at the correct depth, tighten up the screw. If you plan to fill the holes in the wood with wooden plugs, you can countersink the holes, and then drill through with the masonry bit.

This technique prevents any problems with holes being out of line with each other, and also means that you can adjust battens etc. with one screw in place.

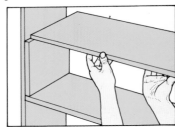

8. The easiest type of shelf unit to assemble has partitions

between the shelves. You can use the partitions to set the height of the shelves and support them while you fix them to the sides.

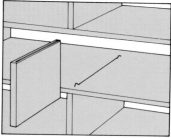

9. Invisible wire shelf supports are a good way to hold partitions

in place as well as shelves. This method also makes it easy to have the partitions in line with each other for a cube effect.

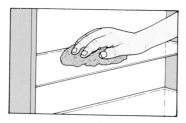

10. Glass shelves need frequent cleaning, so it's a good idea not to put them in hard to reach places.

Safety Tips

1. Make sure your shelves are strong enough for the load.

2. Don't leave a shelf unit temporarily leaning against a wall without making sure it won't fall or that children won't be able to climb on it.

3. Always get the advice of a glass supplier about the thickness and type of glass to use for shelves and have the edges ground and polished.

4. When using sharp-edged and power tools, always keep all parts of your body behind the cutting edge.

5. Make sure there are no electrical wires or pipes in an area of wall to be drilled.

6. Don't leave sharp-edged tools where there are children or pets.

7. Don't wear loose clothing or a tie when using power tools.

An interesting way of dividing open-plan living space is to construct a block-board partition with the required number of spaces and have the whole lot plastered. Additional shelves can be added afterwards and the plaster can be finished to fit in with the general decoration.

FRAME IT

CONTENTS

Introduction

Picture framing is often thought of as something to be left to professionals and, in some cases, this is true. However, with patience and a small amount of preparation, you can frame your own pictures at home. This is not only a very satisfying activity, it can make the difference between having the frames you want and having to settle for what you can afford to have done professionally.

There are many framing skills and techniques that the do-it-yourselfer may never learn – indeed, many of the tools of the professional would be too costly for anyone not wishing to make a living from framing. Nevertheless, all the materials used by the professional are available to the beginner and, by using a few simple tools, a high degree of proficiency can be achieved if you are willing to master a few basic techniques.

There are practical (as well as aesthetic) reasons for framing. You cannot hang a picture on a wall unless it has a support, and the picture will soon deteriorate unless it is protected. This obviously applies to valuable paintings, but a photograph, diploma, or some treasured memento may have just as much, if not more, value for you, and you don't want it damaged.

What else can be framed? There are so many possibilities: embroidered samplers, posters, the children's drawings, stamps, illustrations from old books, old postcards. Three dimensional subjects such as keys, small shells, butterfly collections and coins can work. No matter what it is, framing will protect it as well as show it off beautifully, so that many old treasures can be pulled out of the attic and take pride of place on your walls.

Above *A mixed selection of prints, drawings and photographs have been arranged together to make an attractive display. Before starting to hang any pictures it's a good idea to arrange them on the floor; you will then be able to experiment.*

Right *This original drawing for a newspaper cartoon has been framed, along with the printed version, in a narrow black frame. Hung with other keepsakes, framed in a similar way, they make an interesting display.*

Below *This lovely old
watercolour needed little
enhancement. A plain white
window mount was used with an
old gilt frame.*

Which Frame?

There are no hard and fast rules about which frame suits which type of subject. A good frame is one that you feel looks compatible with your picture, but the following may be helpful as a rough guide.

Watercolours are traditionally framed with narrow, thin mouldings, the size of the mount varying the overall size.

Oil paintings on canvas are not usually framed under glass as the reflection will hide the texture and depth of a medium which should be seen in an unmasked state. Either a generous, large moulding or a simple, thin edge are the most suitable.

Drawings are treated in much the same way as watercolours. Sometimes it is nice to see the edge of the drawing. In this case, do not frame it with a window mount, but stick or 'tip' onto the mount board. This would give a 'free', unrestricted feeling to the picture.

Prints, etchings, lithographs and silk-screen prints are usually framed with a window mount cut just wide enough to show the edge of the print which, if good, should be sharp. Etchings have an indentation running around them made when the damp paper is pressed on the plate. This should also be shown.

Posters and prints of the mass-produced type can be treated in any way, but generally, prints look best with a narrow, simple frame.

Photographs often look very good with a fabric mount and black and white photographs can take quite a bright, strong coloured mount using a 'no frame' frame or a very modern frame.

3-D objects use a 'shadow box' frame.

Tools & materials

All you need are a few inexpensive hand tools to make basic picture frames, and these will last a lifetime. Here is a list of those that are necessary and the materials you will be using.

The first requirement is a place to work. A good, sturdy table with a flat top (such as the kitchen table) is the best surface to work on. If you are able to walk around it, so much the better.

Measuring and Cutting

A mitre box is the basic tool for cutting the 45 degree mitred corners of a frame. You can buy many different kinds of inexpensive wooden mitre box. However, when picture framing, you cannot start sanding and planing slightly inaccurate mitred corners to make them fit, so, unless you are very practised with a saw, you're unlikely to get the best results with this type of box.

The author recommends a metal mitre box (like the one illustrated) which will cost at least twice the price of the wooden one, but will be worth every penny. It will enable you to cut perfect mitres, and will save many hours of anguish and frustration.

The metal mitre box has two screw holes for fixing it to a work bench but, if you're using the kitchen table, screw the box to a piece of wood and then clamp the whole thing to the table with *G-clamps*. This will be quite firm enough, but don't forget to protect your table with a piece of plywood or chipboard (particle board) first. This type of mitre box comes with complete instructions for cutting the mitres.

You will need a *tenon saw* to use with the mitre box. One with a 300mm blade and fairly fine teeth is best. Try not to skimp on the quality of the saw – some cheap ones can't be sharpened.

Cutting mitres requires the saw to be as sharp as possible. When you feel it's losing its 'bite', you can have it sharpened inexpensively by professionals. Most hardware stores provide this service.

G-clamps are useful for holding glued sections together and securing the mitre box to the table.

A metal tape measure is more accurate than fabric ones.

Joining and Nailing

A tack hammer is the best weight for pinning the corners of mouldings together.

A *nail set* (or a blunt nail) for recessing the nail heads.

A small hand drill is needed to bore holes for the pins holding

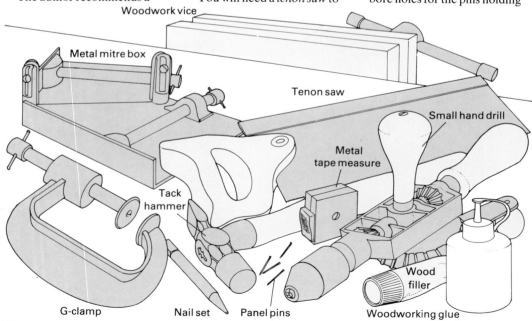

Woodwork vice

Metal mitre box

Tenon saw

Small hand drill

Metal tape measure

Tack hammer

Wood filler

G-clamp   Nail set   Panel pins   Woodworking glue

the frame together when using a very thin moulding. The most useful sizes of drill bit are 1mm and 1.5mm.

Wood filler in various colours is used for filling nail holes and scratches in mouldings.

Woodworking glue is used on the mitred corners before pinning them together.

Panel pins are best for medium and heavy mouldings. Veneer pins are thinner and so help avoid splitting lightweight mouldings. The most useful lengths are 25, 38 and 44mm. A small *woodworking vice* is needed for holding the moulding when joining the corners.

Finishing

Fine glass paper and flour paper are abrasive sheets used to smooth wood mouldings.

Woodstains are for changing the colour or darkening wood mouldings. They are widely available and come with full instructions for using and mixing them.

Sanding sealer is a quick drying clear primer used to prepare wood for waxing, varnishing or painting. By applying thin coats and lightly rubbing down each one, a smooth surface is built up.

Mounting

Use a *craft knife* with replaceable blades, which should be kept razor sharp, for cutting mounts and cardboard. If you're serious about framing, you may wish to invest in a mount cutter. These cut perfect bevelled edges and come with full instructions.

Compasses are useful for drawing circular mount windows.

A metal straightedge ruler is essential for cutting against.

A set square is necessary to establish right angles.

Mountboard is available in different qualities. For hinged mounts that have a window cut in them, use the best quality. This has a white core that shows when the bevelled edge window is cut. A thinner and less expensive mountboard can be used for backing pictures.

Double sided tape is used to attach pictures to the backing mount. As an alternative, you can use stamp hinges.

Assembly and Hanging

3mm hardboard is the best material for the overall backing.

Brown, gummed tape is used to seal the back of the picture.

Picture wire, fastened across the back of the frame to screw eyes or D rings, gives an adjustable hanging point.

Turnclips that hold the backing in the frame are available from art shops.

Clips for the no-frame method hold glass and backing together, and are sold at most art shops.

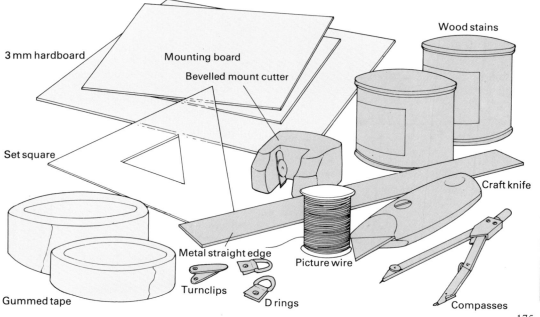

3 mm hardboard

Mounting board

Bevelled mount cutter

Wood stains

Set square

Craft knife

Metal straight edge

Picture wire

Gummed tape

Turnclips

D rings

Compasses

175

MAKING A BASIC FRAME

Before starting, it will be helpful to become acquainted with the jargon of the framer. The most important part of a picture frame is the moulding. It is on this that your success with framing will metaphorically and literally hang! There are hundreds of different styles of moulding available from picture frame shops or timber merchants. Any wood can be used for the moulding, but some are more popular than others. Basswood is common and an excellent choice for the beginner, as it is light and easy to handle and can be stained or painted. There are also aluminium and plastic mouldings, but these need cutting with a hacksaw (unusable with a mitre box) and can be bought ready cut or in kit form.

all the layers snugly.

You can *make your own mouldings* at home by glueing together strips of architrave (used for edging doors and windows).

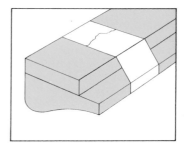

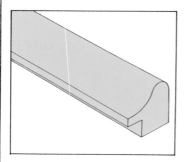

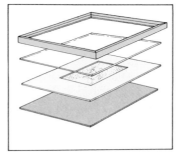

All *ready-made wood mouldings* have a rebate (or rabbet). This is the recess underneath the lip of the moulding that holds everything in place. In the case of oil paintings that need to lie flush with the frame, you won't need a rebate.

Into the assembled frame goes first the glass and then the picture. Finally, the backing board, usually made of hardboard, holds the others in place. When buying your moulding, make sure the rebate is deep enough to accommodate

These won't have a rebate, but you can make your own by glueing a strip of wood to the bottom of the moulding. Hold the strip and moulding together with tape until the glue dries, and then sand the join. This method allows you to make a rebate of any depth. Alternatively, you can ask the timber merchant to cut a rebate into the moulding for you.

Measuring for the Mitred Joints

When cutting the mitres, work from the external measurements

How Much Moulding to Buy

Trim the picture you're going to frame, cutting off drawing pin holes and bent over corners. Then attach it to a piece of paper (see Mounting). To work out how much moulding you need, first add the length and width of the mount and multiply by 2. Now, head for the moulding supplier (with the picture) to try out the various shapes, sizes and colours.

When you've selected your

moulding, add to your first measurement 8 times the width of the moulding chosen (to allow for the overall dimension of the frame) plus a cutting allowance of 200mm.

You may now have an alarmingly long piece of moulding to carry home. Ask the suppliers to cut it in half – the two lengths will always be sufficient for two sides of the frame.

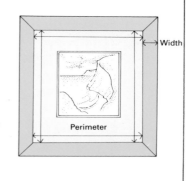

of the frame. To arrive at these, first calculate the rebate size. This is the length and width of the mounted picture plus an allowance of 2mm for clearance. (For instance, the rebate size of a picture measuring 120mm by 100mm would be 122mm by 102mm.)

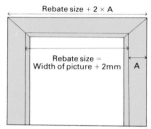

Next, measure the width of the moulding, and from this deduct the width of the rebate. This will give the dimension marked A. The formula for the external measurement of the frame is: Rebate size + 2 × A (the measurement between the edge of the rebate and the outside edge of the frame).

If, for instance, the moulding you've chosen for the picture with rebate size of 122mm × 102mm is 40mm with a rebate width of 10mm, the external frame size would be: 122 + (2 × 30mm) by 102mm + (2 × 30mm).

Cutting the Mitres

If the moulding you've bought has been cut in half for easy

carrying, cut mitres at each of the four ends. Otherwise, cut two mitres at the middle and one at each end.

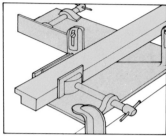

Clamp the mitre box firmly to the table. Clamp the moulding into the mitre box with the rebate side away from you. If you're using a metal mitre box, insert pieces of thin wood or card to prevent the metal from marking the moulding when the clamps are tightened. Also, make sure the moulding is resting absolutely flat on the bottom of the mitre box. If not, the angle of the cut won't be accurate.

Practise cutting mitres with spare pieces of wood and holding them together on a flat surface to be sure you've got the method right before cutting the moulding.

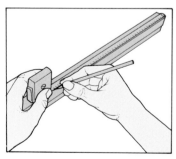

Take one of the lengths of moulding with the mitre at one

end and, using a metal tape measure, mark the external measurement of one of the longer sides on the outside edge of the moulding.

Use a set square to draw a perpendicular line across the edge, making sure the top of the line will be visible when you clamp the moulding in the mitre box. If necessary, continue the line over the edge.

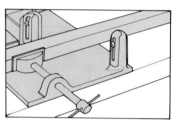

Making sure you will be cutting the mitre in the right direction, clamp the moulding in place and cut the mitre with light, steady pressure.

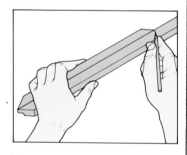

Having cut the first of the longer sides, place it back to back with another piece and mark the length directly. Cut this mitre and check that the two sides are equal length.

Repeat this procedure for the two shorter sides. It's a help to mark the opposite sides of the frame (perhaps one pair as X and one pair Y) so they don't get confused.

Joining and Nailing

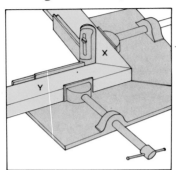

Take one X side and one Y side and position them as if for cutting in the mitre box. Clamp both sides where they form a tight 90 degree corner. Now you will be able to see if they fit well together. At this stage, decide on the position of the pins which, together with the glue, will secure the joints of the frame. For mouldings up to 10mm wide, one pin in each corner will do, but bigger mouldings should have two pins to prevent the joint twisting.

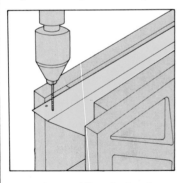

Place the mouldings in the vice and drill holes to prevent the wood splitting – not too near the face or back of the frame, nor too close to the edge of the rebate. Drill the holes in one end of each side only. Lay all

four pieces in the shape of the frame.

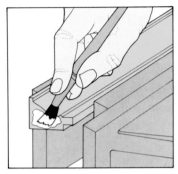

Take one of the longer sides, clamp it into the vice and brush the undrilled end with glue. Butt the end of the adjacent short side (with drilled holes) to the glued end and prop it up so the two sides are level.

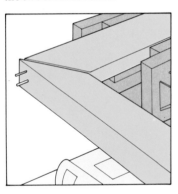

Place the drilled end slightly proud of the other so that the action of hammering in the pins will result in a flush joint. Drive in the pins and sink the pin heads with the nail set or blunted nail. Wipe away any squeezed out glue with a damp cloth and then carefully remove the two joined sides from the vice and place them flat on the table to dry. Repeat with the remaining two sides.

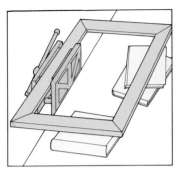

When the glue has set enough to be able to handle, place one of the L shapes in the vice and join the other to it, as before. Be sure to support the free ends so the frame is flat while you drive the pins. Clean off the excess glue and leave the frame to dry on a flat surface.

Making a frame without mitres

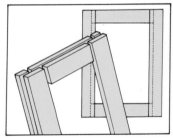

You will need two pieces of rectangular timber moulding, one narrower than the other in order to create a rebate. Glue and pin the two side pieces before cutting them to size. Having then cut them to size, determine the measurement of the top and bottom front pieces. Then measure the narrower back pieces. Glue and pin these together as you did for the sides. You will now have four corners which will butt into each other. These can now be joined in the usual way with glue and pins.

Finishing

If you have made up your own moulding or bought a ready-made (but unfinished) moulding, you must apply a finish to the frame before inserting the glass, picture and mount.

Waxing

If you like a natural finish, waxing is ideal. First, sand the moulding very smooth with fine sandpaper or flour paper. A beeswax furniture polish works well. Rub the first coat into the wood with fine wire wool. When the wax is completely dry, buff it with a cloth. Apply a second coat, this time with a cloth, and buff again until you have a smooth sheen. On carved or beaded mouldings, you can get the wax into the crevices with an old, soft toothbrush and buff with either a soft shoe brush or clothes brush.

Staining

Wood dyes and stains are available in a large range of colours as well as the traditional wood tones, such as walnut, oak, mahogany etc. The colours can be mixed to give in-between shades as well, so a whole artist's palette is available. However, you must stick to one type of stain when you mix them. There are three types: *water based, oil based and spirit based* and they aren't compatible with each other.

Be sure to test the stain on a scrap piece of the same wood before starting on the frame.

After sanding the frame smooth, build the colour slowly, using several coats of diluted stain. This helps avoid more absorbent parts of the wood becoming darker than the rest.

After staining, follow the manufacturer's instructions about finishing with wax, varnish or shellac polish.

Painting

Mouldings that are to be painted should be sanded really smooth. A couple of coats of sanding sealer, rubbed down with flour paper in between, will take up any imperfections in the grain or minute gaps in the mitres. When the wood feels silky to the touch, it's time to apply the first coat of paint. Most types of paint can be used, but make sure it is compatible with the sealer (if in doubt, test on a scrap piece of moulding).

Aerosol cans of paint are very handy for frames as they avoid brush marks in the corners. Follow the instructions on the can and apply several thin coats rather than risking drips and runs.

It isn't always necessary to feel you have to cover the whole frame with paint. A line of paint along a beading or a recess edge picked out in a colour can be just as effective.

When doing this, it's a good idea to mask one or both edges of the line to ensure a good, clean edge. It's sometimes easier to do this before joining the frame together. Silver and gold paint used this way can make an ordinary frame look very expensive.

Spattering is a traditional finish used by framers. This is adding speckles of a darker colour to the final painted or varnished surface.

Dip a toothbrush into the oil paint that is diluted with white spirit (mineral spirits).

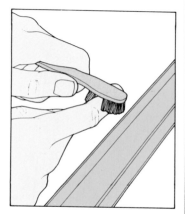

Shake off any excess and then run your fingers across the bristles so flecks of colour are flicked onto the frame. Test the effect on a newspaper first.

There are other special effects which can be achieved with paint, such as rag rolling, sponge stippling, graining etc. These are described in the chapter PAINT IT.

Tips

Whether staining or painting, keep your tones compatible. The frame should not be competing for attention with the subject it is surrounding.

Having made the frame and mounted the picture, all that remains is to assemble them with the glass and the backing.

Glass makes an amazing difference to the finished frame. Besides being necessary for protection, it intensifies the colours of the picture. *Non-reflective glass,* which eliminates all reflection, has a flattening effect; sometimes more obvious than the reflections it is trying to prevent. It is considerably more expensive, so unless you have a problem with reflection where you intend hanging the picture, ordinary *picture glass* is best. This is of a standard thickness and is much thinner than window glass.

For beginners, the simplest way is to go to your local glazier, framing shop or hardware store and let them cut a piece of glass to your exact measurements. This will be the rebate size less 1mm each side for clearance. Although it is not difficult to cut glass, the amateur will probably not have the space to store large amounts of thin glass safely, if there are small children around, the last thing you want is for them to be playing in the glass chippings. Also, there are no large savings from buying large sheets of glass and cutting off what you need.

However, if you have a piece of glass from an old frame and want to cut it smaller, you can buy a glass cutter at any DIY shop. This should be dipped in white spirit before each cut as it helps to keep the wheel running smoothly and the cutter sharp. Smooth the edges of the cut glass with wet emery cloth.

Lay a piece of felt or towel on the table and place the glass on top. Use the set square and straight edge to score a line all the way across the piece. Be sure the scored line goes right to the edges.

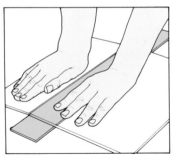

Slide a thin strip of wood beneath the glass with one edge along the line and press down on either side, snapping it in two. It's difficult to cut off edges of less than about 25mm, so if your glass is only slightly too large, it's easier to buy a new piece the right size.

Tips

The cut edges of glass are razor sharp! If you're framing with the no-frame method, ask the glazier to grind and polish the edges.

Having bought the glass, you can now cut a piece of hardboard to the rebate size and you are ready to assemble.

Backing

The backing is easier to buy cut to size by your supplier, as you probably don't want to store a large sheet of hardboard. Most DIY stores will cut neatly and square to your measurements, but offcuts are cheaper, so if you have a piece you want to cut smaller lay it on the table with the smooth side up.

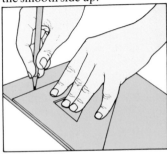

Measure and use the set square to draw the lines to be cut. If necessary, use a longer straightedge with the square.

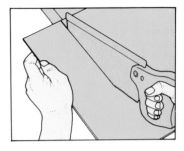

Keep the edge of the table as near to the cutting line as possible, and support the overhanging part with one hand. You can use the tenon saw with quick strokes, being careful not to let the part you're holding sag, or the last part of the cut may tear.

If you find that you can't keep from tearing the bottom surface of the hardboard, don't worry as this edge will be covered by the tape when the frame is assembled.

If the tearing out at the edges is too serious, place a waste piece of hardboard or thin plywood underneath and cut through both pieces. Also, if you're cutting off a large piece, put a piece of wood under the sheet after you've started the cut to help support the work.

Assembly

Clean both sides of the glass thoroughly, using warm, soapy water. Then, rinse off and dry with a clean, lint free cloth.

Clean the mount face and remove all specks. Any pencil marks can be gently rubbed off with a soft eraser.

Place the frame face down on the table, insert the glass into the rebate, followed by the picture and the hardboard. Check to see it's absolutely clean; you may have to repeat the cleaning process to be rid of all the specks.

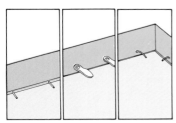

If the rebate is deeper than the sandwich, you can tap veneer pins into the back of the rebate every 75mm to hold everything together.

If the backing is flush with the frame, use turnclips.

Alternatively, drive pins into the back of the frame and bend them over the backing.

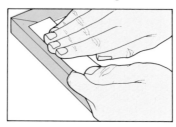

Finally, to prevent dust getting inside, seal the back edges with gummed paper or masking tape.

Hanging

Attach screw eyes or D rings each side, about one third of the way down from the top of the frame. Make sure the screws are long enough to hold, but not so long that they come through the front of the moulding.

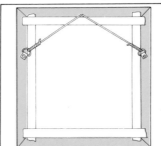

Thread picture wire through the rings twice and twist back up. The wire should come just below the top of the picture when fully stretched.

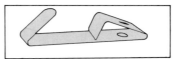

The usual method of hanging is to use picture hooks. These have

hardened pins to be able to penetrate masonry or wood and will support most pictures on most walls. For heavy pictures or mirrors, use mirror plates.

However, if the wall is too hard for the pins, or if it's hollow and the picture is too heavy, there are picture hooks that use screws.

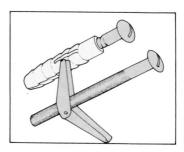

In solid walls, a hole is bored to take a plastic plug, into which the screw is driven; and, for hollow walls, there are fittings that expand behind the wall and grip when the screw is tightened.

To measure where the hook should be, get a helper to hold the picture in the right position and then make a small mark on the wall at the middle of the top of the frame.

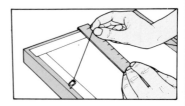

Then place the picture face down and measure the distance from the top of the frame to the wire, when fully stretched. Place the hook on the wall the same distance below the mark and either drive in the pins or mark the hole for the screw.

FRAMING WITH A MOUNT

A mount increases the overall size of picture and also, by giving space between the picture and frame, lets the picture 'breathe'. There are basically two types of mount.

The simplest is a plain piece of card or *mountboard* onto which the picture is mounted (or 'tipped'). This serves as a backing for the picture, as well as leaving an area around the outside.

The other type is a *hinged mount,* in which the picture is seen through a window cut through a second card on the front. Hinged mounts should be used for pastels, drawings and watercolours as they would be damaged if they were in direct contact with the glass.

Mounts are made of special card called mountboard. This is stiff and thick and yet cuts easily. Mountboard is available in a wide range of colours and shades and, when a window with a bevelled edge is cut in it, the white inside of the card creates a miniature frame that gives depth to the picture. There is also a thinner, less expensive mountboard available for the simple mounts that won't have windows cut in them.

Not all small art shops will stock a large range, but a little searching around will usually provide the right colour for your picture.

But, how do you decide which is the right colour? The subject to be mounted must be considered quite carefully. Take the picture with you when buying the mountcard. The colour should tone with one of the colours in the picture itself, or at least be complementary to the overall tone. Avoid a very strong colour that would compete with the picture, the mount should only highlight and enhance it.

Mounts can be decorative in themselves. You can cover them with fabric, paint designs on them or draw simple lines around the windows. Two or three mounts of different colours and with different window sizes can be placed on top of each other to give an even greater feeling of depth to the picture. Also, a single mount card can have several windows cut in it, enabling a number of pictures to be arranged in one frame.

Once you've mastered the basic technique of making a mount, try experimenting with your own ideas.

Left *Limited edition etchings 'tipped' onto dark brown mounting card.*

Above *The blue of the embroidery has been echoed in the mount, on which a fine line has been drawn for further emphasis. The wooden frame has been hand-painted with various shades of blue matt paint.*

Above left *This window mount is covered with self-adhesive shelf paper. White lines have been drawn round both edges of the mount and serve to accentuate the dried ferns, which have been allowed to tumble over the edge of the mount.*

Above right *An attractive and unusual way to display a lovely old lace tablemat and a pretty lace handkerchief. In one case a fabric-covered mount has been used with a simple wooden frame; in the other a simple coloured mount has been framed with a hand-decorated frame.*

Right *A junk shop find. Old watercolours sympathetically treated with oval mounts and dark stained wooden frames. The choice of a dark colour accentuates the delicate painting.*

Making a hinged mount

If you decide to use a hinged mount, then the mount should be your first concern. Choose a colour that is right for the picture and determine the overall size of the mount before buying the moulding.

To give the right effect and show the picture to its best advantage, keep the mount as large as possible, but always remember that about 6-9mm will be lost in the rebate of the frame. Dimensions are, to some extent, a question of personal preference but, as a general rule, narrow margins tend to give a pinched-in, tight look, and very small pictures can benefit from extra wide margins. Usually, the smaller the art, the wider the mount and vice versa. Also, it is best to avoid a repetition of widths, such as the same width moulding as width of mount.

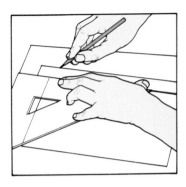

Mark the cutting lines for the window very lightly in pencil on the front of the mount board.

You are now ready to cut the bevelled edge. Don't attempt to do this until you've practised cutting on a spare piece of mount board!

Two L shaped pieces of card are useful for deciding how much of the picture is to show. Make the size of the window slightly smaller than the picture itself, for a neater finish.

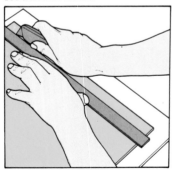

Using an old piece of card underneath so as not to blunt your knife, take your straightedge and cut the mountboard to the area decided on. Use the set square to make perfect, right angled corners. To ensure the board is truly square, measure the diagonals to see they are the same.

Next, cut a mount back of thinner, cheaper card, exactly the same size.

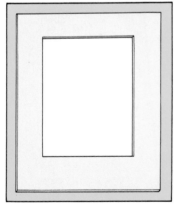

When measuring for the window size, make the bottom margin slightly more than the top and sides. This will make the picture appear central in the frame when it's hung on the wall.

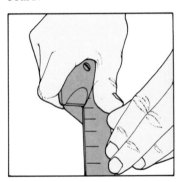

Using the metal straightedge to guide your knife (or mount cutter), score lightly but firmly along the line, holding the knife at an angle of 50 or 60 degrees and pulling it towards you. Then, score again with the knife at the same angle, until you've cut right through. It may be necessary to ease the tip of the knife into the corners to free the cut out part completely. If there is any fuzziness on the bevelled edge, a gentle rub with flour paper will eliminate it.

To complete the mount, hinge the back and front together with sticky tape. Position your picture so that the desired area shows through the window. When you're completely satisfied with its position, attach the picture permanently to the back with double sided tape or stamp hinges. These should be stuck as close as possible to the top edge of the picture.

Tips

Keep your hands clean when touching the mountboard. Wipe the straightedge before cutting. Pencil marks are easily removed with an eraser or bread, but greasy finger prints are hard to remove.

Fabric Covered Mounts

There are times when the texture of a fabric can greatly enhance a painting or drawing. You should always use a hinged mount because of the problems of attaching paper to fabric. Any fairly thin fabric, such as *linen, lawn, moire, gingham, muslin, satin* etc. can be considered.

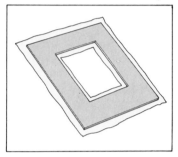

After cutting the window in the mount in the usual way, cut a piece of the fabric a little larger all round. Make sure the grain of the fabric is running straight and glue it to the mount front. You can use ordinary fabric adhesive, but the aerosol mounting adhesive from art shops is best. Spray it over the whole surface of the card.

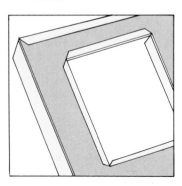

Make diagonal cuts to the corners of the window, and then turn the mount over and glue the

edges to the back of it. You can trim off the pointed ends to leave enough fabric to keep the edge stuck down.

Attach the mount back, position the picture and finish in the usual way.

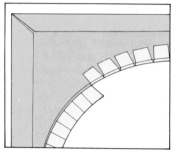

Oval and circular mounts can be covered by making cuts towards (but not quite reaching) the edge of the mount. Then, fold and glue the flaps one at a time, pulling each one to keep the fabric tight and to prevent the ends of the cuts from showing on the edge of the window.

Special Mount Finishes

There are many ways you can decorate a mount. If you intend to do this, it is a good rule to use the 'no-frame' principle (discussed later on) and to use the decorated mount with a simple subject, such as a portrait or a simple drawing.

Painting a mount with a simple pattern can be very effective. Coloured inks are suitable for this. An easy decorative touch is to draw lines around the mount windows with a ruling pen. These are inexpensive and well worth having as some of the thicker inks, such as white, black or gold flow much more easily through this sort of pen. Ordinary fountain pens tend to get clogged. With a ruling pen you can also draw lines of different widths, but this takes practice.

Stencils can be bought ready made or you can make your own. Designs are best kept simple to avoid distracting attention from the subject.

There are shops that sell beautiful *decorative papers – marbled, coarse textured, Japanese rice paper –* any of these, even *wallpaper,* can be stuck to the mount and carefully cut out with the craft knife. If you do plan to cover the mount, you can use the cheaper type of mountboard.

Experiment also with *pressed flowers, sequins, cutouts* from old scrapbooks and *lace.* Whatever decoration for the mount you choose, make sure it is firmly stuck on with the appropriate adhesive.

Circular and Oval Mounts

These are much easier to cut out of paper or thin card than out of mountboard. If you want the bevelled edge that you only get from mountboard, you could ask a picture framer to do the mount cutting for you. Some art shops sell ready-cut oval and circular mounts. The type of mount cutter used by professional framers is not worth investing in unless you intend taking up framing for a living!

To cut mount from paper or thin card, you can use templates supplied from art shops, or look around for anything you might have at home first. The kitchen is a good place to start, a plate or bowl will serve the purpose just as well.

With your craft knife you can cut directly against a template

but if you are using a plate or bowl it is probably simpler to mark the circle in pencil first and then very carefully cut along the line with the craft knife. If you plan on making several circular mounts, you can buy a compass cutter from art shops.

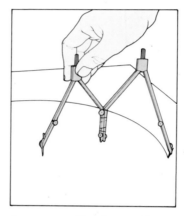

A compass will make a perfect circle, and two compasses, the pointed end of one where the pencil would be in the other, will give a greater span.

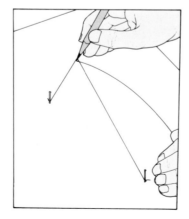

For the oval, two drawing pins and a loop of string will enable you to draw ovals of various proportions.

Mounts with More than One Window

If you have several small drawings, postcards, stamps or photographs, the answer may be to cut a mount with several windows. Any number can be happily incorporated into the frame, but the planning and laying out needs to be done carefully. First, find the best arrangement on a sheet of paper, grouping the subjects for the best effect. Cut the paper to the overall size.

When you've made your final decision, mark the position of the corners of the windows or cut them out of the paper. Then lay the plan on top of the mountboard and keep it in place with clips or small pieces of tape taken around the back. When you're absolutely sure the paper can't slip, prick through the corners of the windows into the mountboard. Then remove the paper and lightly pencil the lines to connect the corners. Cut the bevels as before.'

FRAME KITS

There are several different types of frame kits on the market. The most common are made of aluminium and sold as pairs of sides, so that you buy two packs of two for each frame. They start quite small and go up in size by about 50mm at a time, so you should always be able to find two pairs of sides to suit your picture. Many variations in size are possible, and this could be helpful if you were planning to clad a whole wall and wanted a feeling of unity.

When using these, you will still have to fit your picture to the frame, make a mount and backing and have the glass cut. However, you will have the mitres already cut for you and also the necessary angle plates and screws for joining the corners together. They come with full instructions, are very simple to assemble and very strong at the corner joints.

Various frames for canvases are also avail-able in kit form. There ar￼ come complete with glass an￼ can be made of aluminium or ￼ finished wood to be finished a￼ choose.

No frame frames

Some pictures look better when there ￼ frame to close them in. A frame isn't alwa￼ essential, indeed, why not use the wall o￼ which the picture will hang as the frame! A picture sandwiched between a backing board and glass and held together with clips is particularly suited to today's style of simplicity and high tech. Kits are readily available and can be assembled in minutes. However, they are also easy to make yourself from many varieties of clips and brackets available from art shops, hardware stores and framers. Often this is less expensive than buying in kit form.

Above *A simple aluminium frame which was easily assembled from four pieces and a few clips. The mount was available at the same supplier.*

Above *No-frame frames used in a kitchen to protect simple prints and drawings.*

Above *Perspex box type frames are available in many sizes. Here they have been used to display family photographs. By arranging on a simple grid more boxes can be added as and when they are wanted.*

her frames

se partout and other similar
bes are a quick, inexpensive
d easy way of framing small
pictures or snapshots. Children's
paintings or drawings also are
ideal subjects for this method.
There is no actual frame, but the
tape used to bind the edges
provides the illusion of one. A
'no-frame' kit is the simplest way
to use this method, or you can
buy the glass (be sure to ask for
the edges to be polished). Cut
the hardboard backing piece to
the same size, or have it cut by
the supplier.

The glass, backing and mount
(optional) are held together by
the passe partout tape.

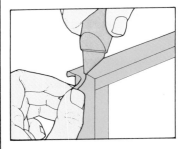

Carefully trim the ends of the
tape flush with the corner,
making sure the glass and
backing won't show.

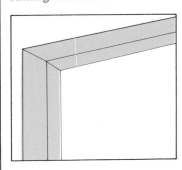

Then, either leave the front
edges overlapping, or use a
straightedge and knife to cut

through both layers of tape.
Remove the off-cuts and you
have a mitred corner.

Strut Back Frames

Strut back frames are most
commonly seen on mantelpieces
or dressing tables. Any ordinary
frame can be made into a strut
back by cutting a tie shaped
piece of hardboard about two
thirds the length of the frame.

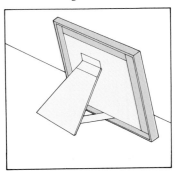

This is attached to the backing
board by either a light cabinet
hinge or fabric tape. A piece of
cord or ribbon is then glued on to
the strut and the back of the
frame top prevents the strut
from opening too far. If the
frame is metal, small pads of felt
can be stuck to the bottom to
prevent it scratching the furniture.

Fabric Frames

If you're good with a needle, you
probably have scraps of
dressmaking material or
furnishing fabric left over. These
can be used to make fabric
frames, perhaps to fit in with
your decor. The method of
doing this is basically the same as
for covering a mount with fabric.

First, cut out the shape of the
frame in thick card. Lay the
fabric on the card and position
the mount over it, and draw

around the window, leaving a
good margin to fold around the
edges. Cut out the window in the
fabric.

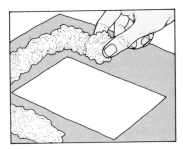

At this stage, you could pad the
fabric with a layer of cotton
wadding to give the frame a bit
more thickness.

Make the diagonal cuts almost to
the corners of the window, fold
the edges around and glue them
to the back of the mount.

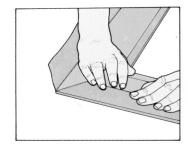

Now, make diagonal cuts to the
outside corners and fold the

edges around, glueing them to the back. Try to keep equal tension on the fabric to avoid creases on the front.

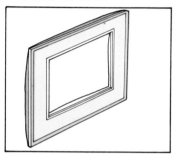

To finish the back, cut another piece of fabric a little smaller than the mount and cut the window large enough that the edge of the fabric won't be seen from the front. This backing can be sewn around the edges, but it's easier to glue it over the whole surface.

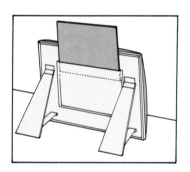

Finally, cut a piece of felt slightly larger than the picture and glue just the sides and bottom edges to the back of the mount. Now you have a sleeve into which you can slide the picture.

To turn this type of frame into a strut back, you could make two struts, and fix them either side of the window.

Another method of making a frame is to make a basic wooden

frame from the plainest moulding, such as clamshell or half round. Using the same method as for covering a mount, glue fabric directly onto the frame using spray adhesive.

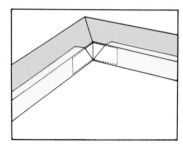

If the frame is deep and you have trouble getting the fabric to cover the inside corners, glue small strips of the same fabric along the edge at the corners before folding the main edge around.

Other Finishes

If you have a frame with a very simple, plain moulding, you can attach a variety of things. *Shells, strips of bamboo,* almost anything goes. It's not unheard of to bake frame-shaped pieces of bread dough in the oven!

Making a Shadow Box Frame

Shadow boxes are used to display three dimensional objects, such as a collection of *butterflies, shells, coins, and old fans, tapestry work, textiles* – in fact anything than won't lie completely flat.

The box is created by using a moulding with a very deep rebate, so that there is a large space between the glass and the back of the frame. Decide the required depth of the rebate as

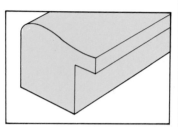

follows: if the object is 12mm thick, add the thickness of the glass (3mm), the thickness of the mount (2mm), and at least 5 mm for the clearance between the object and the glass = 22mm. Add another 6mm for safety.

Measure and cut a piece of mountboard and cover with fabric such as felt or velvet.

Then, measure for the moulding, cut the mitres and make the frame in the usual way. Measure for the glass and insert this into the frame.

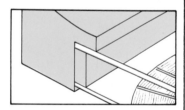

Now, you need four strips or 'fillets' of wood to hold the glass in place and create a second rebate for the mount. Cover the fillets with the same fabric as the backing board, as they will show once the frame is assembled. Glue the fillets to the side of the rebate in the moulding, making sure they touch the glass.

The object can be attached to the mount with pins, glue, small strips of Velcro or it can be sewn.

When the glue has set, insert the mounted object, followed by a backing board, and finish in the usual way.

Old frames

There are many ways you may come across old frames – junk shops, auctions, jumble sales – perhaps there are a few dusty ones lurking in the attic. When you're looking at one, don't be put off by the subject in the frame, try to imagine the frame around a picture of your choice. By now you should be armed with enough confidence and know how to set about making a new mount to fit an old frame or re-cutting its mitres.

A word of caution, if you find one that you think may be valuable, take it to an antique shop, a good picture framer or a valuer for his opinion before you start to chop it up. This could well apply to gilded or carved frames.

Above *A large collection of old frames of various types and sizes look very attractive hung together in a rather random fashion. To achieve something along these lines you must be willing to spend a lot of time planning how the pictures best relate to each other and the whole–there are no hard and fast rules, you must simply experiment.*

Above right *A marvellous way to display school pictures, holiday snapshots, wedding photographs and other personal mementoes. By hanging the pictures very close one gains an overall effect which is immediately interesting, but which also allows any old frames (regardless of style or condition) to hang alongside more modern ones.*

Right *These beautifully renovated old frames are all slightly different; however, hung together they complement each other and are further linked by the flower prints they hold.*

Metal Leaf Gilded Frames

Assuming the frame is in reasonable condition, i.e. with no large chunks missing, a clean up with some acetone or white spirit may be all that's needed. Work on small sections at a time, dabbing the area dry with an absorbent rag to see how things are going. Use white spirit (mineral spirits) if you suspect the frame is painted and you just want to clean it. Use acetone if it is gilded (or you want to find out) as paint will come off, but gold will be unharmed. If you remove a layer of gold paint, you can simply apply another coat. With a gilded frame, a light coat of lacquer will protect and seal its surface, after cleaning. Aerosols of clear lacquer are sold for this purpose.

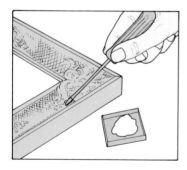

If there are only small bits of moulding missing here and there, these can be filled in with car body filler, which can be shaped and sanded when set.

Wooden Frames

If the frame has been *painted* first clean with white spirit (mineral spirits) and, if it's not too chipped, sand and re-paint. Use a suitable undercoat.

If the frame is *polished* and simply dull and grimy with age,

clean it up with methylated spirit gently rubbed on with fine wire wool. It can then be waxed. If you want to darken the colour, there are tinted waxes you can use.

Remove any old brown paper by sponging with water, but take care not to soak the wood.

It may well be that an old wooden frame has wobbly mitres. Here you may decide to take the frame apart and re-join or even re-cut it. Try to ease the corners apart by hand.

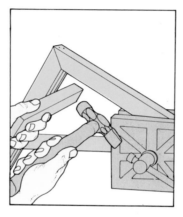

If that doesn't work, clamp one side of the frame in the vice and gently knock it apart with a hammer. Use a block of wood to protect the frame. Try to take it apart in the direction of the old pins, as it is then less likely to split. Unfortunately, it's not always possible to see from which side of the joint they were put in. Have a good look at all four joints; maybe you'll see how one was joined and you can assume the other three were done in a similar way.

Once apart, the nails can be pulled out with pliers, and the holes filled with a mixture of fine sawdust and wood glue.

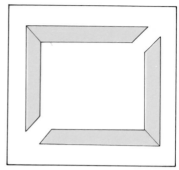

If the mitres are sound, but you want to make the frame smaller, then you need only to cut through two corners diagonally opposite each other. Don't use your tenon saw to cut through the nails at the corners, use a hacksaw instead.

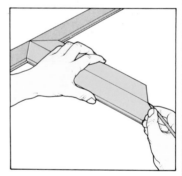

Measure the length of one side as if you were making a new frame, and having cut one mitre, use it to mark the opposite side in the usual way.

Tips

If you are stuck for ideas with an old frame try turning it into a mirror. The size would be no problem as mirror glass can be cut to fit any frame.

Mirrors

Mirrors are possibly the easiest of subjects to frame; they require no mount and can be framed in an endless variety of styles – from heavy ornate gilt to the simplest pine. By their very nature one's eye is drawn to them and this is an occasion where you could safely let your imagination run wild on the kind of frame used. Highly decorated frames, made of fabric or shells, for example, can all be equally stunning. The prettiest mirrors by far are those with a bevelled edge, but unfortunately they are much more expensive.

On a practical note, remember that mirror glass is at least twice as heavy as picture glass and, therefore, a frame for this purpose must be sturdy enough to support the extra weight. It may even be necessary, in the case of a large mirror, to reinforce the mitre joints with metal corner plates attached to the back of the frame.

Above *This simple mirror was made from a square of hardboard, with a circle cut out of the centre, covered with a remnant of printed velvet. A small mirror was then stuck onto the back.*

Right *A simple white painted wooden frame has been made for a mirror and then thin strips of white painted wood have been stuck on top of the mirror, so making it resemble a window. A useful idea for cheering up a dark corner or a small room.*

Left *Tiny shells of different colours have been stuck onto the mirror to make an attractive design and different shells have been used to make the flowers. Any mirror could be embellished in this way – either a modern plain one or perhaps an old one which has begun to lose the silver around the edges.*

Below *The frame of this old oval mirror was too damaged to repair, so velvet was stretched over it and stuck down firmly at the back. A ribbon was stuck to cover the join and add further interest.*

DISPLAY

Sometimes it's hard to place your pictures where they will have the maximum effect. Over the mantelpiece or over the bed are two places where anyone can hang a picture without difficulty but, all too often, they're put up on any bare expanse of wall without much thought as to their size, colour or effectiveness. The result is that they are often 'lost'. A common mistake is that pictures are hung too high – you should be able to look into a picture without cricking your neck. Also, pictures are not for looking at only when you're standing – take care that they're not out of sight when people are seated.

If you have more than one small picture, consider grouping them close together on one wall. They will have much more impact then if they're just dotted around randomly. You can either frame them in a similar style and colour, or let them contrast with one another, some quiet, some vibrant, some narrow, some wide etc. The secret of successful grouping is to form a type of grid into which your pictures will sit.

Taking four or five pictures, for instance, plan an imaginary cross through the centre of your group. The width of the cross should ideally be about the same size as your mounts, and the bottom of the highest pictures will be level with the tops of the lowest. To this system, more and more pictures can be added, keeping the spaces between them the same. Try out your arrangements on the floor first, otherwise someone in the family will end up with aching arms!

Right *These prints have been hung very close together as they complement each other and are more effective hung as a pair. For this reason they were not put in heavy frames, which would have had the effect of separating the subjects.*

Left *A series of modern flower paintings have been simply put behind glass to maintain the uncluttered look and so allow them to be hung close together.*

Bottom *Simple no-frame frames have been used for these colourful graphics, which look good just leaning against the wall.*

Consider hanging pictures in places other than the sitting room. A kitchen or bathroom shouldn't be ruled out because of steam and moisture. Posters, prints or magazine pages (i.e. anything not too precious) can liven up these rooms. Children love pictures in their rooms, but remember to hang them low enough for the children to enjoy them.

Try to balance pictures with objects near them. You may have a piece of wall space that calls for a particular shape of picture, such as a long narrow one in the space between two doors or two horizontal ones along the side of a bath. A small print will be lost on a large expanse of wall, but may be just right in an alcove or between two pieces of furniture. Similarly, a big picture will look dramatic on a large expanse of wall that is uncluttered by other pictures or ornaments.

Stairs offer a picture-hanging challenge. Here they're seen either going up or coming down – a dramatic one at the end of the climb could be stunning; or place a group of quiet ones at the beginning of the stairs to be contemplated while standing still.

Above right *The pictures in this bathroom have been hung in groups of two or three for maximum effect. Don't put anything valuable in your bathroom or kitchen in case the steam damages it.*

Right *A group of pictures hung on a simple grid. The three on the left set the grid and the others, all slightly different, follow it as closely as possible. A nice way to display this type of work.*

Far right *The pictures here have been hung to follow the line of the stairs. This is much easier when they are all the same size, but when they vary considerably do give yourself plenty of time to experiment.*

Top left *Blocks of wood fixed to the wall support a back sheet, mount and glass and allow them to slide out so that the photographs can be changed.*

Centre left *A simple wooden frame with wooden backing makes a perfect display for a collection of metal numbers and signs.*

Bottom left *This simple appliqué has been mounted on a size of board that allows for a small border of the backing fabric to show around the edge.*

Above *The four sides of this wooden frame were covered with satin before the frame was assembled. This makes the frame part of the appliqued satin picture it surrounds.*

TOP TEN TIPS

1. When cutting the moulding, always cut the longest side of the frame first. This way, if you make a mistake, you will still have enough to make the shorter sides.

2. Use short, quick movements of the saw when coming to the end of cutting the mitre. This helps avoid splitting the wood as the saw breaks through the bottom of the moulding.

3. When masking off an area for painting, don't forget to remove the tape before the paint dries.

4. When glueing the mitres, always make sure all traces of excess glue are wiped away with a damp cloth before it dries.

5. Don't use your tenon saw to cut aluminium mouldings or nails in old frames. Use a hacksaw.

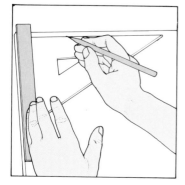

6. Never assume anything is square – even sheets of mountboard. To establish a true square, place your straightedge along the side and lay the set square against it to draw a right angle. You will then have one true right angle from which you can obtain the other three.

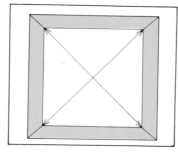

7. To check a frame or mount is square, measure the distance between diagonal corners. They should be the same.

8. Don't hang unglazed pictures over a radiator. The rising dust and dirt will soon affect them.

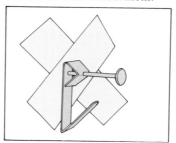

9. When hanging a picture, tape on the wall will help avoid damaging the plaster.

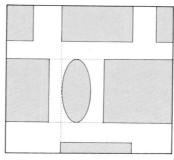

10. If you are grouping pictures and want to add an oval, treat the oval one as a rectangle lining up the widest part.

Safety Tips

1. When using sharp edged tools, always keep all parts of your body behind the cutting edge.

2. Don't leave tools where children could play with them. That goes for nails and pins, too.

3. Always wear heavy gloves when handling glass with rough edges.

4. To minimise fire risk, finishing materials should be stored in clearly marked containers with tight fitting lids, and out of reach of children.

5. Never underestimate the weight of a picture or mirror.

6. Always ensure there is good ventilation when using paints and solvents.

7. If you are using the kitchen as your workroom be extra thorough when sweeping up splinters of glass etc.

8. Don't leave pieces of moulding with protruding nails lying around. Either tap nails out with a hammer or remove with pliers.

9. Never leave glass lying around. Find a safe place to store odd pieces you may wish to use at a later date.

PLUMB IT

CONTENTS

Introduction

There was a time when you had to warn the do-it-yourselfer not to tackle plumbing, apart from simple jobs such as fitting a new washer on a tap; but all that has changed. Several developments are responsible: pipes are now made of easy-to-work materials. Also, new devices have made it easy to join the pipes and connect them up – to taps and cisterns, for instance.

As a result, the amateur plumber can take on a whole range of improvements and installations that would previously have been thought right out of the question.

This is not a manual on how to install a complete plumbing system in an empty house – a task few do-it-yourselfers would ever be called on to face. But the chapter does show you how to care for existing plumbing – how to maintain it, carry out repairs, and extend it to add extra facilities that will give you and your family a better home – and a better life.

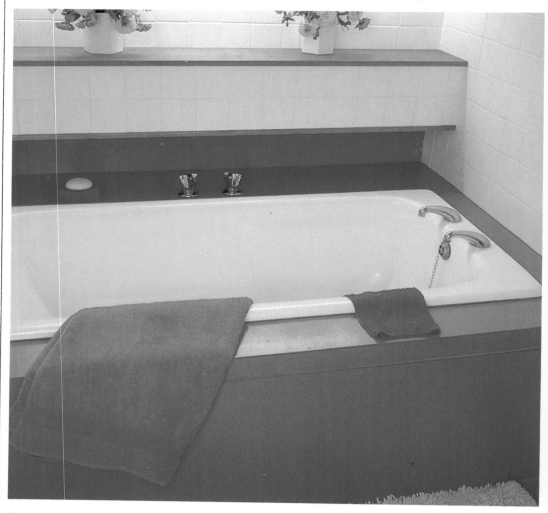

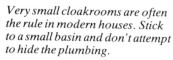

Very small cloakrooms are often the rule in modern houses. Stick to a small basin and don't attempt to hide the plumbing.

Far left *If you are changing your bath for a new one, why not think about an alternative siting for the taps? In this bathroom, hot and cold spouts have been put in place of the taps, with the controls at the side, connected by pipework.*

Above left *It's a good idea to try and keep all your plumbing in one part of the kitchen. Fitting the washing machine next to the sink makes for minimal pipework. Ideally it should be on an outside wall, close to the drain.*

Left *This large nursery room has its own washing machine and sink unit concealed behind folding louvred doors. This seems a very practical solution to the mounds of washing produced by small children, but do keep an eye on the plumbing. A flood on the first floor could prove both inconvenient and expensive.*

HOW A PLUMBING SYSTEM WORKS

Before you can do any jobs on your own plumbing system, you need to understand it. There are, in fact, two aspects to it. You have to bring water to where you want it – the supply; and get rid of it when you're finished with it – the waste. Let us look at both, initially, in terms of a conventional small house built during the last 50 years or so.

Supply

First, the supply. Water enters your property (not necessarily your house) underground, via a branch pipe from the Water Board's main, running under the street. From the point at which it does so, it becomes your responsibility. Near the garden gate or in the street, there should be a *stop tap* to allow you to turn off the supply in an emergency or when work needs to be done. The pipe then continues underground and emerges in the house, usually near the kitchen sink. There should be a stop tap here, too. Just beyond the stop tap, there will be a branch line to the sink's cold tap, so that water used for cooking and drinking will be pure from the main.

The main pipe now continues upwards and is known as the *rising main*. It feeds a tank called the *cold storage tank*, which is usually in the loft (it's the one that freezes up in winter if it isn't lagged properly), but it could be in some other part of the house. Indeed, it will have to be if the house has a flat roof (and therefore no loft).

The Cold Storage Tank

This tank usually supplies all the cold outlets (taps) in the house, except for the one at the kitchen sink. It also feeds with cold water any water heating system powered by a boiler. However, it could be that, in order to save on pipework, a builder has connected some, or even all, cold outlets direct to the rising main. Many water authorities frown on this.

Water rises up to the cold storage tank because of the pressure of the mains. It is then fed to the various outlets by gravity – which is why the tank must be sited high in the house. Water stored in this tank might get contaminated by dust, insects, birds etc, so water from cold taps not fed directly by the mains should not be drunk without first being boiled.

At various points throughout the system there will be other stop taps – the cold feed to a wc, for instance, or to the hot water system – so that these can be isolated when you need to work on them.

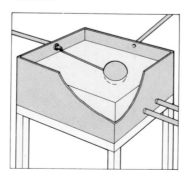

The entry of water into a cistern – on a wc or the cold storage tank – is controlled by what is known as a *ball valve*. The valve has an arm, on the end of which is a metal or plastic ball that floats on the surface of the water. When the level in the tank is low, the ball drops, taking the arm with it, and that opens the valve. As more water is admitted, the level rises, raising the ball and arm, and so the valve is shut off. In case anything should go wrong and too much water comes in, there is an overflow pipe so that the excess water will be carried away safely outside, instead of flooding the house. Such an overflow (the term is used to describe the flow of excess water, as well as the pipe itself) also draws your attention to the fault.

Boilers

The most common form of domestic water heating is by means of a boiler – free-standing, or a back boiler that is part of a fireplace. (Plumbers use the word 'domestic' in this context not as the opposite of 'industrial', but to refer to the water drawn off the household taps, as opposed to the water in the radiators of a central heating system.) The boiler may be fired by gas, solid fuel or oil. The heated water is stored, ready for use, in a tank known as the hot cylinder, that is nearly always located in an airing cupboard.

The system is usually a gravity one, and functions because hot water is lighter (in weight) than cold. Thus, in any container, water that is heated will rise to the top, and cold water will drop to the bottom. How this works in a water heating system is that the heated water rises from the boiler to the hot cylinder by means of a pipe known as the *flow*, and cooler water is pushed down (by gravity) to the boiler via the *return pipe*. Thus there is

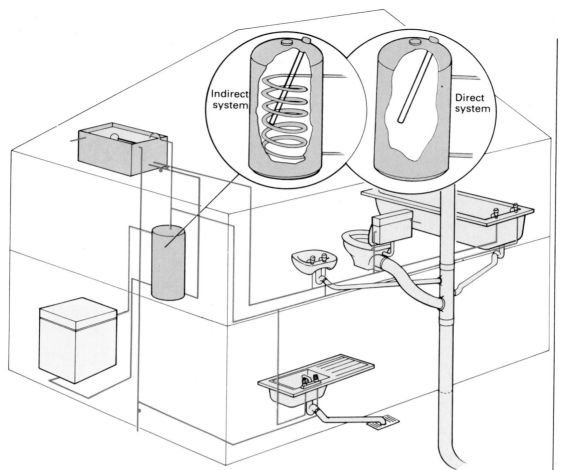

Indirect
system

Direct
system

a continual cycle of flow and
return whenever heat is supplied
by the boiler. The flow and
return pipes are collectively
called *primaries*

For a gravity system to work
properly, the hot cylinder must
be placed higher up than the
boiler. Where this isn't possible
– in one-level homes such as
flats, for instance – the water has
to be forced from boiler to
cylinder artificially, and so you
get *pumped primaries*.

The hot cylinder may well
have an electric immersion
heater. At one time, these were
fitted as the sole means of water
heating, but are nowadays more
likely to be intended to
supplement a boiler during
breakdowns and in summer.

Modern boilers and
immersion heaters are
controlled by thermostats to stop
them from overheating.
However, just in case things do
get out of hand, a pipe (called
the *vent pipe*) rises up from the
top of the hot cylinder to the cold
tank, over which it is bent like a
shepherd's crook, so that any
overheated water is discharged
into the tank. If, as a result, the
cold tank becomes too full,
excess water will discharge via
the overflow.

The draw-off point (the pipe
that carries hot water to the taps
etc) is in the vent pipe, just
above the cylinder. This is where
the water will be hottest. Cold
water to replace the hot that is
drawn off is normally fed from

the cold storage tank into the
bottom of the cylinder.

A drain cock will be fitted at
the lowest point of the system,
usually near the boiler, so that
the water can be drained off
when necessary.

**The boiler system may be direct
or indirect.** In a *direct system*,
the water that is heated in the
boiler goes directly to the hot
cylinder to be drawn off at the
taps. With an *indirect system*,
however, it is fed to a small inner
cylinder or coil inside the hot
cylinder, which thus becomes
hot. It is the heat from the coil
that warms up the water in the
outer cylinder, which will then
go to the taps. This way, the
water in the boiler and the water

you actually use are quite separate. Indirect cylinders are usually confined to homes with central heating, so that radiator and domestic will never get mixed up. However, you do find indirect cylinders in a system that merely heats domestic water.

If you live in an older house (where a modern plumbing system is a later addition), in a house with a rambling complicated ground plan, or in a flat (especially a conversion in an old house), the layout of the supply may not be as neat as that shown in the diagram, but it will be based on the general principles outlined.

Try to get to know your plumbing system. Go round your house, following the pipes, with the book in hand open at the previous page, until you can understand its layout. In particular, try to determine which fittings and sections are controlled by various stop taps. Shut off a stop tap and then see which taps on baths, sinks, basins, lavatories etc will then not work. Beware of drawing off too much water from a hot system with the tap shut off and the boiler working. You should turn the boiler off.

Instantaneous Heaters

In small flats created by converting large houses, and in older homes built without a water heating system, but later modernised on a budget, it may be too complicated to add the sort of system described above. Water may then be heated by a gas or electric instantaneous heater. There is no hot cylinder – hot water is not stored – and thus, no airing cupboard.

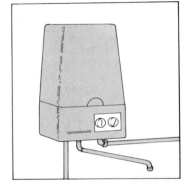

The heater will be connected directly to the mains, and its gas

jets or electric element will come into play only when a tap is turned on, and water flows. Such heaters can be single or multi-point. A single point will be placed over one sink or bath and provide hot water just at that spot. However, pipes will carry water from a multi-point to more than one tap, usually to all those in the home.

Single point instantaneous heaters are sometimes fitted to a house with a full-scale boiler storage system as a means of providing hot water during the summer.

The Head of Water

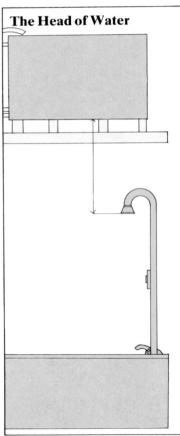

The difference in height between the cold storage tank and the outlet at which the water emerges – tap or wc valve, for instance – is known as the *head of water*. Plumbers usually take the measurement from the bottom of the tank, for the water level in it will often be low. The head of water determines the pressure of water at the outlet, and thus the force with which it will come out. A good head of water is always necessary to give a strong flow – you couldn't, for instance, have a tap higher than the cold tank – but it is especially important when you install a shower. Note that the pressure at the hot taps, just as surely as the cold, is determined by the head of water between outlet and cold tank. The hot cylinder plays no part in determining the pressure; from this point of view it is merely a swollen-up section of pipe through which the water passes on its way from cold tank to tap.

Waste

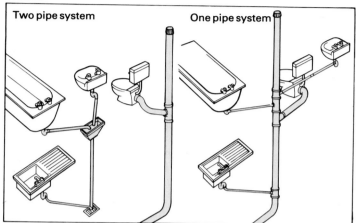

Two types of domestic drainage system are used in British homes: the two-pipe system, and the one-pipe system (sometimes called the single-stack system). Most homes have the former. In this, the waste from the wc is kept apart from the waste from sinks, baths, washbasins, bidets etc (known collectively as 'fittings'). The wc discharges into a soil pipe that connects to the local authority sewer. The soil pipe also extends upwards – well away from windows – to act as a vent for the escape of sewer gas. It is topped by a wire cage to stop rubbish getting inside it and causing blockage.

Gullies

Waste pipes from ground floor fittings discharge into open gullies that are connected to the drains. Baths, basins and other fittings on upper storeys empty into a type of open gulley, known as a *hopper*, fitted to the top of a downpipe. This pipe, in turn, conveys the water to a ground floor open gulley – sometimes the same one into which the ground floor waste pipes discharge.

Modern and high rise homes will have one pipe systems. In this, both wcs and fittings discharge into one pipe (usually inside the building) that carries all the waste to the drains. This pipe (or stack) was at one time made of cast iron, but nowadays only plastic is used.

It is easy to tell which type of drainage system your home has.

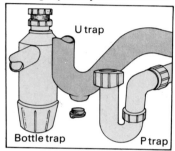

The Trap

One feature of all waste pipes is that they have a trap. This is a device designed to trap a small reservoir of water to stop drain smells from coming up the pipe and into the home. A wc trap is fitted at the back of (or sometimes forms part of) the pan. The trap for sinks and other fittings is a separate item inserted into the waste pipe during installation.

The Rules

Any changes you make to your home's plumbing system must be carried out in accordance with your local water authority's regulations. These will cover the sizes of various tanks and cisterns, plus precautions to stop appliances that mix hot and cold water (eg showers and mixer taps) from sucking water that has been stored in a tank (and therefore won't be fit for drinking) back into the mains, and so on.

You don't have to get permission to carry out plumbing work, as you do with the planning laws or building regulations, but the water authority has the right to inspect your home and to demand alterations.

The rules change from time to time, and vary from one authority to another. You can carry out minor repairs (fitting new washers, stopping overflows, curing leaks etc) without consultation, but you should always check before doing anything major.

Building regulation approval is needed if you want to alter or extend the waste water system. Consult the Building Control Department of your local authority.

Kitchens

A few plumbing improvements can make your kitchen a much easier place in which to work. For instance, you can fit new, better taps in place of the old, change two taps for a mixer, and so on.

Most important of all, you should make sure that *washing machines* and *dishwashers* are properly plumbed in. You will find it much more convenient than constantly having to wheel the machine out, attach a hose to the taps, and clip a waste to the edge of the sink (with the risk of the pipe coming adrift and causing a flood).

Above right *A modern stainless steel sink unit has been set into a tiled work surface. The mixer tap unit swings to reach both sinks, and there is a spray attachment and waste disposal.*

Above *An old pine cupboard has been converted to hold a brightly coloured, square sink. Taps have been matched to the sink and mounted behind.*

Opposite *The space under the stairs outside this basement kitchen has been used as a laundry area. Maybe you too have some unused space like this, that could get the washing out of the kitchen.*

INSTALLING A SUPPLY

Whenever you want to install a new fitting, or plumb in an electrical appliance, you have to lay on a supply of water to it. At one time water supply pipes were made of lead (the word plumb comes from the Latin word for lead) and between the wars steel pipes were used. Modern plumbing, however, uses copper pipe and, increasingly, plastic.

If your home has lead or steel supply pipes, the system is obsolete and needs complete renewal. You might even qualify for a home improvement grant. Copper pipe is the most usual, and it is easily worked by the do-it-yourselfer.

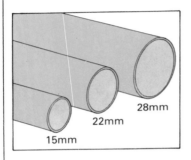

Domestic copper supply pipe is sold in metric sizes, and there are three main diameters–28mm for the primaries, 22mm for main runs, and 15mm for *branch lines*. If your existing installation is 12 or more years old, the pipes will be in the imperial sizes of 1 inch, ¾ inch and ½ inch. These, of course, are not direct translations of the metric, but this doesn't matter. The metric figures refer to the external diameter of the pipe, while the imperial ones refer to the internal diameter. The 28 and 15mm sizes are directly interchangeable with the 1 and ½ inch sizes, and when you wish to connect 22mm to ¾ inch pipe, you must use an adaptor.

Working Copper Tube
There are four different operations to be carried out on plumbing pipework. When you want to install a water supply to a

fitting, all, or most of them, will be necessary.

The pipe must be cut to length; it will need to be joined (eg to make two short lengths long enough, or to take a branch line at an angle from a straight run); it may have to be bent to go around corners; and it will need to be connected to fittings, such as taps or a cylinder.

Cutting
As copper is a soft metal, the supply pipes can easily be cut to length with a hacksaw. However, there is a tendency for the cut end to flatten slightly, and this makes it difficult to make a waterproof joint. Also, the cut end must be truly square, and it is not easy to ensure this with a hacksaw.

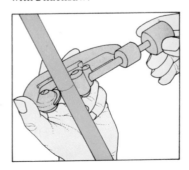

It is better to use a proper *pipe cutter* that will not flatten the end, and will make a cut you can

be sure is square. Small portable cutters, intended for the do-it-yourselfer, are not very expensive.

However, when you are cutting into pipework that is already installed and fixed close to a wall, there is often not enough room to wield a pipe cutter. Then you must use a hacksaw.

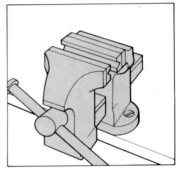

Never hold pipe in a woodworker's vice: use a proper **pipe vice** (or a Workmate) instead. This will prevent the pipe being dented and impeding the flow of water in use. Always aim to avoid this.

When the pipe has been cut, use a file to get rid of any 'burr' on the ends, and also to make any final adjustments needed to ensure it's square.

Joining Pipe

Supply pipes may need to be joined – eg to make two runs long enough, or to fit a branch line at an angle to a main run. Two types of joint are used – *compression joints* and *capillary joints*. The compression joint is easier for DIY use, but it is bulkier and more expensive (though this is not so important for small jobs).

Compression Joints

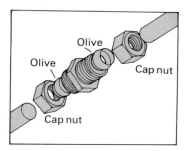

A compression joint consists of a threaded body, a small copper ring (called an *olive*) and a *nut* (cap nut). Slip first the nut and then the olive on to the end of the pipe. The chamfers of the olive are unequal; the longest should point towards the body.

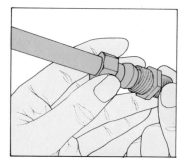

Insert the end of the pipe into the body as far as it will go, and slide the olive and then the nut to the body. Tighten the nut. The action of doing this crushes the olive, making the joint watertight.

You must tighten the nut by just the right amount. Too little and the olive will not be crushed sufficiently; too tight and it will be crushed too much. Either way, the joint will leak. To avoid it, tighten the cap nut as far as you can by hand. Now give it one complete turn with a spanner. When the work is completed and the water supply restored, inspect each joint in turn to see if it is watertight. If it weeps slightly, give the nut a series of quarter turns with a spanner, until no more water oozes out. You can, if you wish, use a jointing agent (see *Threaded Joints*) to help ensure watertightness, although the makers of joints always insist this isn't necessary.

Capillary Joints

These work by means of solder, a small ring of which is fixed inside the joint.

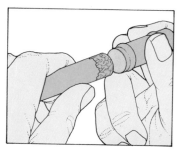

Apply flux to the end of the pipe, push the pipe fully home into the joint and twist it around so the flux is evenly spread. Now play a blowlamp flame on the joint. The heat will melt the solder, which will flow out and surround the end of the pipe, making the joint watertight.

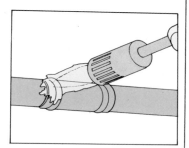

There are, however, a few points to watch. Everything must be spotlessly clean, so rub both the end of the pipe and the inside of the joint (don't disturb the ring of solder) with fine steel wool until the copper is really burnished. Then take care not to touch the cleaned parts with your hand.

Secondly, it is impossible to apply the flame to one end of a joint without the heat flowing along to the other and melting the solder there, too. So, all ends of a capillary joint must be made up at one go.

Thirdly, if you apply heat for too long, the solder will flow out too far; too little and it won't flow far enough. The trick is to

Tips

When testing a joint for weeping, don't use your fingers; skin is always moist anyway. Instead, wipe the joint with a tissue and look to see if it's damp.

Sometimes, one end of a capillary joint is defective, and doesn't have enough solder. You should have a small stick of solder handy in case this happens.

watch the joint you're heating very carefully, and remove the flame the instant a ring of bright solder appears. Then allow the solder to cool off and harden before disturbing the joint.

If a capillary joint weeps when you restore the water supply, you will have to drain off, allow it to dry (solder won't take on wet surfaces), and then reheat the joint and feed in more solder. If this doesn't work, you will have to break the joint, throw it away and fit another. This is another example of how much more convenient compression joints are.

Threaded Joints

These are used mainly for connecting pipes to taps and boilers, but you do come across them elsewhere.

Threaded joints consist of a threaded fitting – the male part – that is inserted into a threaded hole – the female part. The joint has to be sealed with PTFE tape, or plumber's hemp, and a jointing compound, such as Boss White.

Dealing first with plumber's hemp (it is not as neat as PTFE

tape, but it is more effective on the deeper threads you find on boilers).

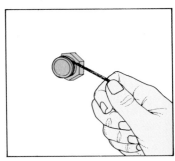

Smear a little jointing compound on the male thread and then pull off a few strands, and wind them around the threads of the male fitting in the direction that it will turn when it's being tightened up. This is to ensure it is pulled into the fitting rather than scraped off during tightening. Smear a little more jointing compound onto the hemp, insert the fitting into the female, and tighten up as hard as you can with a spanner.

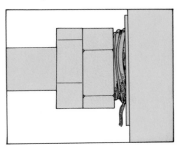

The hemp should have travelled well into the female fitting. If it's piled up outside, you have put on too much hemp, or you have wound it in the wrong direction, or perhaps not wound it tight enough. In any case, you must break the joint (unscrew the fitting) and start again.

PTFE tape looks neater than hemp, and is also easier to use. It comes in rolls like sticking plaster, although the tape itself isn't sticky.

Wind it on in the same way (and same direction) as for hemp, two or three times around the fitting, allowing it to overlap. Smear jointing compound on the female thread, insert the male and tighten.

With both hemp and tape, some thread should still be visible after tightening. If not, the joint will probably not be watertight and you'll have to start again, adding more tape or hemp.

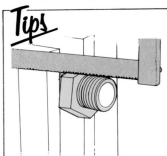

Draw a hacksaw lightly across a threaded joint to form a burr that will grip the plumber's hemp and keep it in position as you tighten the joint.

Bending

One way to take a pipe around a corner is by bending it. Plumbers have bending machines, but it's hardly worth buying one for DIY. You can bend 15 and 22mm pipe by hand.

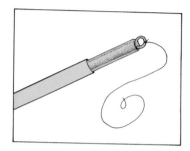

To stop the pipe from flattening, use a *bending spring*. These are available from hire shops, and you should specify one to match the diameter of your pipe.

Smear a little oil or grease on the spring, tie a length of string to one end of it and then push the other end into the pipe until the halfway point of the spring is roughly at the centre of the required bend.

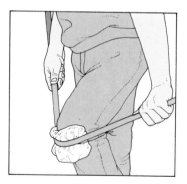

Grip each end of the pipe, place it across your knee, and give a sharp tug. If this hurts your knee, tie a protective rag pad to it.

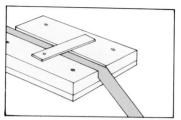

Another way to bend piping, is to use a wooden former. Nail two lengths of batten to a piece of board, the gap between them equal to the diameter of the pipe. Hold the pipe between the battens with one hand, and pull the free end to the required shape with the other.

As it is impossible to make a bend near the end of a length of pipe with either of these methods, you must bend the pipe before cutting it to length.

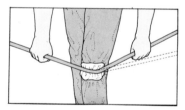

Bend the pipe slightly more than you need, then bend it back to the required angle. Twist the spring clockwise, and you should then be able to pull it out.

28mm pipe is too rigid to be bent by hand, so a bending machine must be used. However, few amateur plumbers need to use this diameter pipe – or to put bends in it. If you do, the answer is to use *elbow couplings*. These are not used generally because of their cost, and the fact that any joint introduces the possibility of a leak. However, for a small job that requires few bends, use elbows on any size of pipe.

Support

Long runs of supply pipe need to be supported.

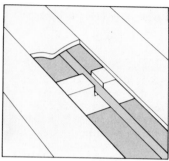

Any pipes that run beneath a timber floor, in the same direction as the floorboards, can sit in notches cut in the tops of the joists. These notches should be positioned directly under the middle of a floorboard, so that nails driven in the board won't pierce the pipe.

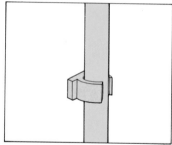

Pipes above the floor should be held to a wall or skirting board by clips and this applies to pipes under the floor at right angles to the floorboards. Use stand-off clips that space the pipe clear of the wall, rather than the saddle type that hold it close against it.

The recommended spacings between clips on 15mm pipe are 1.8m on a vertical run and 1.2m on a horizontal run; for 22 and 28mm pipe, they are 2.4m and 1.2m respectively.

INSTALLING A WASTE SYSTEM

When you are installing a new fitting or appliance, it will require a waste system. Modern waste systems are always in plastic. Four plastics are used – **UPVC** (unplasticised polyvinyl chloride), **MPVC** (modified polyvinyl chloride), **ABS** (acrylonitrile butadiene styrene), and **PP** (polypropelene).

There are two main sizes of plastic waste pipe for sinks and baths – 43mm (1½ inch) and 36mm (1¼ inch) – and as with supply pipes, the imperial dimension is the internal diameter, and the metric, the external.

Like copper, these need to be cut to length, and sometimes to be bent, although, even more than with supply pipes, it is more convenient to use an elbow joint.

Cutting Plastic Waste Pipe

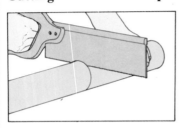

Plastic pipe is cut with a saw. This can be a hacksaw but, to help keep the end square, a fine-toothed general purpose saw is better. Measure carefully the length you need, and be sure to allow for the overlap inside any joint.

After sawing, clean off the burr, inside and out, with fine glasspaper, and then file the end of the pipe to a 45° chamfer all round.

Joints

Two methods of jointing are used: the *push-fit* and *solvent* welding. However, PP can't be solvent welded.

Manufacturers' instructions vary, so it's best to stick to one brand and follow the instructions exactly. In this section, however, we give a general guide.

Solvent welded joints

The joints used in solvent welding are smaller and neater than the push-fit kind. However,

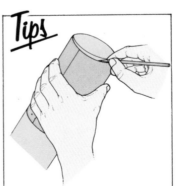

Tips

Test the cut end of a pipe for squareness by folding a length of paper around it and joining the ends. Mark any protruding edge and use a file to remove it.

they cannot compensate for the expansion of the pipe caused when hot water passes through it. A 4m length of PVC will expand by 13mm when heated above 20°C so, on long runs, you must introduce expansion couplings at 1.8m intervals. Such long lengths rarely happen in homes. Push-fit joints allow for expansion.

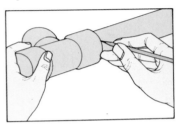

Push the end of the pipe into the socket of the joint as far as it will go, and draw a pencil line all around it. Withdraw the pipe and you will see at a glance how much fits inside the joint. Roughen this section with a file, and the inside of the socket with fine glasspaper, to provide a key for the solvent. Clean the end of the pipe and inside the socket with a spirit recommended by the manufacturer.

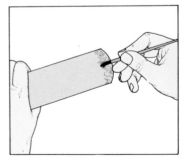

Apply the recommended solvent cement with a clean paintbrush, both to the end of the pipe and the inside of the socket. Brush it on in the direction of the length of the pipe, and make sure the whole surface is covered.

Now push the pipe into the socket (some manufacturers recommend doing this with a slight twisting action), and hold the joint securely for about 15 seconds. Wipe off any solvent that has oozed out and let the joint set for 24 hours before allowing hot water to pass through it.

Push-fit joints

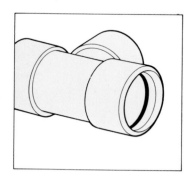

Push-fit joints work by means of a rubber sealing ring inside the body of the joint. With most brands, the ring is fitted during manufacture, but it might come separately for you to fit yourself. In either case, make sure the ring is seated properly.

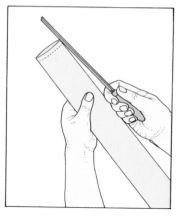

Draw a line around the pipe about 10mm from the end and chamfer back to this line with a file. Clean the end of the pipe and the inside of the socket, and smear petroleum jelly (or a silicone jelly recommended by the manufacturer) on the end of the pipe.

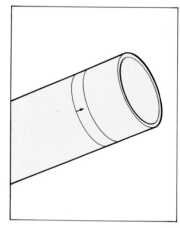

Push the pipe home and make a pencil mark where it meets the edge of the fitting. Then withdraw it 10mm as an expansion allowance.
   This will ensure that the joint is watertight.

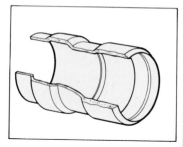

The expansion couplings that you have to fit in long runs of pipe joined with solvent cement method, have a solvent weld joint at one end and a ring seal at the other.

Support

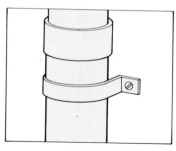

Plastic waste pipe needs to be supported by clips. These should be fitted at least every 750mm.

Tips

In modern plastic waste systems, the trap is held in place by large nuts. A washer is fitted to make a watertight seal. If a leak develops there, place a bucket underneath to catch spillages, and unscrew the nut(s). Take off the old washer and replace with a new – you might have to take the existing one to the shop.

215

Connecting to the Drains

You will have to make arrangements for the waste pipe to discharge water to the drains properly.

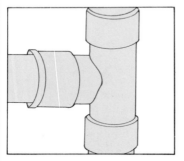

If there is an existing waste system nearby, you can often connect up the new pipe to it by means of a T fitting. Where this isn't possible, you must adopt other methods.

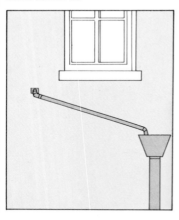

If you have the open gulley type of drainage, the waste pipe can pass through the house wall to reach it. The necessary hole should be made with a club hammer and cold chisel.

You will find it best to work from both sides of the wall. Begin gently on the plaster on the inside to avoid damage, and take care to clear out all the rubble from the hole as you break through cavity walls. Otherwise, debris might fall into the cavity and lodge, making a bridge that will lead damp from the outer to the inner leaf.

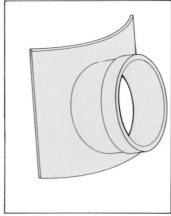

If your house has the one-pipe drainage (single stack) system, your new waste can be connected to the stack. The connection is made by means of a special device, known as a *boss*.

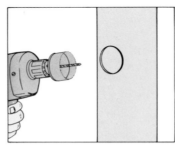

A hole must be cut in the stack using a hole saw (you can usually hire it) fitted to a hand or electric drill. The hole must not be within 200mm of a wc connection on the opposite side.

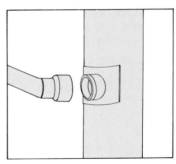

Boss

Various types of boss are made, most needing solvent welding to the stack. Then the waste pipe is connected to the boss by either a ring seal or solvent weld joint. Ask when you buy it, to make sure you get the one suitable for your needs.

One big problem with single stack systems is that water rushing down it can cause siphonage (suction) that can empty the water out of the waste traps.

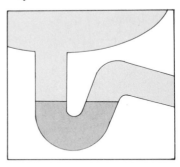

To prevent this, deep seal 75mm traps must be used, and the waste pipes laid with as short a run as possible and very shallow falls. In the case of washbasins, it may be necessary to connect a 38mm waste (instead of the usual 32mm) or fit anti-siphon traps. All these are points to be discussed with your local authority.

Installing taps

There are more taps in a plumbing system than the familiar sink, basin and bath taps. *Stop taps* positioned at strategic points will allow you to isolate various appliances when maintenance is called for, without shutting down the whole system. There should be stop taps in the supply pipes from the cold storage tank (to save draining it during maintenance) and, if there is a separate pipe to supply the hot cylinder, it's very handy to be able to turn it off separately, too. Few homes have enough; it is a good idea to fit extra ones.

Stop Taps

A stop tap is fitted by means of a compression joint at each end. Select a suitable position for it, and measure how much of the supply pipe will have to be removed to accommodate it. The pipe will have to fit right up to the shoulder inside the joint socket, so measure inside there.

Turn off the supply. Cut out enough pipe to take the stop tap. There probably won't be enough room to wield a pipe cutter, so use a hacksaw, taking care not to flatten the ends of the pipe. Clean up the ends and slide on the nuts and olives.

Place the tap in position with the arrow on its body pointing in the

same direction as the water will flow. You will be able to spring the pipes far enough apart to do this.

Tighten the compression joint at each end of the tap, restore the supply and check that the fitting is watertight.

Mixer Taps

Mixer taps can be fitted in place of two single taps at a kitchen sink. Or a shower fitting can take the place of bath taps. The only pre-condition is that the holes in which the present taps sit must be at a distance that allows the two 'tails' of the mixer to be inserted. In modern baths and sinks there should be no problem as the holes are at a standard distance. In any case there is often some leeway over this as the two legs of some mixers can be swivelled to vary the distance between them. Measure the distance between the centres of your single taps before you buy.

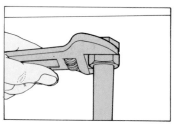

After shutting off the supply, disconnect the supply pipes from

the taps – by unscrewing the cap if it's a compression fitting, or sawing through it if it's a capillary joint.

The biggest difficulty will be removing the old taps, as they may be so corroded it will be hard to loosen the nuts that hold them in place.

There will not be enough room to wield an ordinary spanner, so you should use the type known as a *crow's foot spanner*. If the nut still sticks, try squirting penetrating oil (or other products designed to free corroded joints) around the nut.

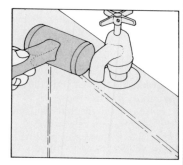

One trick that works is to get a helper to hold the tap while you turn the spanner, or hold the spanner tightly while your helper gently taps the spout of the tap to unscrew it. Be careful not to

Sinks & basins

damage the sink or bath.

With the old taps out of the way, fitting the new is easy.

There should be full instructions, but usually the tap legs are bedded in putty (scrape off the old putty first). There is a washer underneath and a back nut holding everything in place. Sometimes a washer is fitted both above and below, and there may be a second locking nut.

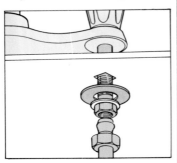

The mixer is connected to the supply by means of a *tap connector*. This fits to the tail of the tap by means of a threaded joint, and to the supply pipe with a compression joint.

New Taps

New taps for old are an easy way of modernising an old washbasin or bath. The procedure for fitting them is the same as for a mixer.

A basin can be sited where none is fitted at present (for instance a bedroom) provided it can be conveniently connected to the drains.

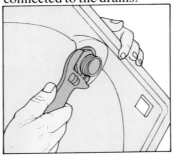

To install a new washbasin prepare it by installing the waste outlet fitting, which is held in place by a back nut underneath the basin, and made waterproof with the washers supplied, or mastic. Do not over-tighten the nut, or you may damage the basin.

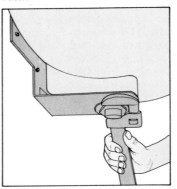

Fix it to the wall with brackets of the correct size, or on its pedestal according to the instructions supplied with it. If the basin is to be set into a worktop, use the template (supplied by the manufacturer or make one yourself from card) to mark, then saw out, a hole to receive it. Mastic is used to make a waterproof seal between basin and worktop.

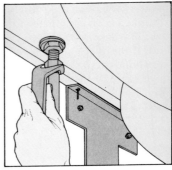

Fit taps to the basin, tee into the hot and cold supply at a convenient point, and connect supply pipes to the taps.

Connect a trap to the waste outlet, and run a plastic waste pipe to discharge into a convenient drain.

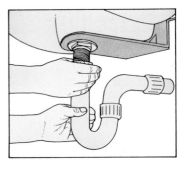

If the basin is to take the place of an existing one, turn off the supply and disconnect or saw through the supply pipes to its taps. Disconnect the trap, if the waste is plastic, or saw through it if it's metal.

Lift the basin clear, and remove the pedestal or brackets. Replace a metal waste system with a new plastic one.

Sinks are dealt with in a similar manner.

Washing machines

Some machines need both a hot and a cold supply; others only cold. Follow the maker's instructions. There are two ways of connecting up to the supply.

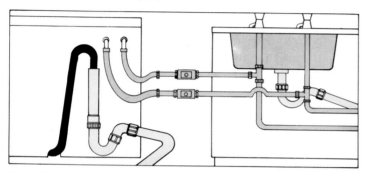

Supply

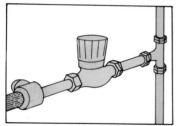

Find a convenient point, cut into the supply pipe, and fit a T junction. To the branch of the T, connect a short length of pipe and either an ordinary stop tap or one purpose-made for washing machines. The stop tap is essential in case the machine has to be removed for maintenance, or a leak develops in the hose or machine itself. Some manufacturers recommend that the supply is turned off at the stop tap whenever the machine is not working. At the end of the pipe, fit the coupling to which the flexible hose of the machine can be connected. This is the method professional plumbers usually adopt.

Do-it-yourselfers may prefer a simpler method:

you can use what is called a *self-cutting tap*, made especially for plumbing-in appliances.

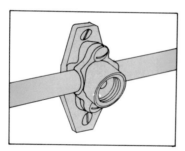

First fit the tap's *saddle clamp* at a convenient point on the supply pipe, and tighten the screw that holds it in place.

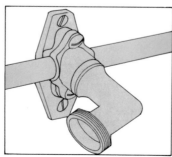

On the side of the clamp is a threaded socket, into which you

screw the main body of the tap. This has a special tip that cuts into the pipe, so connecting with it. No water can escape during the fitting, so you don't even need to turn off the supply. Tighten the tap with a spanner, and you have your stop tap ready to connect to the supply hose of the machine.

Waste

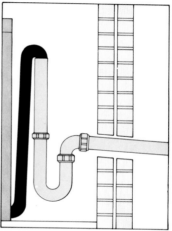

Construct the machine waste system in pipe of the diameter recommended by the manufacturer. The machine has a flexible hose waste pipe that has a bend at the end of it. This end hooks into a vertical pipe that is fitted near the wall close top the back of the machine. The top of the pipe must be left open, and the height above the floor will be specified in the instructions.

From the vertical pipe, a plastic waste pipe can be run to an outside gulley, or joined to the main stack (see page 216) or connected by means of a T junction to an existing waste pipe. Also, a trap must be fitted somewhere in the run.

219

Showers

Electric Showers

Electric showers are connected directly to the rising main and, since the pressure of the main ensures that water comes out of the rose with sufficient force, there is no need to worry about the head of water. The appliance has an instantaneous heater that warms up the water as it flows out when the tap is turned. No hot water is stored.

To install one of these showers, fix it to the wall at a suitable spot according to the manufacturer's instructions. The shower can discharge into a bath, or you can site it near a basin, so that it can be used for hair washing.

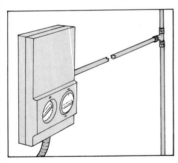

Run a supply pipe from the shower to a convenient spot on the rising main, and connect it by means of a compression T joint.

There are special regulations regarding the wiring of electric shower units. Instructions for electric wiring are given on page 256.

Conventional Showers

You can also install a shower which is fed from the hot cylinder and cold storage tank. This can be either in place of, or in addition to, the existing cold and hot taps on your bath.

Two basic types of shower unit are available. Firstly, there is the *thermostatically controlled unit*, which will maintain the temperature you've selected throughout your shower. These units are, however, very expensive, and most people settle for a *mechanical unit*, with which the temperature can vary.

The main disadvantage of a mechanical unit is that it may suffer from what plumbers call an *auxiliary draw-off*. This means that in the middle of your shower, someone may turn on a tap or washing machine, or even flush a wc, and so cut down the flow of water to your shower. If the tap is a hot one, it will be the hot supply that is reduced, and you will get a sudden cold douche, an unpleasant shock perhaps, but nothing else. Much more dangerous, however, is when it is the cold supply that is restricted, giving you a scalding hot shower.

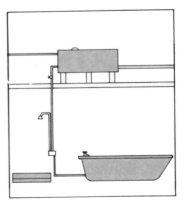

To prevent this happening, you should give the shower its own cold supply pipe directly from the cold storage tank – not joining on to a conveniently placed existing cold supply. You can arrange the hot supply by teeing into the supply to the bath's hot tap.

The other point to watch with a shower is that you must have a sufficient head of water to give enough pressure (see page 206). The maker's instructions will tell you the minimum head required (usually about 1m), but the more you can exceed the minimum, the better your shower will be. If you can't get a sufficient head of water, it is possible to boost the pressure with a pump. Most people, however, would settle for an electric instantaneous shower unit that gets its pressure from the mains.

Shower Cubicles

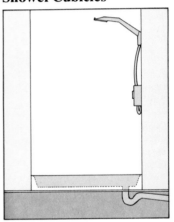

Installing a shower cubicle in a bedroom, landing or under the stairs is an inexpensive way of increasing your home's bathroom facilities. Basically, it is fitted just like a sink or basin. The big difference is that, since the waste outlet is so low down, you may have problems getting a sufficient fall in the waste run. It should be 25mm per 300mm for a short run of 600-900mm, but only 12mm per 300mm where the run will be 3-4.5m. Also, the trap may have to be fitted under the floorboards.

Right *A vanity basin fitted into a counter in any bedrom is a practical luxury.*

Far right *Designed for someone confined to a wheelchair, this simple, easy-to-maintain bathroom has all the plumbing concealed behind a tiled box. The washbasin has both taps easily accessible, and has been plumbed-in at a low level to enable it to be used from a wheelchair.*

Centre *Why not put your own bathroom at one end of your bedroom, divided off by sliding screens?*

Below left *How about fitting an extra shower under the stairs? Ideal for a sporting or gardening family, and when the door in front is closed, no one would know it's there.*

Below right *To help ease the strain on an overworked family bathroom, see if you can add a shower on your landing.*

REPAIRS AND MAINTENANCE

Quite a few things can go wrong with your home's plumbing system, and various parts can deteriorate and need renewal. Here we look at some of the more common jobs.

Taps

Taps are made of a non-rusting metal (usually brass, or chrome plated on the outside) although plastic taps are now being introduced.

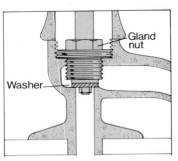

Two metal surfaces pressed together can't provide a perfect water seal, so a *washer* is used to make everything watertight. Washers were once made of leather or fibre, but nowadays are rubber or nylon.

When you close a tap really hard and it still drips slightly, the washer needs to be replaced. This is how to replace the washer on a domestic tap – and the method is the same for stop taps.

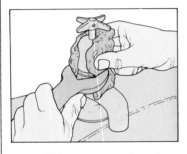

Turn off the water supply and open the tap. Then unscrew the *shield*. If corrosion stops you doing this, use a spanner, protecting the shield with a cloth. Still no success? Try pouring boiling water on the shield to make it expand.

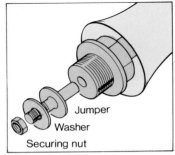

Loosen the hexagonal head with a spanner and lift the top clear of the body. The washer is fixed to the jumper plate with a small nut. Remove the nut and replace the washer with a new one of the same diameter – the maker's name should face downwards. Reassemble the tap.

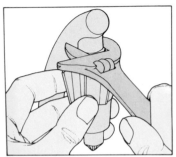

Supataps are treated differently. There is no need to turn off the supply. Loosen the gland nut with a spanner and unthread the nozzle, checking that the valve that stops the flow of water has dropped into position.

The supatap has a combined jumper and washer, housed in its *flow straightener*.

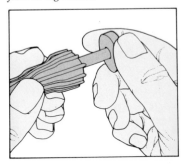

Take out the flow straightener – one way is to push it with a pencil from the other end – and replace the washer. Clean the flow straightener before reassembling the tap.

Leaks

If water oozes out from the top of the shield, the fault lies with the gland unit.

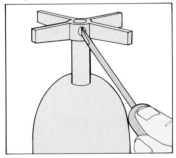

Begin by removing the top. A cross top will be fixed by a small grub screw. Remove this and place jaws of a spanner underneath and lever the top upwards.

With modern-style taps, prise out the H or C button in the middle of the top and withdraw the screw underneath. You will now be able to pull off the head.

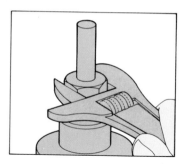

In both cases the gland nut will now be accessible. Tighten this half a turn with a spanner. Temporarily replace the head and check that the tap is easy to turn. If it's too tight, slacken the gland nut slightly.

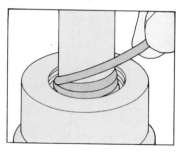

Check, too, whether the tap still leaks. If it does, remove the gland nut and re-pack with string smeared with petroleum jelly around the spindle.

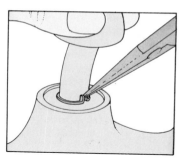

If there is a leak at the bottom of the swivel nozzle of a mixer tap, raise the shroud at the base – some you merely lever up, others have to be unscrewed.

Prise up the circlip that will now be revealed, and expand it. Slide it up the nozzle, and lift the nozzle clear.

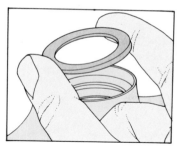

Replace the seals in the base, and wet the base before re-assembly.

Shower Mixers

If there is a drip from a shower mixer, a defective O ring is the likely cause.

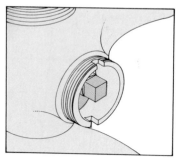

Take off the shower-bath diverter by withdrawing the screw that holds it. You will now see a slotted connector.

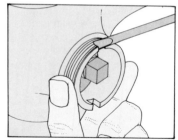

Remove this by inserting a screwdriver in the slot and pushing.

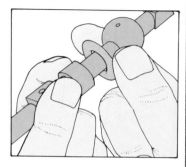

Remove the old O ring, slide on the new, and re-assemble.

Turning off the Supply

When you want to work on a tap or cistern, you must shut off the supply of water to it. When it isn't controlled by its own stop tap, this involves turning off the stop tap on the rising main (so that the whole system is closed down) and draining the cold storage tank. Before doing this, either switch off (or lower right down) the thermostat of any boiler or heater that supplies hot water. Solid fuel fires and boilers should be damped right down.

Once you have turned off the raising main, open the tap on which you want to work – or in the case of a lavatory, repeatedly flush – until no more water can be drawn. Then you can start work. Restore the water supply as soon as you've finished.

223

Overflowing Cisterns

A cistern overflows when the ball valve doesn't shut off the supply when the water reaches the correct level – usually about 12mm below the overflow pipe. This may be because the arm isn't set properly.

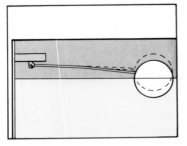

If the arm is metal, try bending it so the ball (or float) rides lower, and the valve will shut off the water before the level reaches the overflow.

If the ball is submerged, instead of floating on the surface, it is punctured or damaged in some way. Don't bother trying to mend it – you could never get rid of all the water inside. Better to replace it – a new ball is inexpensive. Simply screw the new ball onto the thread end of the arm.

You will have to shut off the water while changing the float.

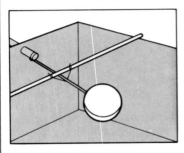

If there's no stop tap handy, place a stick across the top of the

tank and loop a string around arm and stick to keep the arm raised.

There is another possibility. If the valve still drips when you raise the arm as high as it goes, then it needs a new washer.

First, turn off the supply to the valve. Several types of ball valve are fitted, but the most common is the *Portsmouth*.

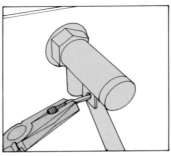

With the **standard Portsmouth,** take out the split pin holding the float arm, and remove the arm. Place a screwdriver in the slot under the valve, and lever out the piston.

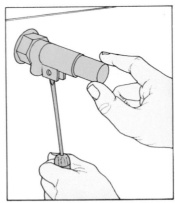

Push your screwdriver in the slot in the piston and unscrew the washer retaining cap. Fit a new washer, lightly grease the components, and reassemble.

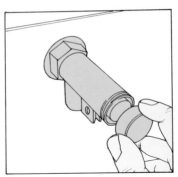

With a **Portsmouth equilibrium valve**, you have to unscrew the valve's end cap before you can remove the piston.

If fitting a new washer is not successful, the washer seating may be damaged. You can hire a re-seating tool to smooth it down, but as a last resort you may have to fit a new valve. Check with your local plumber's merchant to ensure you get one suitable for the water supply.

If you're working on an existing installation (rather than a new one) turn off the supply to the cistern and push the ball down until no more water comes out. If this could cause an overflow, lower the water level in the cistern by turning on a cold tap or, if it's a lavatory cistern, flushing the wc.

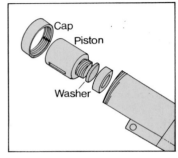

Cap
Piston
Washer

Remove the fixing nut, and take out the old ball valve. Slip one of the washers provided over the threaded tail pipe of the valve, and push the tail through the hole in the side of the tank.

Fit the other washer on the outside and tighten up the back nut. The supply pipe is then connected to the tail pipe by a compression joint.

Freeze-ups

If your supply pipes are not protected by lagging, the water in them will freeze in really cold weather. Not only does that mean the inconvenience of not being able to draw water; water expands as it turns into ice, and that can fracture a pipe or force a compression joint apart. So, when the thaw comes, you will get a flood.

As soon as you realize you have a freeze-up, try to thaw it under controlled conditions, so as to avoid a burst. Turn on the affected tap (keep a watch so the sink doesn't overflow) and work backwards from it looking for signs of the freeze-up – the pipes will feel at their coldest where the ice has formed.

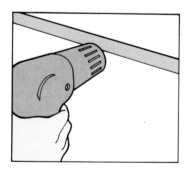

Turn off the supply and apply heat to the affected part. The most convenient way of doing so is with a hairdryer, but an electric fan heater will do. As a last resort, wrap rags soaked in

warm water around the pipe. Eventually you will melt the ice, and the water will flow again. Resolve immediately to lag the pipes so that you never suffer such trouble again.

The next section on how to cure a leak will tell you what to do if your remedial action is too late, and the pipe is damaged.

Curing Leaks

A leak may occur at a compression joint because the nut has not been tightened enough. Tighten it by a series of quarter turns until the leak stops. If the reason is that the nut has been tightened too far, you will have to drain off, dismantle the joint, and fit a new olive.

A leak in a capillary joint always means draining off, breaking the joint and fitting a new one. It will have to be a compression joint unless you're prepared to wait for everything to dry out completely, as solder won't work on damp surfaces.

When you find a threaded joint leaking, you can try tightening the nut further. If this doesn't work, you will have to drain off and refit the joint.

A leak can arise in the middle of a pipe run because of frost or physical damage, such as a nail being driven into it.

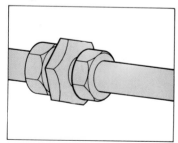

If the fracture is small, merely cut out the correct length of pipe

and fit a compression joint there This is done in the same way as fitting a stop tap.

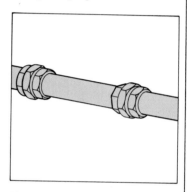

If the damaged area is too long to be covered by a joint, fit a short length of pipe by means of a compression joint at each end.

Blocked Traps

Two types of trap are found on the fittings of British homes. The *bottle trap* is found on modern plastic waste systems. It is usually held on by a knurled nut, with a rubber or plastic washer under it to ensure a watertight seal.

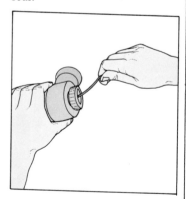

When a bottle trap becomes blocked, the easiest thing to do is to remove it and take it to another sink or basin to wash it out. You may have to poke wire through it in stubborn cases.

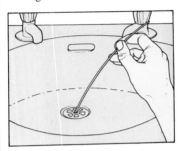

The second, older type of trap is formed simply by a bend in the pipework and is known as a *P trap* (sometimes *U trap*) because of its shape. Older types are not easily removed and it is better to get rid of the blockage from the sink end. You can try poking wire down it to clear things out, or pouring down a solution of caustic soda (be sure to follow the safety instructions on the tin).

If this isn't successful, use a plunger or rubber suction cup. In both cases, bung up the overflow with rags before you begin.

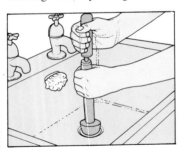

A plunger looks rather like a cycle pump. You pump the handle up and down while the other end is inserted in the waste outlet. Since water can't be compressed, it forms a column that pushes the blockage out of the way.

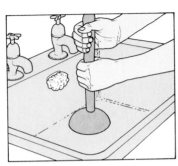

A suction cup operates on the same principle. It consists of a rubber or plastic flexible cup, attached to a handle. Place the cup over the outlet and move the handle up and down.

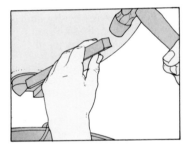

If this does not work, place a bucket under the trap and remove the cap at the bottom. The cap may take the form of a large nut that you turn with a spanner or wrench, or it may be a recessed nut with two small projecting lugs. To turn the nut, take a scrap length of wood, place one end on one of the lugs, and tap the other end with a hammer.

With the nut removed, the fall of water may bring the blockage with it. However, once again you may have to free it with a length of wire. Once the blockage is clear, replace the nut, making sure you keep the bucket underneath until you're sure it's watertight.

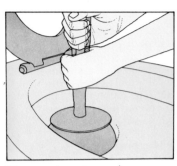

Wcs, too, have traps. A blockage can be cleared by a special plunger that has a metal plate above the rubber cup. This is to stop the cup being inverted as you work. Try to hire such a plunger. Place it in the pan and work it vigorously to force water round the bend and so clear the blockage. Once you're successful, flush the wc to re-fill the trap. If this doesn't work, call in the plumber.

Blocked Gullies

If the blockage is above the grating, scoop out as much as you can, then remove the grating and scrape it clean. Finally, wash everything in a solution of household soda, flush out with clean water and treat with disinfectant. Wear rubber or plastic gloves throughout. Treat hoppers in the same way

For blockages below ground, raise the grating and scoop out.

You may have to do this by
hand, so it's even more
important to wear protective
gloves. Flush out clean
afterwards.

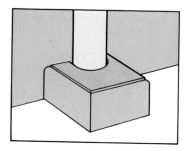

Where blockages are persistent,
consider making a protective
timber cover for the gulley, or
perhaps having a metal one
made for you.

Air Locks

If, instead of flowing freely,
water splutters and hisses out of
a tap, the likely cause is a bubble
of air trapped somewhere in the
pipe – an air lock.

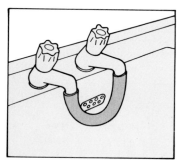

This can often be cured by
running a short length of hose
between the kitchen cold tap
(which operates at high
pressure because it is connected
directly to the main) and the
affected tap. This is easy enough
when the affected tap is the
adjacent hot tap, but it's still

possible in other cases. Turn on
both taps and leave for a few
minutes, and then turn off – the
affected tap first. The pressure
from the mains should have
cleared the air bubble.

Note that this dodge is
frowned on by many authorities,
because they say there is a
danger that impure water could
be sucked back into the mains.
Others say that the mains
pressure is so much stronger that
this just won't happen. It's best
to check with your local
authority.

Radiators

Radiators are normally
trouble-free, but minor
faults can develop.

When a radiator feels
cold, check that the boiler is
working, the room
thermostat is calling for
heat, and that other
radiators are warm.
Nothing wrong there? Then
the probable cause is air in
the radiator. You get rid of
it by opening the air vent – a
process known as 'bleeding'
the radiator.

The air vent is in one side
of the radiator at the top.
Open it with a special
radiator key – plumbers'
merchants sell them. With
the boiler operating, open
this vent. Any air inside will
hiss out. You will know all
the air has been released
when water starts to spurt.
Keep a cup handy to catch

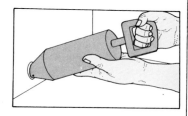

Another remedy, where the
affected tap is supplied by the
cold storage tank, is to use a
pump. You should be able to
hire one. With this, you force air
down the cold tank outlet, and
thus dislodge the bubble.

this; it is dirty and might
stain floor coverings. At
the bottom of the radiator
on each side is a valve – the
wheel valve, or hand
control, for turning the
radiator on and off, at one
side, and the *lockshield
valve*, used to balance the
flow of water when the
system is first
commissioned. The valves
are supplied in two parts for
installation – the radiator
insert, a male fitting that is
threaded into a female
tapping in the radiator
itself, and the main body of
the valve, which is fitted to
the insert. Threaded joints
are used in both cases. The
valve is usually connected
to the pipe by a compression
joint.

If a leak develops at one
of the connections, try
tightening the joints with a
spanner – but beware of
overtightening the
compression joint. If this
does not work, the system
will have to be drained off,
and the joints re-made.

Fitting a new cold tank

At one time, cold storage tanks were made of galvanised metal. But their life is limited, and eventually they have to be replaced. The replacement should be plastic or glass fibre, which won't corrode. Also, plastic ones can be squashed to go through a small loft opening.

Your local water authority will have regulations about the size of tank you must have. The size will probably be expressed as something like 50/60 gallons. The higher figure refers to the amount of water it would hold filled to the brim. The lower one is the amount it is designed to contain in practice. Usually there is a mark on the side to indicate the correct water level.

Your house will have to be without water while the work is going on, so do as much as you can beforehand.

Your first job is to take out the old tank. Turn off the rising main, and drain the tank by opening or turning on one or more of the cold taps that it feeds. Don't bother trying to free the tank by taking apart the joints connecting it to the rising main and the various supply pipes. They will probably be so corroded that you cannot turn the nuts. Anyway, it is almost certain that the pipe runs will have to be modified, no matter how slightly, to suit the new tank.

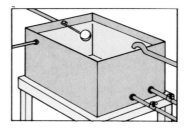

Saw through the pipes near the tank, making sure the cuts are truly square. A pipe cutter would be better for this than a hacksaw.

Be careful as you lower the old tank down from the loft. Draw-off points are positioned slightly above the base of the tank so that

sediment settling at the bottom won't find its way into the supply pipes, so there will be some water left in it. The old tank may be too big to go through the loft opening; jokes about DIY plumbers who have enlarged loft openings, even removed part of a roof, to get an old tank out of the loft, are part of the plumber's folk lore. You shouldn't bother; just empty the tank and leave it up there.

Your new tank can go in the same position as the old. However, if you have a shower, remember that the pressure of water at the rose will be determined by the head of water. So, it's a good idea to consider siting the tank on a raised platform.

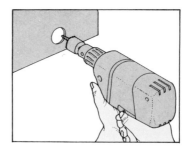

A tank full of water is very heavy, so the platform will have to be strong. Also, a sheet of

thick plywood should be fixed under the flexible plastic tank.

The new tank will be supplied without holes for the pipes, since the manufacturers couldn't possibly know where these will be required. You will need at least three – one for the inlet to the ball valve, one for the overflow, and one (or more) for the outlet to supply the various cold points throughout the house. Also, the vent pipe from the hot cylinder must be positioned so that it can, if necessary, discharge into the cold tank.

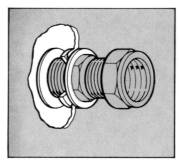

The necessary holes in the new tank should be made with a brace and bit or a hole saw in an electric drill. They should match the diameter of the pipes that have to be connected to the tank.

Pipes are fixed to the tank by means of *tank connectors*. These have a threaded sleeve with a

Fitting an outdoor tap

back plate that goes on the inside of the tank. Push the sleeve through the hole, with a washer either side of the tank wall, and tighten the fixing nut. Pipes are connected to the outside by compression joints.

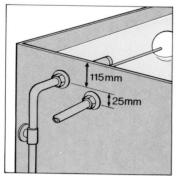

Your local water authority may have rules about the position of the holes for the pipes. However, it is normal for the ball valve inlet to be about 115mm below the rim of the tank and the overflow to be 25mm lower still. This is to prevent water from ever covering the inlet valve, with the consequent risk that it could be siphoned back into the main. The various feeds for the supply pipes should be 50mm above the bottom of the tank.

Incidentally, it is a good idea to fit stop taps to the supply pipes, so that parts of the system can be isolated when maintenance is necessary. These taps can be near the tank or, more conveniently, where you can reach them without having to climb into the loft.

The flow of water to the cold tank can often be heard throughout a small house. Cut down on the noise by closing the stopcock slightly.

An outdoor tap can be a very useful addition to the amenities of your garden, and it's easy enough to install. Remember to discuss your plans with your local water authority, who will probably want to put up your water rates.

First, choose the site for the tap – one that will be convenient in use, but not involve a complicated pipe run indoors.

The type to use is known as a *bib tap*, which you can buy complete with hose connector. It leans away from the wall, so that you will not bang your knuckles when using it. The tap is fitted, by means of a threaded joint, to a tap connector, which is screwed to wall plugs.

Fit a 15mm T joint in the rising main, between its stop tap and the branch line to the kitchen sink. From this run a pipe to the tap connector outdoors, bending the pipe or using elbow couplings to follow the necessary route. You will certainly have to use couplings to get through the hole in the wall, for it will not be possible to push a bent pipe through it.

The hole should be slightly higher than the tap, so the pipe run outside slopes downwards. Make the hole with a club hammer and cold chisel, or you can hire an industrial electric drill and masonry bit. Work from both sides of a cavity wall, making sure dust doesn't get into the cavity.

A stop tap must be fitted in the pipe run, close to the T joint. In winter, close this tap and open the bib tap to drain off all the water from the run, so there will be no freeze-up during frosty weather.

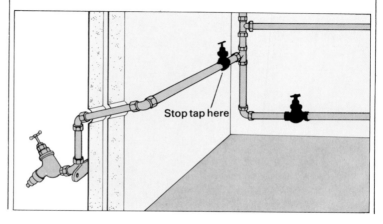

Stop tap here

TOP TEN TIPS

1. To free a badly corroded nut, you can use heat. Depending on the situation, either wrap hot rags around the nut, pour boiling water over it, or play a blowlamp flame on it for a second or so (not plastic pipes, of course). The heat causes the metal to expand, and the movement frees the thread.

2. It's a nuisance when you want to work on a supply pipe leading from the cold storage tank, and there's no stop tap to shut it off. Well, there's no need to drain off the whole system.

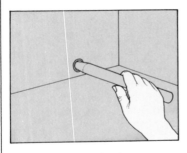

Take a short length of broomstick, sharpen it to a point at one end and push it into the outlet to the pipe inside the tank. It will act as a bung, and save you depriving the whole system of water when you want to work on just one pipe.

3. Here's how to prevent stop taps from jamming. Every six months, turn them off and on several times. Finally, open the taps fully and close them a quarter of a turn. This will restrict the flow of water slightly, but not enough to matter, and make the taps less likely to jam in future.

4. Even if your plumbing system is well lagged, frost can still strike at a waste pipe outside the house. It is no use introducing hot water into the sink or basin – heat rises and so will not go in the direction of the ice. Better to pour the hot water on the base of the pipe outside the house, so the heat will rise towards the cause of the trouble.

5. When cutting copper pipe, don't risk flattening the ends by over-tightening the vice.

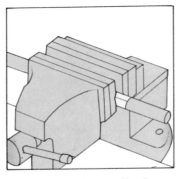

A way of ensuring an effective grip is to wrap glasspaper around the pipe before inserting it in the vice.

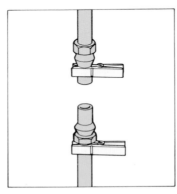

6. When fitting a compression joint in a vertical run of pipe, use spring clothes pegs to stop the nuts and olives from sliding down.

7. You may sometimes need to empty, or partly drain off, the hot storage cylinder – easy enough when the cylinder has a drain tap, but these are not always fitted. You then have to siphon the water out. Shut off the water supply, then open up all the taps to drain off the pipes.

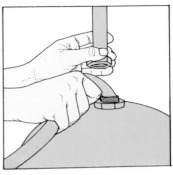

Undo the nut that connects the vent pipe to the top of the cylinder, but have a bucket and cloths ready, there will be water in this pipe.

You now need a helper. Fill a garden hose with water, pinch both ends of it so the water can't get out, and ask your helper to carry one end to a convenient discharge point. Thrust your end deep into the cylinder., Your helper can now open his end of the hose, and the water flowing down will draw the tank's water after it.

This dodge can be used for emptying many types of closed tanks. In the case of a small tank – or where a small amount of water needs to be extracted from a large one – you can use a small diameter hose.

Place one end in the tank, then suck on the other end until water starts to flow. Lower the other end, and the water will be siphoned out of the tank.

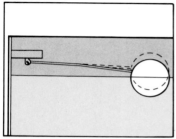

8. When a wc cistern does not give a strong enough flush, it may just be that there is not enough water in it, because the ball valve cuts off too soon. Look inside. If the water level is way below the mark, try bending the ball arm (providing it's metal) so that the ball will ride higher and admit more water.

9. Keep a quick repair kit ready to hand. A screwdriver for any grub screws in the handles, spanners for gland nuts and washers of the right size for every tap in the house.

Aim to get a tool kit that includes a spanner to fit every nut in your home's plumbing system. It is tempting to go for just one adjustable spanner to cover every situation, but these (as distinct from wrenches) are never so effective.

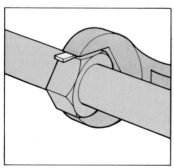

When you don't have a spanner of the right size, place a too-large

spanner on the nut, then drive small pieces of wood as wedges between the jaws and the nut. They will help you to get a firm grip.

10. If a radiator valve is weeping around the spindle (not the threaded joints to the radiator or the supply pipe), there is no need to drain the system to cure it. There are two types of radiator valve (not including thermostat valves); those with O rings, and those without.

Turn the valve off, remove the handle and place cloths around the base of the pipe to catch the small amount of water that will dribble out. Remove the gland nut and turn the shaft clockwise to pull it out.

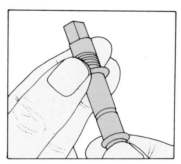

Working quickly, remove the O ring (or both if there are two) fit a new one, smear some petroleum jelly on the shaft and replace it in the valve body (twisting anti-clockwise). Replace and tighten the gland nut.

If the spindle won't come out by turning clockwise and pulling, then the valve doesn't use O rings and all you need to do is repack the body around the spindle with string and petroleum jelly. Then replace and tighten the gland nut.

WIRE IT

CONTENTS

Introduction

Anything to do with electricity is thought to be difficult and dangerous. The usual advice is 'leave it to a qualified electrician'—and this attitude is encouraged by all competent authorities. The truth is, however, that many electrical jobs are well within the competence of the amateur who takes the trouble to understand the subject and who takes obvious precautions, such as first switching off at the mains before starting any work.

Read this chapter carefully and try to understand the basics of home wiring before planning any changes. If you find yourself still baffled, leave the job to a competent electrician. Do not try to tackle anything like a complete home wiring until you have first successfully completed some of the simpler jobs.

Care and accuracy are most important. 'It looks right' or 'that will do for now' might be acceptable for some jobs around the home, but this certainly does not apply to electricity. Everything must be exactly right. You must check everything carefully before completion and switching on.

There are regulations about the supply of electricity to the home. The electricity board can refuse to connect your home to their supply if they consider the wiring to be unsafe but, in practice, their interest is limited to making sure you have an effective earth system so that, if there should be a fault, your wiring is not likely to jeopardise their equipment or the supply of electricity to other homes.

There are also rules for electric wiring safety in the home. These are contained in the *Regulations for the Electrical Equipment of Buildings* (fifteenth edition), published by the Institution of Electrical Engineers, and better known to all professional electricians who follow them as 'the IEE Wiring Regs'. Following 'the Regs', a copy of which can be found in any reference library, is not only advisable in the interest of your own safety but it also means the work will satisfy the electricity board.

The Regulations are not too easy to understand—even for the professional—but we have tried here to simplify them, as they apply to home wiring.

Left *A peaceful monochromatic colour scheme has been brought alive by touches of yellow and good lighting. If you don't want to embark upon the individual wiring of ceiling lights, you could use a track system connected to the* ceiling rose. *You can then have as many fittings as you want.*

Above *In planning this galley-type kitchen, it was essential to have sufficient outlets for all-electric appliances.*

ELECTRICITY IN THE HOME

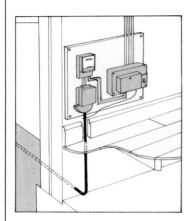

The Meter

Electricity comes into the home through a thick, armoured, two-core service cable made up of the live and neutral circuits. The cable goes to the meter through a box containing a fuse (service fuse). This is sealed by the electricity board and must never be touched. If this fuse fails call the emergency service of the electricity board (it is in the telephone directory but it's a good idea to write the number on the wall, close to the meter). Check all the other fuses in the house first, as it is very rare for this fuse to 'blow'. Check with neighbours that it isn't a power cut.

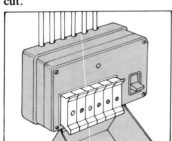

The Mains Switch

From the electricity meter the electricity supply goes to the

mains switch which controls the electricity supply to the house. In houses 30 or more years old it is still common to find the mains switch in a separate box. In modern homes it is part of the fuse box, where the main circuit is split into a number of separate circuits — power, lighting, cooking and so on — each with its own fuse.

The electrical equipment and wiring from the meter onwards is the responsibility of the householder. The householder also has to make sure there is an effective earth wiring point to which all the other wires in the home are connected.

Modern wiring practice for effective earthing is to fit an

electro-mechanical earth—a *residual current circuit breaker* (*RCCB*). These are also known as *earth leakage circuit breakers* (*ELCB*).

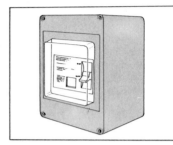

An RCCB is designed to keep a constant check on the live and neutral circuits, which normally operate in equal balance. If the

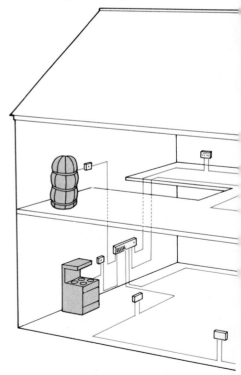

RCCB notices a sudden change in the current flow, it instantly and automatically switches off the current. RCCBs are sometimes incorporated with the mains switch in the consumer unit. More often they are used as separate units to protect one circuit — especially the one for outdoor sockets or switches where the risk of electric shock is always greater.

From the *fuse box* (sometimes called a *consumer unit*), cables form separate circuits, each containing a *live, neutral,* and *earth* wire. In these cables the *live* is coloured *red* and the *neutral, black* (flexes have different colours: see page 240). The earth wire is usually bare.

All three wires are encased in a grey or white insulating material. In most homes the cables are imbedded in the plaster on the walls or run in steel, aluminium or plastic tubes. Older homes may have cloth or rubber covered cables, black or red.

The Ring Circuit

The circuit supplying the socket outlets and plugs is the ring circuit. The ring circuit has the 13 amp socket (with square holes) to fit a square, three-pin plug that can supply an appliance up to 3000 watts. This type of socket has safety shutters that close automatically when the plug is withdrawn so children

can't poke anything in to touch the live terminals.

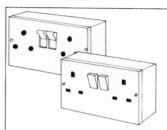

Modern homes use the ring circuit system of wiring for sockets that have shuttered square entrance holes for the matching square pin plugs. Earlier systems use round pin plugs and sockets. These systems should be replaced.

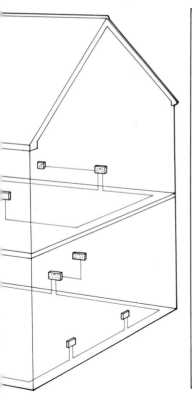

Tools

There are only a few extra tools, in addition to normal DIY items, that are needed for home wiring jobs.

Wire cutters (or diagonal cutters) for cutting cable and flex to length.

Wire strippers are used to remove the insulation from individual wires, not the outer sheath of cable. There are several types available and they adjust to accommodate different thicknesses of wire.

A *sharp knife* is necessary to score the outer cable sheath. Be careful not to cut through the insulation of the wires inside.

A *thin-bladed screwdriver* is best for the brass terminal screws in many electrical fittings.

Fuses

The cartridge fuse in the 13 amp plug is designed to protect the flex by being a deliberate weak spot in the electrical circuit. If more current flows than the flex is designed to carry, it could get dangerously hot. To prevent this, all fuses are made of weaker material than the rest of the circuit, so that it melts (or 'blows') when overloading occurs. This stops the flow of current and prevents further trouble.

Main Fuses

The fuses in the main fuse box (consumer unit) operate on the same principle. There is one for each circuit, eg lighting, power sockets, cooker etc.

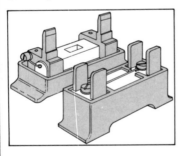

The most common form of fuse for the consumer unit has a fuse wire held in position by brass screws.

A modern alternative to rewirable fuses are *Miniature Circuit Breakers (MCBs)*. These look like ordinary switches or push buttons and they automatically flick themselves off if the circuit they're protecting is overloaded. The

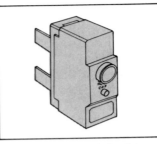

circuit can be brought back into use simply by pressing the switch down (or pushing the button in) to reset the circuit breaker.

Do not get confused between an MCB and an RCCB. The MCB operates only in the case of overload (too much current), while the RCCB operates in the event of current flowing to earth (out of the circuit — perhaps through a faulty appliance).

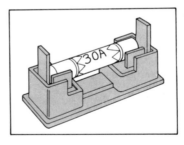

Another type of fuse for consumer units is a *cartridge fuse*. This is similar to the cartridge fuse in the 13 amp plug and may be replaced as easily.

Replacing a Rewirable Fuse

Get a torch (keep one near the fuse box). Switch off the main switch. If possible, find out the cause of the fuse blowing. Switch off the faulty appliance or lamp and unplug it, otherwise the new fuse may blow.

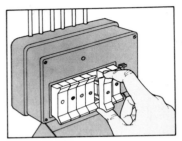

Find the blown fuse by taking out and inspecting each one in turn. It is usually obvious which one has blown — not only will the fuse wire be broken, but often there will be scorch marks around the fuse carrier.

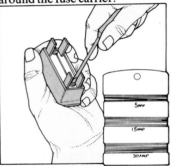

Replace the old wire with a fresh piece of the correct amp rating. Don't stretch or strain it when tightening the screws. Replace the fuse carrier, close the box, and then turn on the switch. If the fuse blows again, or if there is any doubt, send for an electrician.

Tips

You can make the job of finding blown fuses easier by labelling each fuse in the consumer unit. That way you can see quickly which fuse belongs to which circuit, eg upstairs lighting, ground floor power, etc.

Reading the meter

How Electricity is Measured

The 'flow' of electricity is measured in amperes (amps or A); the 'pressure' is measured in volts (V), and its power (the work it can do) in watts (W). The standard voltage in Britain is 240 V (Northern Ireland 230/240V). All fuses and fuse wires are marked in amps.

1000 watts used continuously for one hour is equivalent to one kilowatt hour (*kWh*). This is the *unit* by which electricity is measured and is stated on the bill.

A metal rectangle, called a rating plate, is usually found at the rear of an appliance. It shows the maker's name, the model number (which is quoted for servicing) and the amperage, the voltage and, usually, the wattage. Multiplying the amps by the volts will give the watts $(A \times V = W)$ — the amount of power the appliance uses, and so a guide to the running cost.

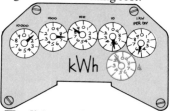

The dial meter has six dials. Each pointer goes round in the opposite direction to its neighbour. The dials record units: tens of thousands, thousands, hundreds, tens, and singles. Ignore any dials that register tenths or hundredths of a unit. These are usually coloured red.

Start by reading the dial showing single units, and write down the figure. Then read the dial showing tens of units, then the one showing hundreds, then thousands and then tens of thousands, working from right to left and writing them down in that order. Always write down the number the pointer has passed (this isn't necessarily the nearest number to the pointer). So, if the pointer is anywhere between 3 and 4, write down 3. If the pointer appears to be directly over a figure, say 7, look at the pointer on the dial immediately to the right. If this pointer is between 9 and 0, write down 6. If it is between 0 and 1, however, write down 7.

This is the *digital meter* that shows units of electricity by a simple row of figures. Subtract the previous reading from the new reading to see the number of units (kWh) used.

Running Costs

The Major Popular Appliances

Cooker Uses about 4 units a day cooking for a family of four.

Dishwasher Washes a family's dinner dishes for about 3 units.

Freezer Uses about 1.5–2 units per cu ft per week.

Electric fires and fan heaters With a loading of 2 kw, 2 units per hour.

Refrigerator The table-top height size uses about 1 unit per day; the larger sizes 1.5 units per day.

Shower 1 unit for 2 showers.

Iron Irons for over two hours for 1 unit.

Spin dryer Spins about five weeks' laundry for 1 unit.

Tumble dryer Uses about 2 units for one hour.

Automatic washing machine About 2 units of electricity for one wash load on prewash and hot wash.

Smaller Appliances	For 1 unit of electricity you can:
Air conditioner	run for 1 hour in summer
Blanket (over)	all night for 2 or 3 nights
Blanket (under)	use every evening for a week
Blender	make 500 pints of soup
Coffee percolator	make about 75 cups of coffee
Floor polisher	polish for 2½ hours
Food mixer (stand model)	mix 67 cakes
Hair dryer	use it for 3 hours
Health lamp (infra red and uv)	use it for about 4 hours
Kettle	boil about 12 pints of water
Lawn mower	do 4 hours' grass cutting
Power drill	have about 4 hours' drilling
Sewing machine	sew 11 childrens dresses
Shaver	have over 1,800 shaves
Television (colour)	have about 5 hours' viewing
Toaster	make 70 slices of toast
Vacuum cleaner	clean for about 2 hours
Video recorder	have about 10 hours' use
Waste disposal unit	grind about 1 cwt of rubbish

CABLES & FLEXES

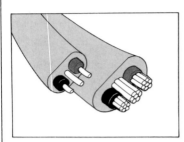

Cables

The supply of electricity depends on cables and flexes. *Cables* are oval and are meant to be permanently fixed, held flat by special clips. Cables are made of three conductors (wires). One covered with *red* insulation (the *live*, one covered with *black* *(neutral)* and a bare wire called the *earth continuity conductor*.

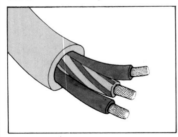

Flexes

Cables have relatively few, but thick, strands of wire while *flexes* are made of many finer strands to give them the flexibility needed to run between plug and appliance. The insulation on the three conductors is coloured differently from cables. The *live* is *brown;* the *neutral* is *blue;* and the *earth* is *green yellow*. The outside insulation of most three-core flex is plastic but it may be rubber with a braided linen cover for appliances such as irons. Also, some heaters and immersion heaters require a heat-resistant insulation.

Double-insulated appliances only need a *two-core flex*. This is because they are made in such a way that no current could leak to the outside of them and cause electric shock to the user. Double insulated appliances all bear a symbol of one square inside another.

Two-core flex is also used for standard and table lamps unless they are made of metal.

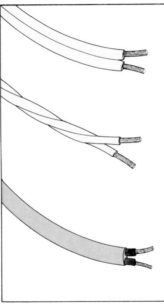

There are three types of *two-core flex. Parallel twin flex* has two wires, each in its own insulation cover, joined together and not surrounded by an overall covering. Although the insulation on both wires is the same colour, there is usually a small rib along the side of one wire. If possible, you should use this wire as the live conductor.

Twisted flex has a braided fabric cover which makes it better for use with table lamps.

Finally, *two-core sheathed flex* with colour-coded insulation is made in different forms and amperages.

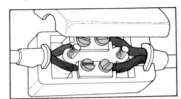

Never try to extend a flex by joining on an extra length using insulating tape. Purpose-made flex connectors in tough plastic are sold, but it is usually cheaper to buy a complete length of flex and connect it to the appliance.

Avoid long flexes as it is all too easy to trip over them. It is even worse if they have to be run under a carpet where they can be damaged and may even cause a fire. The best solution is to install extra sockets (see page 242).

When fitting a flex to a plug or appliance, only remove enough insulation to enable the wires to be connected to the terminals. There should never be any bare wire exposed. Also, never stretch the insulation, and be sure to use any flex grip in the plug or appliance so that an accidental tug on the flex will not pull out the conductors.

Only fit flex of the correct amperage. Check the wattage of the appliance or lamp, and divide it by the voltage (240) to give the amps $\left(\dfrac{W}{V} = A\right)$

Wiring a 13 amp plug

Ring Circuit

All modern homes have their socket outlets wired on ring circuits or loops of 2.5 sq mm twin-core and earth PVC sheathed cable that starts at the consumer unit, 'visits' each socket in turn and returns to the consumer unit. Each ring is protected by a 30 amp fuse. Each ring circuit is limited to supplying socket outlets and fixed appliances over an area of 100 square metres, but the number of sockets on a ring is unlimited. Because the maximum load that can be taken at one time is about 7200 watts, it is usual to have two ring circuits, one concentrated near the kitchen area.

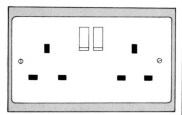

It is best to install double sockets rather than single, and they should have switches.

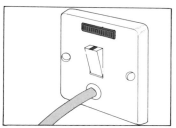

A fixed appliance should be supplied from a *fused connection unit (FCU)* rather than a socket. Appliances such as freezers should be connected by a plug and socket (or FCU) fitted with a red neon indicator to show that the electricity supply is connected and working.

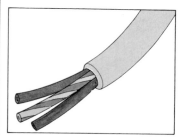

Cut away about 50 mm of the sheath on the flex, without cutting the insulation on the individual wires.

Open the plug by undoing the screw, and remove the cartridge fuse. Cut the wires off so they are just the right length to go through the fixing holes or around the clamping screws. Strip off just enough insulation and no more.

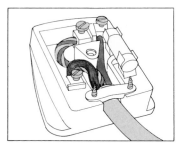

The *green or green yellow* is the *earth wire,* and goes to the larger of the three pins—marked 'E' or 1. The *brown lead* goes to the pin marked 'L' (for *live*). The *light*

blue lead goes to the pin marked 'N' (for *neutral*). A two-core flex can be connected to a three-pin plug, but leave the earth pin unconnected.

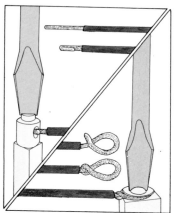

Clamp the wire ends firmly in the terminal connections, as shown. The outer sheath of the flex must be gripped firmly under the clamp where it enters the plug. This prevents the wires pulling out of the terminals.

Replace the cartridge fuse. Most plugs are supplied with a 13 amp (brown) fuse, but a 3 amp (red) fuse should be used for lamps and appliances rated up to 720 watts. See the appliance rating plate or the maker's instructions, if you're in doubt about which fuse to use.

Before screwing the cover on to the plug, make sure there are no stray strands of bare wire and that the terminals are tightened hard down—not just finger tight.

Replace the plug cover and screw it into place. There should be no looseness or rattles of any kind when you've finished, and all screws or nuts holding the plug together should be firmly tightened.

Adding extra sockets

Extra sockets can be added to the ring circuit. These are added on a *branch line* from the ring called a *spur*. The spur is wired from the back of an existing socket and can supply two singles or one double socket. Sockets should be placed not less than 150 mm from the floor.

To connect a spur to the ring, turn off the power at the mains switch and ease an existing socket from the wall by undoing the screws in the faceplate.

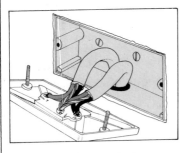

Behind the faceplate is the *mounting box* containing up to three cables. Check whether this socket is on a ring or on a spur. (Leave spur sockets alone.) *One-cable* sockets are always spurs; *three-cable* sockets show that a spur has already been added to the ring and these also should be avoided. *Two-cable* sockets are probably on a ring, but they just might already be part of a spur, so it is a good idea to check with a **circuit tester** (see opposite).

Next, decide where you will run the cable. In many homes you can run the cable under the floor but, where there is a solid floor, the cable will have to run in the plasterwork of the wall. Alternatively, you can use hollow metal or plastic skirting to conceal the cable. The cable could also be run along the surface of the skirting, but it

should always be covered in plastic conduit to protect the cable and also to disguise it.

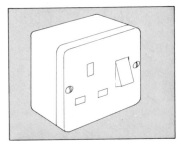

The new socket can be mounted on a plastic surface box, but flush-fitted metal (or plastic) boxes are the neatest.

Cutting the plaster to hide the cable is not as difficult as it might seem, especially if redecoration of the wall is planned.

Using a sharp knife, score two lines 25 mm apart along the proposed route. Use a club hammer and a brick bolster to chip out enough plaster to allow the cable to fit comfortably.

Another method is to use a plaster router bit fitted to an electric drill or router, after first drilling a series of holes along the proposed route. Check carefully that you are not going to interfere with or damage any cables already in the wall.

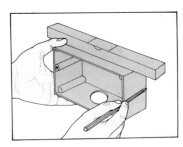

The hole to take the metal box usually needs to be cut deeper than the depth of the plaster. First place the box against the wall and trace the outline with a pencil.

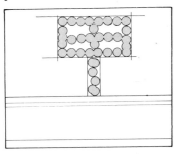

Use a masonry bit (marked with tape to a level a little deeper than the box) to cut a series of holes along the lines, and then drill holes over the whole area.

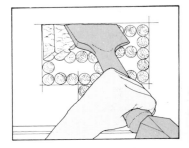

Now the bolster will remove the plaster and brick easily. Check that the mounting box fits and then knock out the required holes in the box for the cable.

Always fit a *grommet* (a rubber ring) into each hole to prevent the cable from rubbing against the metal. Place the box in the hole and mark the wall for a screw, take out the box, drill a hole and insert a wallplug. Finally, fix the box, making sure it sits level—a crooked socket always looks untidy.

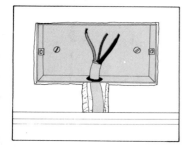

Take the end of the length of cable (2.5 sq mm PVC sheathed twin-core and earth) through the new box's knockout hole and leave about 75 mm protruding from the box.

Now run the cable to the existing socket, either in a channel in the plaster or under the floor. On a ground floor the cable can normally be placed in the void beneath and clipped to the joists.

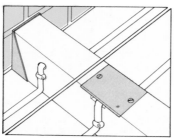

On an upper storey, where the cable runs at right angles to the joists, pass it through holes drilled at least 50 mm below the joist's top edges. Otherwise, you could cut notches in the top edges of the joists to take the cable, but stiff metal plates must cover the cable and be fixed to the joist.

Take the cable to the socket on the ring where it is to be connected. Remove this socket from the cable and unscrew the box. Now complete your channel to give access for the new cable. This will probably mean knocking out another

circular metal blank in the box and fitting another grommet. Pass the cable through the grommet and screw back the box. Cut the new cable to leave about 75 mm protruding.

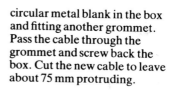

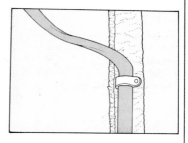

Clip the cable along its length where necessary, to hold it in place. There are clips made for the purpose—be sure to use clips of the correct size and shape for your cable.

Now mix your plaster, fill in the channel and around the new box, and leave to dry.

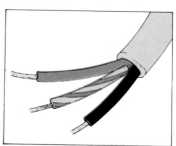

Next prepare your cable ends, stripping away the outer insulation with a sharp knife. Take the red and black covered wires and remove 12 mm of insulation from each with the wire stripper. Cover the bare copper earth wire, where exposed, with green or green and yellow PVC sleeving.

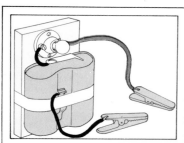

A circuit tester can be made from a 9 volt battery, some bell wire, a pair of crocodile clips and a miniature bulb and bulb holder. Use the tester to link the cables' red wires. If

the bulb lights, the socket is on a ring circuit.

You can also use the circuit tester to do an earth test. Place one clip on the metal part of the appliance, and the other on the earth pin of the plug on the appliance (this won't work on double insulated appliances). If the bulb is bright, the earth is safe; if it's dim, the earth is weak and should be examined. If the bulb lights when the clip is placed on either of the other two pins, there is a serious fault.

Cookers

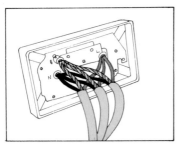

In the existing box, the three red, three black, and three copper (earth) wires are matched and each group of three connected to the appropriate terminal on the socket (see illustration).

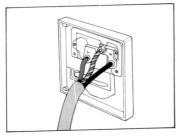

In the new box, one wire is connected to each terminal (see illustration). Screw each terminal tight, making sure all the wires are fastened under the screws.

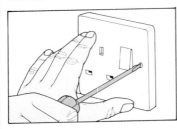

Replace the sockets by holding the faceplate against the box and pressing the cables in carefully. Fix the sockets to the boxes with the bolts provided, switch on, and test.

Double Socket for a Single

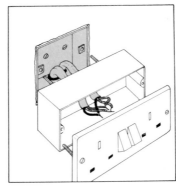

It is sometimes possible to fit a new double socket on to an existing flush box using a slim surface mounting *pattress*. This is about 19 mm deep and fits over the existing box. There is a mounting hole at each side so that it can be screwed to the wall. The double socket is then fixed on to the pattress in the same way as onto a surface mounted box.

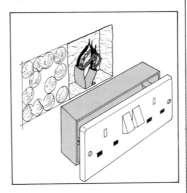

The more usual method is to remove the old mounting box and cut out a hole to take the new mounting box. The method of cutting the hole, mounting the new box and connecting the socket is the same as described in *Adding Extra Sockets* (page 242).

Fitting an Electric Cooker

The cooker must have its own circuit—30 amps for cookers up to 12 kw and 45 amps for those above 12 kw, such as the large split-level ovens and hobs operated on the same circuit.

The cable is run from the consumer unit to the cooker control unit mounted on the kitchen wall.

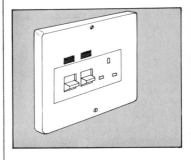

The cooker control unit has a *double pole switch*—one that controls both the live and neutral conductors.

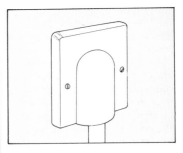

With a free-standing cooker, it is usual to fit a *terminal outlet box* about 600 mm from the floor. This is joined to the control unit with a second length of cable. Finally, a length of flex joins the cooker to the terminal outlet box, allowing the cooker to be drawn away from the wall for cleaning.

A split-level cooker can be controlled from one unit, but neither the hob nor the oven must be more than 2m from the switch. The cable supplying both is divided in the cooker terminal, or else taken first to one unit and then on to the other.

Plan the route for the cable either under the floor or through the kitchen ceiling to above the consumer unit. Channel out the walls to take the cable. The 6 sq mm or 10 sq mm cable is heavier and thicker than the 2.5 sq mm used for the ring circuit, so a deep channel will be needed. If you choose to run the cable on the surface, use cable clips every 200 mm or else conceal it in plastic channelling or conduit.

Open up the floor or ceiling space and cut holes in the joists to take the cable if it has to pass across them.

Mark the position of the metal *mounting box*. If it is to be recessed, remove a portion of the wall to take the box. Knock out the blanks for the cable entry holes and fit grommets into the holes. Screw the box to the wall.

Insert the cable into the box and strip off about 200 mm of outer cable sheath. Fit a length of green yellow sleeve on the earth wire. Remove enough of the insulation on the live and neutral wires so that they can be connected to the terminals on the unit. Repeat this operation with the cable to the cooker. With a split-level cooker there may be two cables to connect to the outlet terminals of the unit. Make sure the red wires go to the live and the black to neutral. The terminal screws must be tightened to hold the cable ends effectively. There should be no loose strands of wire. Check that the earth connections are tight.

Fit the unit into its box and fix the retaining screws.

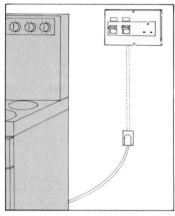

Free-standing cookers
The terminal outlet unit for the free-standing cooker has a metal frame with a terminal block that fits into a mounting box. This box must be sunk into the wall. Channel the cable into the wall up to the cooker control unit. Complete any replastering.

Prepare the ends of the cable in the same way as on the control unit and connect to the terminal block. Fit the terminal block on the mounting box followed by the front plate cover.

Now the other end of the cable has to be connected to the consumer unit and this is a job best left to a professional electrician or the electricity board. You will have to arrange a temporary disconnection. If there is no spare way to the consumer unit, a separate double pole switch unit with a 30 or 45 amp fuse will have to be installed. The unit is mounted next to the consumer unit and needs two 3 m lengths of 16 sq

mm, one red, one black and a 6 sq mm earth cable of the same length for connection to the terminal block by the electricity board.

To install a free-standing cooker, first find the *cable connection point* at the rear of the cooker. This is usually located behind a metal plate with a cable clamp. The cable connecting the cooker to the terminal outlet box should be of the same size and capacity as the circuit cable. About 2 m should be sufficient.

Prepare both cable ends for connection, leaving more bare wire at the cooker as it usually has to be wound around a screw and clamped down with brass washers and screws.

Switch off at the mains and at the cooker control box. Open the terminal and make the connections. Replace the terminal cover, switch on and test.

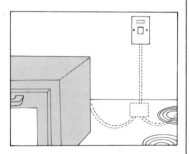

To install a split-level cooker, the cable connection is taken from the cooker control unit through a flush mounting placed behind the hob and oven. The cable is clamped inside the mounting box and a terminal outlet front plate fitted. Connection is then made to the oven and hob at the terminals provided.

IMPROVING YOUR LIGHTING

There are plenty of good ideas that will help you to improve your lighting, and many need little or no structural work or rewiring. Changing a light switch to a *dimmer*, for instance, allows you to create mood lighting and is a job that takes only a few a minutes. For any of these jobs, though, switch off at the mains first — not just the switch at the door — or else remove the lighting circuit fuses from the consumer unit.

Light Fittings

Rise and fall ceiling roses allow the height of the shade to be adjusted simply by finger touch. A circular box with a spring balance replaces the ceiling rose. The fitting should suit the weight of the shade.

Lighting track is one of the best ways of getting more light without rewiring or tearing into walls and ceilings. The track can be mounted on to a wall or ceiling and a variety of small, neat light fittings can be clipped into the track anywhere along its length. It is particularly useful for mounting small spotlights that concentrate their light on to nearby walls, furniture or pictures.

Spotlights produce a beam of light of different sizes and intensity. One of the best methods of using them is to conceal them in the ceiling so that only the bulb can be seen.

The ceiling space in most homes is sufficient to take this kind of fitting. The average recessed depth is usually less than 125 mm. A circular hole must be cut in the ceiling and the cable connection can be taken through the space between the joists to the nearest lighting point. The hole should be cut carefully, although any rough edge will be hidden by the trim on the fitting.

As many as four of these fittings can be run from an existing centre ceiling point, the four cables being connected together within the ceiling rose or a new junction box. It is a good idea to control all these with a dimmer.

The *'eyeball'* is the most versatile of the recessed fittings. The housing that holds the

A row of recessed spots give directional lighting, making this corner ideal for sewing or reading, whilst not over-illuminating the whole room. They are easily fitted, provided you have sufficient height in the ceiling space; check this before buying your fittings.

lamp swivels to direct light at any angle. The smallest eyeball (for mains voltage) needs a hole of only 100 mm diameter and a depth of 115 mm. Eyeballs that take a larger lamp need holes of 200 mm and the recessed depth is about the same.

Cones, tubes and squares create pools of light of different sizes, depending on design. Some can be adjusted or only partly recessed in the ceiling, making the fitting suitable for shallow ceilings. One version has the lamp set at an angle to throw light sideways on to the wall, like the eyeball:

Circular glass fittings have a lens that hides the lamp and spreads the light. Some fit flush

This large basement kitchen/dining room relies on a well thought out plan that provides light only where it's wanted, by means of strategically placed spots. The fitting over the dining table is separately switched.

with the ceiling, some are slightly recessed (which tends to narrow the spread of light) and others have the glass and trim surface mounted. Clear, milk and sculptured glass covers are available and most are designed for the tungsten filament (GLS) lamp. These light fittings are suitable for bathrooms and kitchens.

Lamps are the first essential of any lighting. Popularly called 'bulbs', there is a wide choice.

Pear-shaped bulbs are known in the trade as GLS (general lighting service). Pearl coated and white (argenta) give a diffused light, while clear are for clear and tinted fittings where the undiffused light adds a sparkle. 60 and 100 watts are the most useful sizes. Long-life bulbs give a little less light and cost a few pence more, but they last for 2000 hours instead of the usual 1000.

Most bulbs have bayonet cap fittings (BC), but many continental fittings use screw cap (ES) bulbs.

Decorative bulbs are variations on the pear shape, usually for situations where the bulb is visible. Candle flame shapes are for wall lamps. Coloured bulbs are for parties and at Christmas, and those with pink pearl coating give soft background lighting or create a welcoming glow in the hall or on the patio. There are also specially shaped bulbs with the white (argenta) coating. Some of the decorative bulbs have cap fittings that are smaller than normal — called SBC or SES.

Crown silvered bulbs have the front silvered so the light is then thrown backwards against a reflector, to give a glare-free spotlight beam. These are used in special fittings, some of which need special small bulbs — 40, 60 or 100 watts.

Internally silvered bulbs (sometimes called reflector lamps) are silvered at the back so all the light is reflected forward (like a spotlight). There is a choice of narrow or wide beam and different sizes to suit special fittings — 40, 60 or 100 watts.

Pressed glass (PAR38) are strong spotlights made of toughened glass and are capable of being used outdoors as well as indoors. They are usually ES (screw cap) and need a special fitting. These bulbs have a long life — 5000 hours — and are made in 100 and 150 watt sizes.

Linear filament bulbs are tube-shaped ordinary bulbs (not to be confused with fluorescent tubes). They are usually used in wardrobes and under worktops and may have double-end fittings or single, to match the fitting — 35, 40 or 75 watts.

Fluorescent lamps give five times as much light for the same number of watts as filament lamps. They cost more, but they last much longer — about 7500 hours. Their sizes range from miniature tubes, 300 mm long (only 8 watts) to the most popular home sizes — 1200 mm (40 watts) and 1500 mm (65 watts). The colour of the light they produce is called 'warm white' but you can ask for de luxe warm white (sometimes called by a brand name such as Homelite). The colour of the light from these is more like the light from a filament bulb and not the rather white, cold tone of most fluorescents.

Almost all tubes can be disguised with a *baffle*. There are various translucent plastic covers for ceiling use in the kitchen. There

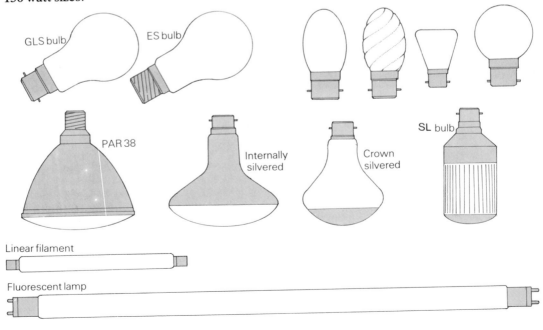

GLS bulb ES bulb SL bulb
PAR 38 Internally silvered Crown silvered
Linear filament
Fluorescent lamp

are also circular tubes with covers for use in the centre of the ceiling in a living room or bedroom.

New thin fluorescent tubes that are twisted into a compact shape and fitted into a glass jar are threatening to replace conventional lamps. The smallest of these uses only 9 watts of power, but gives the light of a 40 watt GLS bulb, and the 18 watt version gives the same light as a 75 watt bulb. These new lamps fit into conventional bulb holders and, although they are far more expensive to buy, they last for 5000 hours and offer very reduced running costs. There is also a type — the 2D — that has a futuristic shape.

Dimmers vary the amount of light given out by a bulb. Most dimmers can be fitted in place of an existing switch, or there are free-standing models for table lamps. Several dimmers can be mounted together on a twin-switched plate. Always suit the loading of the dimmer to the lighting load (see maker's instructions). Fluorescent lamps need special dimmers. Connection of a dimmer switch is the same as for a rocker switch.

Other Devices

Pullcords are needed in a bathroom for safety; they are also useful in a bedroom where the pullcord can hang down close to the pillow, making it easier for the elderly and invalids.

Timers are usually plug-in and are useful for turning equipment (such as a table or standard lamp) on and off when you are away from home (an anti-burglar device).

A Besa box is a circular mounting box for some pendant wall and porch lights that have a circular base. They are recessed into the wall in the same way as square boxes.

Terminal blocks, made of white or black plastic, have pairs of screws for connecting cables inside mounting boxes. They are purchased in lengths and cut off in strips of two or three. They are often used to connect light fittings to the cable inside the Besa box.

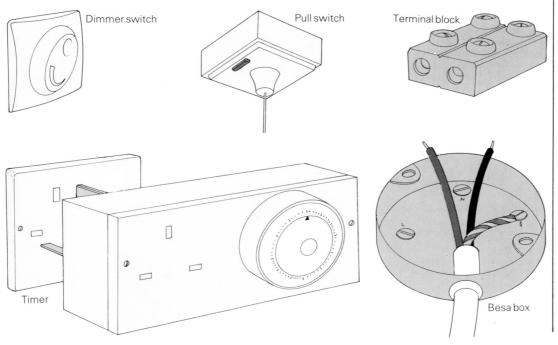

Dimmer switch

Pull switch

Terminal block

Timer

Besa box

Fitting ceiling roses & holders

Before beginning any work on ceiling roses or lamp holders, be sure to switch off the electricity at the mains switch—it is not enough to switch off just the light switch.

Lamp Holders

A lamp holder is needed for all lamps. To fit a new one, first unscrew the cover and slacken the flex from around clamping grooves on the centre pillar. Unscrew the terminals and remove the flex ends. If the flex is rubber insulated and cotton braided and has been in use for some time, it will almost certainly require replacing with twin-core, heat-resistant flex.

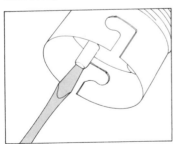

Push each terminal plunger up and down to see if the tension is still good. If not, or if the moulding is damaged, replace it with a new lamp holder. Thread a new cover on to the flex and remove the insulation from the ends of the wires, twisting each bare end neatly to keep the strands together.

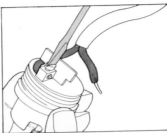

Place the flex ends into the terminals and tighten firmly. (If a flex with brown and blue conductors is being used it will not matter which terminals are chosen.) Place the flex in around the pillar in the grooves provided. Screw down the cover, keeping the flex slack.

Ceiling Roses

A ceiling rose connects pendant (hanging) flex to mains. Multi-outlet versions allow you to suspend up to five pendant fittings from one ceiling outlet. They are useful in a stair well or over a coffee table in a corner; or the flexes can be looped through hooks to spread light over the ceiling.

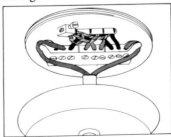

To replace a ceiling rose, switch off at the mains switch. Undo the cover of the rose. If it is an old porcelain pattern, or one that has been much painted over, it may be necessary to smash it. Undo the flex connections and remove the pendant flex to the lamp. Loosen the terminals that grip the cable ends. Fit on the new base and tighten the terminal screws.

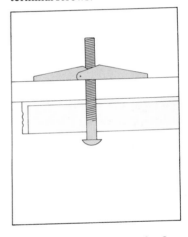

Insert the fixing screws and refix the base to the ceiling. If the ceiling is weak or damaged or the screws won't hold (important if the light fitting is heavy) then use new screws linked to an appropriate anchor fitting. The toggle plug is one used for hollow ceilings.

Renew the pendant flex and, if necessary, the lamp holder. Use heat resistant (silicone) .5 sq mm flex. Insert the flex through the rose cover and fix the wires to the terminals. An earth terminal is provided in the ceiling rose to which the earth wire is connected, if there is one. Older lighting circuits do not have them, but they are now installed for metal encased light fittings that have a three-core flex. Screw on the rose cover.

Switches

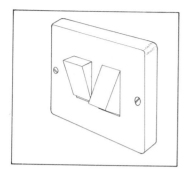

Rocker switches that you just push top or bottom to turn the light on or off are easy for the young, elderly or infirm to operate. Several switches can fit on one plate. Replacement of a switch is quite simple. Switch off at the mains first.

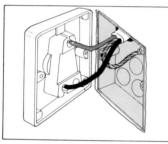

Remove the screws in the switch cover and lift the switch from the wall box. Unscrew the wire from the terminals, using a screwdriver with a fine blade. Fit the new switch by placing the wires to the correct terminals and screwing them firmly into place. The terminals are usually marked with 'COM' (common) and '1' and '2', so identification should be simple. The red conductor goes to 'COM' and the other wire to '1'. The earth wire is normally connected to the terminal in the mounting box. Screw the new switch on to the box, switch on the mains and test.

Two-way switches allow the light to be turned on or off at two points. This is useful for stairs, and also in bedrooms for the bedside and by the door. Many switches can be converted to operate 'two-way', but it needs an extra wire between the two switches—three in all.

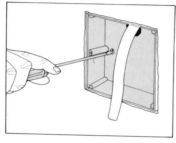

Begin by fitting a mounting box where the new switch is to go. You can use either a plastic box screwed to the surface of the wall, or a metal plaster depth box screwed into a hole cut out of the plaster.

A length of 1 sq mm three-core and earth, PVC sheathed and insulated cable is needed. The insulated wires are coloured red, blue and yellow. Feed this cable into the box through one of the knockout holes (fitted with a grommet if the box is metal).

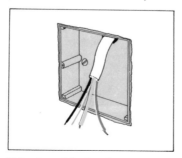

Trim the cable, leaving enough to connect to the terminals (don't connect it yet).

Strip off about 50 mm of the outer sheathing, and 10 mm of the insulation from the ends of the three wires. Place PVC sleeving on the bare earth wire.

Next, run the cable up the wall in a channel cut into the plaster and then above the ceiling, and back down the wall to the original switch. Above the ceiling, if the cable runs in the same direction as the joists, rest it on the ceiling. If there is a chance of it being disturbed (for example in an unboarded loft) fit it to the sides of the joists with cable clips. Where the cable runs at right angles to the joists, pass it through holes drilled at least 50 mm below the top edges of the joists.

Turn off the power at the mains and remove the old switch. Feed the cable into the mounting box and prepare the cable as with the other switch.

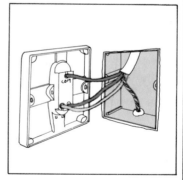

Each of the two-way switches has three terminals, normally marked COM, L1 and L2. On the new switch, connect the red wire to the COM (common) terminal, the yellow wire to terminal L1 and the blue wire to terminal L2. Place the wires in the box and screw the switch to the box.

Extending a lighting circuit

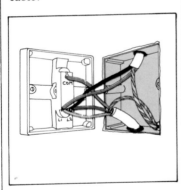

At the original switch, fit a PVC sleeve to the earth wire on the new cable and connect it to the earth point on the box, joining it with the earth from the mains cable.

Connect the red to the COM terminal of the switch. Connect the yellow wire, together with one of the existing insulated wires, to terminal L1. Connect the blue wire, together with the remaining existing insulated wire, to terminal L2 of the switch. (The two existing wires will be red and black respectively, but either may be connected to the L1 or L2 terminals.)

Screw the switch into the mounting box, restore the power, and check everything works.

Lighting has a different kind of circuit from a ring circuit. The cable connects the lighting points and there is a branch cable from each to connect with the switch. Most homes have two lighting circuits, each protected by a 5 amp fuse. Each circuit can supply a maximum of twelve 100 watt lamps (240 volts × 5 amps = 1200 watts).

The cable is 1 sq mm two-core and earth, flat, PVC sheathed cable. In older houses the lighting circuit is often single core PVC or rubber insulated cable inside metal pipes (conduit).

The lighting circuit is wired either on the **loop-in system** or the older **junction box system,** or a mixture of both. *[Normally, extra light fittings should not be added to the older junction box lighting circuit unless expert advice has been sought.]* Study the diagrams, noting carefully how the switch forms a branch line on the live conductor.

Plan the position of the lights and the most convenient switching points. More than one switch can be operated from the same position, and a single switch can be replaced by a double switch in the same box.

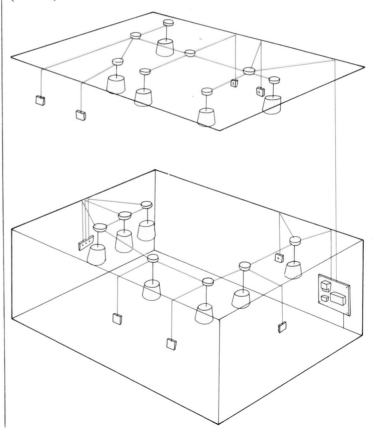

Loop-in Ceiling Rose

A loop-in ceiling rose has live conductors connected to the centre bank of terminals. Compare this with the junction box method and make sure you understand the difference.

In a loop-in rose, the cable runs directly from the main consumer unit to the rose, which has four main terminals, each with a number of screws. Three of these terminals are linked to take the live, neutral and earth wires respectively. A wire is taken from the live terminal on the light switch and a wire from the other switch terminal returns to the four terminals on the ceiling rose. A wire is also taken from the earth terminal on the rose to the earth terminal on the switch plate or mounting box.

The *two leads* for the *lampholder* are connected to the *fourth terminal* and the *neutral terminal,* so the switch operates on the live side of the circuit. If a *metal lampholder* is connected, an earth wire must be connected to the earth terminal on the lampholder casing.

The wires to the next light fitting and switch in the circuit are taken from the *live, neutral* and *earth* terminals in the ceiling rose, continuing around the circuit until the final ceiling rose position is reached.

Mount the new switch and the cable to the switch following the same procedure as for mounting a new socket outlet (see page 242), except that the mounting boxes will be only plaster depth. Take the cable from the switch to the new ceiling rose. Remove the rose carefully, marking each of the connections.

Pass a *new cable* through the hole in the ceiling alongside the

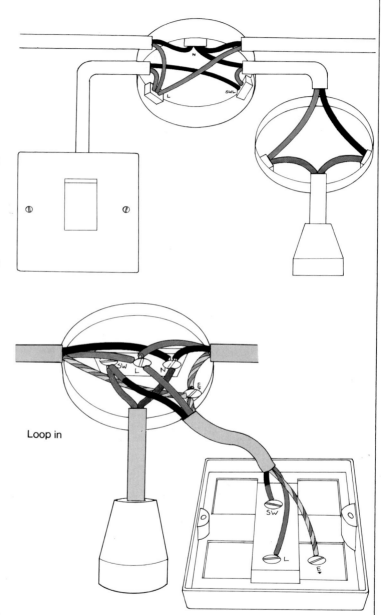

Loop in

existing cables, and take it to the position of the new rose. Prepare the ends of the cables.

At the old ceiling rose, connect the *red* wire to a *centre terminal* in the rose, the *black* to

the *neutral terminal,* and the *earth* (in a green yellow sleeve) to the *earth terminal.* At the new rose, make the connections for the supply cable and switch. Refix ceiling rose and test.

BATHROOMS

No electrical heaters (or appliances such as washing machines or dryers with heating elements) are allowed in the bathroom unless they can be permanently fixed out of reach of anyone using the bath or shower. The only exception permitted in the Regs is the purpose-designed electric shower or pump. No power sockets are allowed, and no switches, except of the pull-cord type.

The only socket allowed is the special one used for shavers, and this must be the type for use in bathrooms, either on its own or with a light. These are made to British Standard (BS) 3052 and have an *isolating transformer* and earthed metal screen, so that the user is effectively isolated from the mains.

The transformer has two sets of windings so that it can be switched either to standard mains voltage or 115 volts for American or continental razors. The socket is usually made to take both the round and flat-pin plugs. These sockets are unsuitable for other appliances, and they can be wired as an extension to the bathroom light.

A room (other than a bathroom) that has a shower cubicle may have a socket, but it must be at least 2.5m from the cubicle.

A *washing machine* or *tumble dryer* cannot be sited in a bathroom, unless the room is very large and the machines can be isolated behind permanent screening (such as louvred panels) so that, effectively, they are in a room of their own.

Above *Electric fires can only be used in the bathroom if they are fixed out of reach and are of the correct design, with the obligatory pull switch. On no account be tempted to fit a power socket in the bathroom, as it is very dangerous.*

Right *This attractive and functional bathroom has a well appointed shaver socket and concealed lighting both above and below the mirror. Extra light is provided by a spotlight.*

A heated towel rail must be correctly fitted with a terminal outlet box and not an adapting socket.

Above *This well lagged tank is correctly fitted with a 20 amp double-pole switch with neon indicator.*

Left *This creative use of industrial fittings is both novel and safe. Note the water heater is also connected via conduit.*

Connecting a Bathroom Towel Rail

The simplest way to fit an electric towel rail in the bathroom is by a *spur* taken from the ring circuit to a fused, switched *connector*. Choose a connector with a red pilot light to show when it's in use and site it outside the bathroom.

From the live and neutral terminals on the connector (usually marked 'out'), take a cable through the wall to a second mounting box placed next to the heater. The heater must be mounted on the wall or floor, out of reach of anyone using the bath or shower.

Connect the flex from the heater to a *terminal block* in the box, through a surface plate with a flex entry hole. Join the flex and cable to the terminal block (including the earth wires) and then secure the block to the mounting box and screw the cover plate on.

Wall Heaters

The same method can be used for heaters mounted high on the bathroom wall and operated by a pull-cord switch. The flex is connected to a fused connector unit mounted alongside.

Wiring an Electric Shower

An electric shower is basically a water heater that heats the water rapidly as it passes over the elements. When the cold water inlet valve is opened, the pressure of the water closes an electric switch that operates the heating element. The water passes over the element and is heated—the temperature varying with the rate of flow; the slower the flow, the higher the temperature, and vice versa.

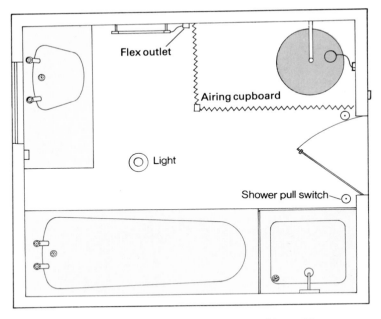

Flex outlet

Airing cupboard

Light

Shower pull switch

As the water is only briefly in contact with the element, the loading (electric power) must be high—6 kw or even higher. This means that the circuit supplying it must be 30 amps capacity and the fuse the same.

The shower unit must have its own circuit, just like the electric cooker. If there is no suitable way (spare fused circuit) on the consumer unit, it must have its own mains switch and 30 amp fuse as with cookers. (See page 245 for instructions on fitting.) This must be connected to the meter by the electricity board. A 6 sq mm cable is normally used although, if a cartridge fuse or miniature circuit breaker is used, the cable can be reduced to 4 sq mm.

The *ceiling switch* must be a pull-cord, double pole (one that switches off the live and neutral connectors). It must have a 30 amp rating and a red pilot light

to show when it's on. The connection from the shower unit can sometimes go direct to the switch via concealed cable, but some have a flex that needs to be connected inside a *terminal box* similar to that used for the towel rail. The terminal block must have a 30 amp rating. The pull-cord switch must be sited so it is in easy reach of those using the shower.

The route for the cable will be up the wall above the consumer unit, and through the ceiling to a point above the bathroom or shower cubicle. If the bathroom is tiled, or you don't want to redecorate, the cable from the switch to the shower unit can be enclosed in plastic trunking. Choose the shortest route, but don't sacrifice convenience. Make sure the cable is secured and follow the advice about cutting holes through joists (see page 243).

Immersion Heaters

An electric immersion heater can provide hot water throughout the year, or supplement a gas, oil, or solid fuel boiler system during the summer months, when a central heating boiler is switched off. To conserve energy (and save money) the hot cylinder must be well lagged (insulated) with a purpose-made lagging jacket at least 75 mm thick.

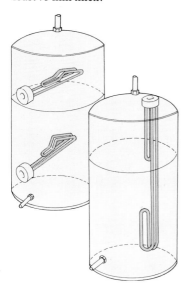

Standard immersion heaters are made in different lengths to suit different size tanks. They can be mounted vertically or horizontally. Two heaters, one near the base of the tank and one near the top, can save money. The *upper heater* is left switched on all the time to ensure a continuous (but small) supply of hot water. It just heats up the water at the top of the tank (which is drained off first). The *lower heater* can be switched on an hour or so before larger quantities are needed, eg for baths or laundry. This heater can also be controlled by a time switch.

The electricity board will connect this lower heater to their Economy Seven tariff meter, so that it uses electricity at less than half the normal price to heat the entire tank at night. This can be a real money saver for a family, and free information about how it works can be obtained from any electricity board.

The dual element immersion heater is fitted into the top of the tank, and combines the features of two heaters in one. The long element heats up the whole tank; the short element just the top part.

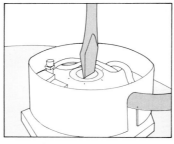

The thermostatic control on immersion heaters can be found under the metal cover on the outside casing, but switch off the heater before undoing the screw holding the cover. The thermostat can be adjusted using a small screwdriver to turn the pointer to the required temperature setting.

In soft water areas, the recommended setting is 70 degrees C, but for hard water areas the recommended setting is lower—60 degrees C. The lower setting prevents the build up of scale in the tank. Most homes find this setting sufficient for their needs, and there are savings in running costs.

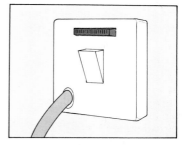

A 20 amp, double pole switch with a neon indicator is needed for immersion heaters. There are dual switches for the dual element heaters.

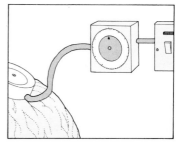

A time switch can also be fitted into the circuit, so that you can arrange for the heater to switch on and give you hot water when you arrive home. Used with a dual heater (of either kind), a time switch (without the Economy Seven tariff) may not offer big savings but it does give added convenience. Follow the maker's instructions for wiring, and switch off at the mains before installing the timer. It should be sited well clear of the hot water tank so that it won't be affected by excess heat. The flex from the switch or the clock to the immersion heater must be of the heat resistant type and 20 amps rating.

OUTDOOR WIRING

A portable cable reel connected to an indoor socket may be easy for an electric hedge trimmer but, if you want garden lights, a fountain in an ornamental pool, or you plan to make profitable use of a greenhouse, then a permanent outdoor supply is needed. The garden circuit should have its own main switch and 20 amp fuse close to the meter. An RCCB (residual current circuit breaker) should be included in the circuit.

Above left *A metal clad, switched socket outlet has been used in this workshop, complete with splash-proof switch.*

Above *A specially designed outdoor light correctly fitted on a garden wall. Remember it is unsafe to fit ordinary lights outside.*

Left *Another use for electricity in the garden is to operate pumps for ponds and pools. Here, the supply has been run from the workshop at the bottom of the garden, and the pump is concealed by greenery.*

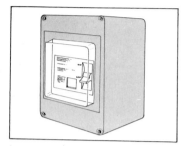

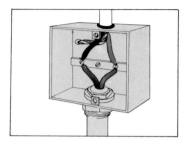

At the meter, the main switch unit with fuse and RCCB will be connected to the meter by the electricity board, once the circuit has been installed.

Underground Cables

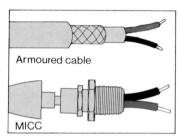

Armoured cable

MICC

Standard 2.5 sq mm twin and earthed PVC *sheathed cable*, as used for a ring circuit, can sometimes be used outdoors, provided it's carefully protected. However, it is more usual to use a special *weatherproof* one, such as 1.5 sq mm copper sheathed twin-core cable (MICC). A third type, especially suitable under a patio or for a supply to a pond, is *armoured PVC sheathed cable*. This two-core insulated cable has ribbons of galvanised steel (acting as the earth conductor) wound around the two cores and encased in an outer sheath of PVC. For both types of outdoor cable, special cable clamping glands are needed at each end to grip the metal sheathing and form the earth conection.

Earth continuity is essential. The outer sheath must be clamped into the terminal or mounting box. Then special clamps, that are made in sections, screw on to the cable and, after it has been inserted into the metal box, the clamp is locked into the hole by a washer and a second clamp passes over the cable and screws down on the first. This not only forms a water-tight seal, but also completes the earth link to the box. The box must then be linked to the earth conductor in the wiring circuit in the house, using any convenient terminal. The cable is buried about 500 mm below the surface. Standard 2.5 sq mm must be protected by galvanised steel conduit.

Cable Wells
If the house has solid floors, or access is difficult and conduit is being used, a 500 mm deep cable well must be dug against the outside wall of the house and the cable run into it. There should also be a cable well at the greenhouse or garage end, and both must be covered to prevent them collecting water. Different methods can be used, including filling with earth or gravel, since PVC cable is unaffected by any chemicals likely to be present in the soil.

With MICC or armoured PVC cable, the task is simpler. The only protection needed is where the cable is exposed. The cable is clipped to the wall using clips designed for the purpose. Additional protection can be given by galvanised covers screwed to the brickwork or greenhouse. Both clips and covers are sold by electrical contractors. Any covering fixed vertically must be covered to prevent water collecting, and there are metal covers and waterproof compounds made for the purpose.

In a *greenhouse* or *garden shed* the cable should terminate in a *control panel*. This must be designed for the purpose or made by an electrician, using standard electrical accessories. The component parts are a mains switch (usually with a

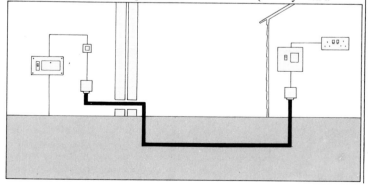

Wiring a door bell

fuse), and from this switched points and socket outlets are wired separately.

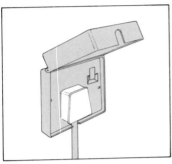

Special sockets are made for outdoor use and in protected places, such as covered car ports and patios, there are *weather-proof plastic covers*. For lighting, there are weatherproof switches.

Connector units, switches and sockets used in greenhouses and outbuildings should be installed 1200 mm from the floor. Ideally, they should be wired with MICC cable, but you can use 2.5 sq mm PVC twin and earth. The cable is taken from the outlet to each point in turn, so they are like links in a chain.

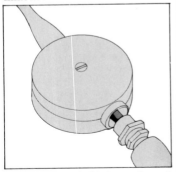

A garden pond with fountain and lights can have direct connections to a waterproof junction box concealed under a poolside stone or a covered cavity in the rockery.

A door bell or chime works on a very low voltage. This may be supplied by dry batteries, or by a small transformer that is connected to the mains and reduces 240 volts to 8, 12 or 24 volts.

A trembler bell is traditional and very reliable. A tiny amount of current causes a hammer to vibrate rapidly against a metal dome, making the familiar clear ringing tone.

A buzzer has a magnet that is vibrated by a metal rod. The pitch and volume of the buzz can be varied on most models.

A door chime uses a double-ended plunger that is mounted on a spring. This is drawn through a magnetic coil and strikes the metal chime bars to give a double note. Some models can be wired to a second push button that produces only a single note, so you can tell which door to answer.

A sonic musical door signal can be set to produce a variety of tunes, pre-programmed into the unit.

Bells and buzzers work on 3 or 4.5 volt long-life batteries. Chimes and sonics usually need 8 or 12 volt batteries. All except the sonics can be wired to a

transformer as an alternative.

A *transformer system* is needed if you want a bell push with a light, otherwise you will be constantly replacing the batteries that should normally last 3 or 4 years.

The *bell push* is simply a spring-loaded switch. When you press the button, two contacts touch to complete the circuit. The batteries are usually fitted inside the case of the bell or chime. Connection to the push is by a thin, twin-core cable called *'bell wire'*. This is sold in white, black and other colours so it can be left exposed along the edge of skirting boards, around door frames and even along the edge of coving. Tiny 'U' shaped plastic cable clips (each with their own pin) secure the wire to the surface. Take care not to sever the wire when driving the pins. The bell wire should be secured at about 300 mm intervals, with enough clips near corners to keep it tidy.

If the distance between the bell and the push is more than 9 m, you may need to increase the voltage of the batteries or the thickness of the wire (see maker's instructions). The electrical resistance of the wire

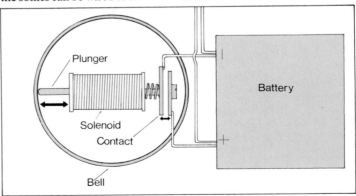

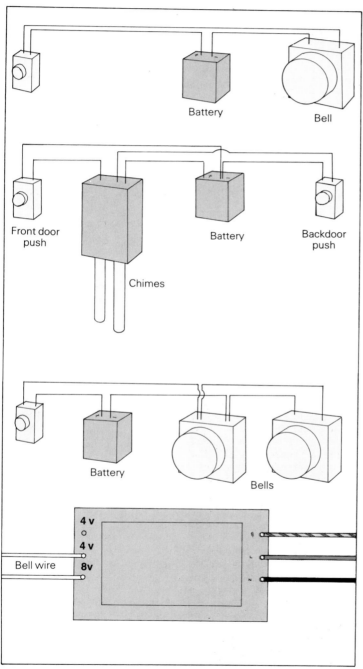

Battery

Bell

Front door
push

Battery

Backdoor
push

Chimes

Battery

Bells

4 v

4 v

Bell wire   8v

reduces the effective voltage.
There is a loss of about one-half
volt for every 9 m of wire. This
may not be noticeable when the
batteries are new, but after a
while the bell or chime will
sound weak and then stop.

It is a simple matter to have a
bell push at the back and front
doors, and some of the chimes
give a single or double note to
distinguish which push is being
pressed.

Wiring a second bell
You can also fit a second bell or
chime to work from the same
push. This is useful upstairs in
large houses, or for someone
with hearing difficulties.

Two methods can be used to
wire a second bell or chime. The
parallel method is for a pair of
matching bells or matching
chimes. The series system uses
twice the voltage, but it can't be
used for trembler bells. All the
manufacturers supply wiring
diagrams, but the basic principle
is a simple circuit that is
completed when a bell push is
pressed.

Where a *transformer* is fitted,
it must be connected to the
mains using 1 sq mm twin core
and earth cable. It can be
connected as a spur from a ring
circuit, but most consumer units
have a 5 amp fuse way designed
for this connection. If you take a
spur from the ring, use a fused
connector unit with a 3 amp fuse.

Most transformers have three
connections on the output side.
If the bell wire is taken to the
outer terminals, this gives a 12
volt supply. The middle terminal
and one outer gives 8 volts, and
the middle and other outer gives
4 volts. These combinations are
clearly marked on the case.

Top Ten Tips

1. Know where your fuse box is, and keep fuse wire, spare fuses and a torch nearby.

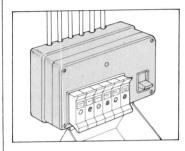

2. Label all the fuses in your fuse box, eg upstairs lights, downstairs power etc. This will save you looking at each fuse for the one that has blown.

3. If a fuse keeps blowing, there is a serious fault in the circuit or in an appliance. Disconnect likely appliances and try again. If that doesn't work, disconnect the circuit by removing the fuse. Then switch on at the mains switch to activate the other circuits. This allows you to have light for replacing the fuse or checking for the fault. Never remove or replace a fuse without first turning off the mains switch.

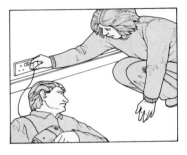

4. There is always the risk of electric shock so be sure to switch off at the mains before attempting any rewiring or electrical repairs. If you encounter any one receiving a shock the first objective must be to break the contact, switch off, remove the plug, or wrench cable free. Do not touch the person while he or she is still in contact with the electrical appliance or cable.

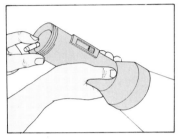

5. A cartridge fuse can be tested using a metal cased torch. Switch on the torch and unscrew the

Hall landing lights should be controlled by two-way switches at the top and bottom of the stairs.

Left Pyjama cords tied together make an attractive pull for this bathroom light switch, and satisfy the regulations.

base. Place one end of the fuse against the case, and the other touching the base of the battery. If the fuse is blown, the bulb won't light.

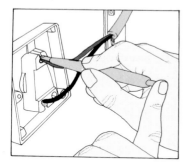

6. Some small screwdrivers have a neon tester incorporated into the handle. The neon will glow when the tip of the screwdriver is touching a live conductor and your finger is touching the metal contact on the handle. The glow is rather faint, so don't rely on it as a sure guide.

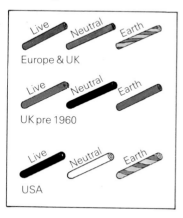

7. In Europe (including the UK) and many other countries, the standard colours for 3-wire flexible cords on appliances are *brown for the live wire, light blue for neutral and green/yellow for earth.* Other coloured wires may be encountered on appliances brought into the UK, particularly those of American origin where a common arrangement is black for live, white or natural grey for neutral and green/yellow for earth. Older (pre 1960) appliances and lamps may have flexes with red for live, black for neutral and green for earth—the same colours as used for the cable wiring in the home.

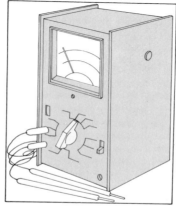

8. A multimeter is a professional, but inexpensive, instrument that is worth buying if you plan to do a lot of electrical repairs. It will measure voltage, current (amps), and resistance. Also it will check batteries and circuits.

9. It's better to add extra sockets than to use adapters for several appliances.

10. When having electrical work done professionally, always use a member of ECA (the Electrical Contractors' Association) or NICEIC (National Inspection Council for Electrical Installation Contracting).

INDEX

Numbers in *italics* refer to illustrations